VIRTUAL MEMORY

VIRTUAL MEMORY

TIME-BASED ART AND THE DREAM OF DIGITALITY

HOMAY KING

DUKE UNIVERSITY PRESS ::: DURHAM AND LONDON ::: 2015

Designed by Amy Ruth Buchanan
Typeset in Chaparral Pro by Tseng
Information Systems, Inc.

Library of Congress
Cataloging-in-Publication Data
King, Homay, [date] author.
Virtual memory : time-based art and the dream
of digitality / Homay King.
pages cm
Includes bibliographical references and index.
ISBN 978-0-8223-5959-3 (hardcover : alk. paper)
ISBN 978-0-8223-6002-5 (pbk. : alk. paper)
ISBN 978-0-8223-7515-9 (e-book)
1. Art and motion pictures. 2. Time and art.
3. Computer art. I. Title.
PN1995.25.K54 2015
791.43′684—dc23 2015014081

Cover art: Christian Marclay, installation view of *The Clock*, 2010. Single-channel video with sound; twenty-four hours. © Christian Marclay. Courtesy Paula Cooper Gallery, New York, and White Cube, London. Photo by Todd-White Photography.

CONTENTS

ACKNOWLEDGMENTS

This book began with a talk on Agnès Varda's *The Gleaners and I* that I gave at the Society for Cinema and Media Studies conference in London in 2005. Coincidentally that conference was also where I first met Ken Wissoker, who has been a marvelous editor and friend. The many years that it took to get from conference paper to book were essential to the ideas expressed here, not because these ideas are necessarily better for having taken longer to develop but because, as Henri Bergson puts it, the time taken up by the invention is one with the invention itself. The people with whom I spent this time—discussing ideas, collaborating on projects, sharing space at lecterns and in print, or just being sociable in person and online—were even more essential. They have shaped this book's contents and facilitated its creation. They include Farid Azfar, Eric Baudelaire, Leo Bersani, Emma Bianchi, Duncan Black, Aviva Briefel, Victor Burgin, Israel Burshatin, David Campany, Tim Corrigan, Drew Daniel, Julie Davis, David Eng, Jim English, Rodney Evans, Jonathan Flatley, Saïd Gahia, Johanna Gosse, Guo-Juin Hong, Sarah Kessler, Maura King, Alex Klein, Simon Leung, Erica Levin, Aaron Levy, Heather Love, Mara Mills, José Muñoz, John Muse, Nguyễn Tân Hoàng, Joshua Ramey, Rebbie Ratner, Sascha Russel, Martin Schmidt, Bethany Schneider, Todd Shepard, Henry Sias, Gus Stadler, Jill Stauffer, Rea Tajiri, Kate Thomas, Sharon Ullman, Patricia White, Ming Wong, Eric Zinner, and my fellow *Camera Obscura* collective members, Lalitha Gopalan, Lynne Joyrich, Tess Takahashi, and Sharon Willis. Extra special thanks go to Rosi Song and Karen Tongson for camaraderie and adventure around the world, and to Kaja Silverman, who always lights the way of intelligence and friendship. Finally I thank Elizabeth Ault for skilled editorial assistance, and the two anonymous readers of the manuscript for their remarkably detailed, thoughtful reports, which wowed me in every way and moved me with their level of intellectual generosity and care.

This book was supported by a University of Pennsylvania Humanities Forum Regional Fellowship, a Bryn Mawr College Faculty Research Grant, and a fellowship from the Mellon Foundation Distinguished Achievement Award held by Keith L. and Katherine Sachs Professor of Contemporary Art Kaja Silverman, Department of History of Art, University of Pennsylvania. An excerpt of chapter 3 was previously published as "Matter, Time, and the Digital: Varda's *The Gleaners and I*" in the *Quarterly Review of Film and Video* 24.5 in Fall 2007. A version of chapter 4 appeared in *Projective: Essays about the Work of Victor Burgin*, ed. David Campany (Geneva: Musée d'Art Moderne et Contemporain, 2014). A portion of chapter 5 appeared in the essay "Anabasis," *October* 142 (Fall 2012). A portion of chapter 6 was previously published under the title "Antiphon: Notes on the People's Microphone," first as an excerpt in *Machete: Occupy Philadelphia*, Marginal Utility Gallery (December 2011), then as an essay in the *Journal of Popular Music Studies* 24.2 (Summer 2012).

INTRODUCTION

THE BLUE MARBLE

Hannah Arendt begins *The Human Condition* with a parable about the launch of the Soviet *Sputnik 1* satellite, the first man-made object ever to break free from Earth's surface and enter its gravitational orbit. The launch occurred on October 4, 1957. Arendt writes, "For some time, the satellite dwelt and moved in the proximity of the heavenly bodies, as though it had been admitted tentatively to their sublime company." It was a moment of encounter with the seemingly miraculous, a technological achievement on the grandest of scales, and a symbolic reversal of the Copernican Revolution. It was also a military event modeled on imperial conquest that heralded the beginning of the cold war space race. Before this race was under way, though, Arendt noted a collective sigh of relief from Earth's inhabitants at the satellite's dispatch: a general sense of optimism in the face of this "first step toward escape from men's imprisonment to the earth."[1]

As a staunch advocate for her home planet who argued in favor of accepting the limitations that had thus far defined the human condition, Arendt found this reaction troubling. The longing to escape the planet and the idea that earth's inhabitants were imprisoned or shackled to its surface went hand in hand with the degradation of tangible, incarnate, sensory experience, along with the kinds of thought, speech, and action that are made possible by embodied perception. For Arendt, the launch of *Sputnik* was troubling insofar as it served as a metaphor for

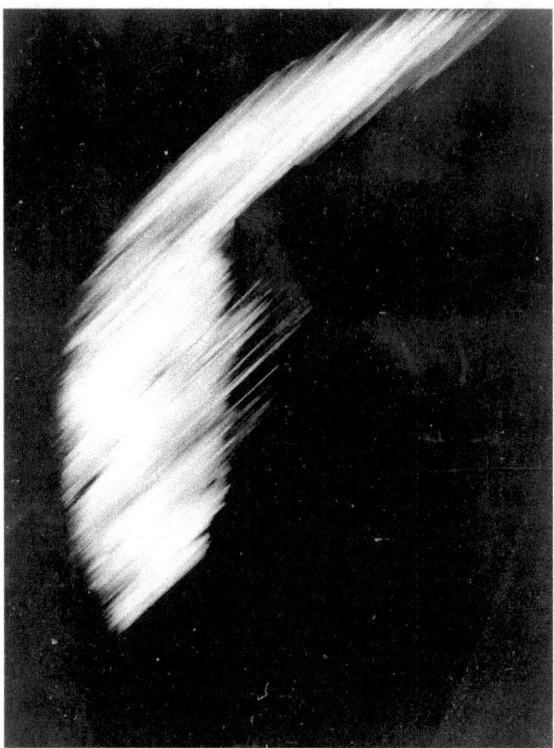

I.1. Photograph of Earth taken by the U.S. *Explorer IV*, August 14, 1959, from approximately seventeen thousand miles, showing the sunlit area of the central Pacific Ocean and its cloud cover. Image courtesy of NASA.

the upward gaze of the scientist or idealist philosopher. It allegorized the victory of the notion that knowledge and power require extraterrestriality, or a similar route to freedom from the web of relations by which the living are bound on Earth.

Two years later, on August 14, 1959, a much-anticipated image began to circulate: the first photograph of earth taken by satellite from outer space (figure I.1).[2] The photograph was made by the U.S. *Explorer IV*, whose flight was made possible in part by the integrated circuits developed at Fairchild Semiconductor, a start-up company located in what would later be known as Silicon Valley. *Explorer IV*'s photograph was heavily abstract. It revealed that from the satellite's point of view, Earth resembled a curved crescent without precise outlines, blurred as if by rapid motion.

Its face was cast mostly in shadow, having been upstaged by the moon. A blizzard of similar photos followed in quick succession. Many of them were likewise dim, inchoate, and creatively framed, as if the mechanical photographer had not yet learned the concept of figuration. Such pictures, in spite of the fact that they were taken from outer space, lacked what Arendt called the "Archimedean standpoint": a position aspiring to a "truly universal viewpoint . . . taken, willfully and explicitly, outside the earth."[3] Earth, in a manner of speaking, had not yet had its mirror-stage.

In 1966 Stewart Brand—a writer, environmental activist, and technology entrepreneur from California—suggested that it was high time to cross that developmental bridge. He made buttons bearing the slogan "Why haven't we seen a photograph of the whole Earth yet?" Brand wrote letters posing this question to luminaries and dignitaries he had selected, including Marshall McLuhan, Buckminster Fuller, a few U.S. senators, and members of the U.S. and Soviet space programs. The only one to reply was Fuller, who wrote, "Dear boy, it's a charming notion but you must realize you can never see more than half the earth from any particular point in space."[4]

On November 10, 1967, though, a photograph appeared that made Brand's wish come true—or rather, half-true, according to Fuller's flawless logic. Made by the U.S. ATS-III satellite, the image showed the earth as a nearly perfectly round disc, in color, surrounded by a black void. The planet was now visible from its good side, its face an evenly illuminated, vivacious circle, beautifully centered in frame. Earth had finally assumed what Jacques Lacan, in reference to the baby in front of the mirror, called the "orthopedic form of its totality."[5] Brand eagerly adopted this image for the cover of the fall 1968 issue of the *Whole Earth Catalog*, for which he served as editor (figure I.2). This catalogue offered "access to tools," a collection of product reviews and short texts, and its audience was the community of tech-savvy, ecologically minded, vaguely Libertarian, countercultural enthusiasts that was beginning to form in the mid-1960s in northern California. Located in and around the San Francisco Bay Area, this community of proto-hackers brought together the curious paradoxes of the "Californian ideology": a fusion of "hippie culture and cybernetics, nature romantics and technology worshippers, psychedelia and computer culture," as it has been described.[6] Rather than sell merchandise directly, the *Whole Earth Catalog* offered a

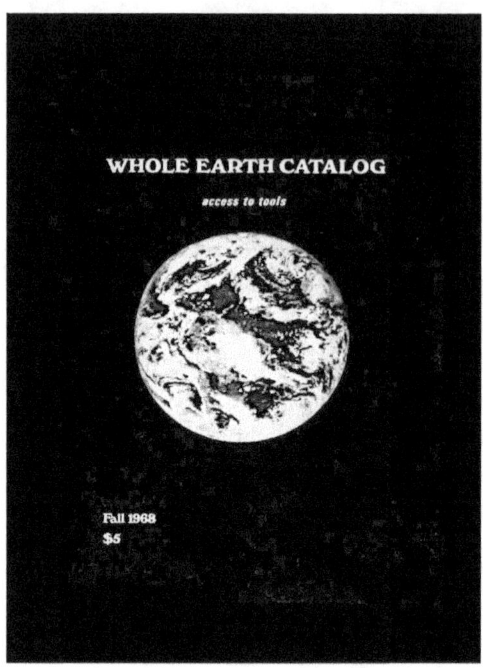

I.2. Cover of the *Whole Earth Catalog*, Fall 1968, featuring a photograph of Earth taken by the U.S. ATS-III satellite.

curated directory of product endorsements, pointing users to vendors who could supply tools and materials for DIY projects by mail order alongside essays by Brand, Fuller, and others. As such, it was in some ways a precursor to the crowd-sourced reviews and linking practices found some forty years later on the Internet.

For Brand, the color photograph captured the planet's fragility. Earth had finally appeared in the form that would earn it the nickname "the Blue Marble," as it was affectionately called in captions of similar pictures taken from space. This photo, in Brand's view, had the potential to solicit an attitude of care and concern for Earth: to promote worldly stewardship, environmentalist practices, investment in local planetary resources and infrastructure, and harmony across differences that, from an intraplanetary perspective, now seemed extraordinarily minor. It expressed not mankind's jubilant conquest of outer space, nor a triumphant escape from Earth's shackles, but rather the world's smallness and delicateness relative to the cosmos as a whole. In an interview Brand described how the earth appeared to him in these images as a "little blue, white, green, and brown jewel-like icon amongst a quite featureless

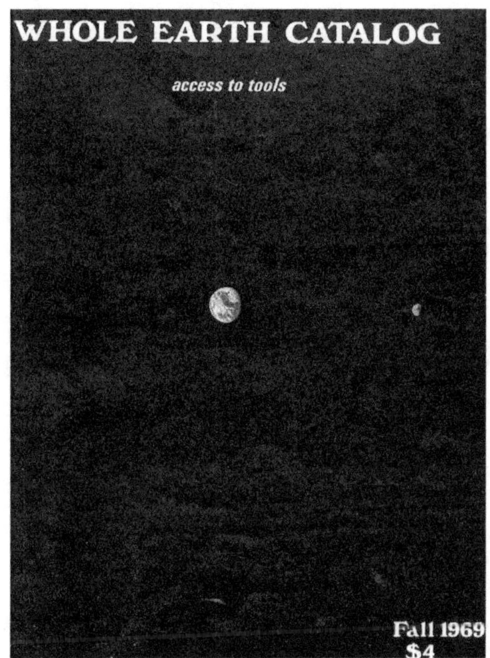

I.3. Cover of the *Whole Earth Catalog*, Fall 1969.

black vacuum." In Brand's view, this image conveyed the precariousness of the planet and its occupants. It looked like an island, with all the accompanying associations of desert island prudence. "Islands know about limitations," he remarked; nevertheless "people still think the earth is flat. . . . They act as if its resources are infinite. But that photograph showed otherwise. Unless and until we find other flourishing planets, this is all we've got and we've got to make it work. There's no backup."[7]

The fall 1969 issue of the *Whole Earth Catalog* bears a similar "whole earth" photograph on its cover (figure I.3). In this image the planet appears smaller and more marble-like. The moon sits to its right, providing a reference point of size and distance. Whereas the 1968 cover's composition and framing suggest a portrait—the world as a familiar face in close-up—the 1969 cover adopted a decidedly Archimedean point of view. Here Earth and its companion satellite appear as lone figures in a vast, inhospitable landscape. The picture offers an intriguingly contradictory set of options for the viewer. On the one hand, if we identify with the small world represented by the blue dot, the image might invite the kind of caretaking attitude that Brand and his cohorts espoused. On the other hand, if we identify with the eye of the camera and the perspectival point from which the image was taken, we find ourselves at a great distance from the planet: exiled and painfully alone perhaps, or, alternatively, larger than life, a deity who could crush the little planet with just a thumb and forefinger.

The remote perspective is traditionally associated with a quasi-theological capacity to appraise, possess, and control. As Arendt writes in *The Human Condition*, "The greater the distance between [man] and his surroundings, world or earth, the more he will be able to survey and to measure and the less will worldly, earth-bound space be left to him." This perspective is also associated with disembodiment. The spatial distance becomes a metaphor for disconnection and indifference. The point of view in which the world appears as a distinct, independent entity is like that of the mirror stage, insofar as this viewing position, while joyful and satisfying to occupy, also entails an alienation or separation. As Arendt puts it, the flight from the planet inserted "a decisive distance between man and earth, alienating man from his immediate earthly surroundings."[8]

The space race has now come to an end, more or less, to the disappointment of many youth of that era. But the longing to escape Earth did not vanish when the race was over. It went elsewhere. It was channeled into digital futures, dot-com bubbles, and the information superhighway, whose netscapes would be navigated, explored, safaried, and homepaged not by astronauts but by new armchair Magellans who took their legacy from Brand and his peers. Digital media universes seemed to promise an alternate place of refuge from the weight and restrictions of Earth-bound existence. It was a virtual refuge, which would likewise require great feats of technical engineering, the assistance of the military-industrial complex, and the consumption of vast natural resources, but it would put the dream of disincarnation vicariously within reach of more than just the astronauts.

SILICON DREAMS

The term *virtual reality* first appeared in print in a 1987 issue of the *Whole Earth Review*, a companion journal spun off from the *Whole Earth Catalog*.[9] It was the title of a short essay about utopian depictions of technology in advertising imagery. The author was Yaakov Garb, a doctoral student in mathematics and science education at the University of California at Berkeley. Garb was not writing about virtual reality in the sense of an electronically simulated, computer-based environment. Rather he used the term to describe computer interfaces and end-user operating systems in general; he called them "masks" that layer on top of hardware. "The source of much of the myth which [computers] weave," Garb wrote, "is achieved through multiple maskings, the creation of 'virtual realities.' One on top of another, levels of symbols are built . . . each level further simplifying the material intricacies which underlie and support it." For Garb, "virtual reality" was the result of an abstraction away from and occlusion of the machine's complex material hardware in favor of its friendly textual and skeuomorphic graphical interfaces. The magazine advertisements added another layer to this virtual reality, and they tapped into a set of fantasies that had begun to crystallize around the image of the personal computer. Garb called these fantasies "the dreams our culture has inscribed in silicon." Above all, and to Garb's dismay, the dream involved "an uninhibited celebration of the separation and transcendence of mind over body."[10]

Some of the images Garb analyzes in this essay feature gridded landscapes reminiscent of early Atari video games or the original Disney version of the movie *Tron* (1982). The images are strikingly dystopic by twenty-first-century standards: today technology industry advertising tends to adopt a more pastoral, agrarian aesthetic, in which the computer user has left the Kubrickian clean room and has gone to the beach with her tablet computer, or perhaps she smiles amid a harvest of fair-trade, organic coffee beans. In the 1980s advertisements, though, anonymous hands manipulate controls at personal computing base stations, giant heads generate reams of text and geometrical forms, and investors use dial-up modems to manage invisible soybean farms by remote control (figure I.4). Garb's commentary on them is prescient. He quotes Descartes describing himself as a thinking entity "whose being requires no place and depends on no material thing." In answer to this fantasy, Garb asks, "Who plants the soybeans, Gentleman Farmer? . . . And where does the irrigation water come from?" He issued an early reminder that someone, somewhere, is always "scurrying to support our virtual reality. . . . Our machines are fed a tremendous amount of

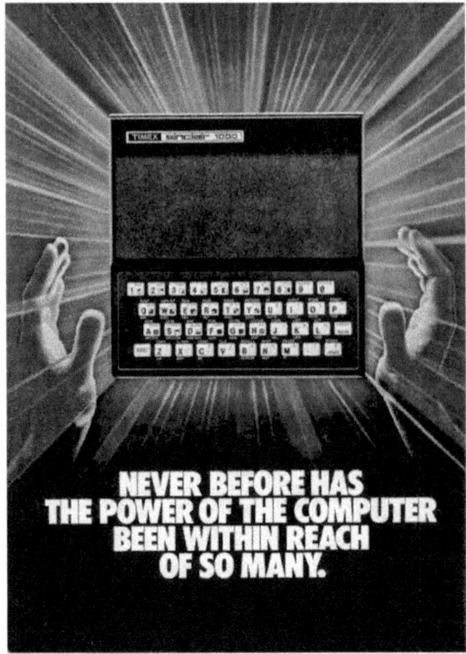

I.4. “The Power Is within Your Reach.” Advertisement, Timex Corporation, 1982.

Life so that they may whisk symbols around.” Among the things that support this virtual reality, he listed “the labor of Taiwanese women in microchip factories, the toxins flushed into our rivers, the dams, mines, and factories,” all of which churn invisibly to power “our pristine alphanumerics.”[11]

In the image of the computer user as a gigantic flying eye or head, we are invited to assume the iconography and perspective of a deity. The 1960s-era photographs of Earth seen from outer space split our consciousness in two: we are this god-like, extraterrestrial eye, but we are also unimaginably small specks on the blue marble in the distance. In the graphical images that Garb analyzes, though, there is no longer a blue marble to identify with—and no stories or accompanying information reminding us that there was once a photographic lens there or an uninterrupted continuum of space between that place and the world that we currently occupy. The Cartesian silicon dream would have it that digital media, the Internet, and virtual worlds free us from the constraints of physical, sensory, and space-bound reality. They allow us to become someone else or to overcome geographical divides, all at seemingly little cost to, and perhaps even to the benefit of, the environment, worldly action and concerns, and the fabric of social relations.

This dream, as Garb and others have claimed, is a myth, similar to those that have accrued to the purportedly uncharted frontiers of earthly and outer space. Howard Rheingold, a former editor of the *Whole Earth Review* and *Millennium Whole Earth Catalog*, says as much with the title of his book *The Virtual Community: Homesteading on the Electronic Frontier*. The myth of digital media as immaterial, abstract, and unworldly allows us to paper over the reality of embodied, lived experience (including experiences of gender, race, sexuality, disability, and economic hardship), as well as the reality of Earth-bound, time-bound, limit-bound existence in general. The myth emerges in tandem with the increasing association of knowledge with data and information and of thinking with their processing. This association is in turn predicated on the idea that computational, quantitative ways of thinking—ways of thinking that can be expressed by a mathematical notation system and rendered in what Alan Turing called "computable numbers"—are the best or the only truly accurate ways of thinking.[12]

:: :: ::

These short parables about the Blue Marble and the silicon dreams that followed, alternately cherished and critiqued by pioneers of the information age, are here to set the stage for an inquiry into the relationship between digital media and alienation from Earth-bound and time-bound experience, perception, and thought. Like the early adopters of computing technology, many of whom expressed skepticism about the effects of widespread digitalization at the same time that they celebrated its potentials, in this book I approach digital culture in an extramoral sense, offering neither a purely utopian nor strictly dystopian account of it. On the one hand, I elaborate a critique of digitality, specifically of the notion that everything can be rendered in numeric, encoded, and computable form; on the other, I claim that contemporary artists and practitioners who use digital media have often rejected this dream, in many cases actively subverting it, and that it is in no way endemic to the matter that supports these works' continued existence. My primary interlocutors for establishing the first point are the British mathematician and computer pioneer Alan Turing and the French philosopher Henri Bergson, best known for his theories of matter, perception, and duration and for his cryptic yet sustained elaboration of the concept of the virtual. The digital media makers through whose work I develop the second point are diverse in kind: they include Agnès Varda, grande dame of the French New Wave, as well as lesser known figures like the artist Erin Shirreff, the electronic music duo Matmos, and the largely anonymous participants of the Occupy Wall Street movement. These figures do not form a coherent set in terms of their geographical origins or current whereabouts nor in terms of their modes of practice or the extent to which they are expressly identified with computing, new media art, or digital culture. What unites the practitioners in this group is that they are denizens of the twenty-first century who have all attempted to grapple with the relationship between analog and digital technology and who make works of digital media that cannot be understood without recourse to earthly, time-bound matter and concerns.

In addition to these figures who form the book's substantive archive, there are a number of contemporary scholars whose work has been inspirational for this study. N. Katherine Hayles established for the emerging field of new media studies an idea similar to that of Garb's "silicon dream": that "the great dream and promise of information is that it can be free from the material constraints that govern the mortal world" and "achieve effective immortality."[13] In *Reading the Figural, or, Philosophy after the New Media*, D. N. Rodowick observed that the digital arts are "the most radical instance yet of an old Cartesian dream: [that] the best representations are the most immaterial ones, because they seem to free the mind from the body and the world of substance."[14] These scholars provided my initial access point to the notion of a digital Cartesian dream, widespread as a symptom in popular media and culture, an idea that Rodowick also touches upon in *The Virtual Life of Film*. In her book *Carnal Thoughts*, Vivian Sobchack cautions against digital media's promise to liberate its users from "the pull of what might be termed moral and physical *gravity*"; she also describes how electronic technologies invite the viewer into a "spatially decentered, weakly temporalized and quasi-disembodied (or diffusely embodied) state." What is lost, Sobchack asks, when digital media promise to liberate users from the limitations of space and time, or indeed when spatiotemporal finitude is understood as a form of imprisonment rather than as the very precondition for perception, thought, and action? For Sobchack, as for Arendt, the overcoming of gravity risks devaluing "grounded investment in the human body and enworlded action."[15]

Some of the most relevant current scholarship on Bergson comes from film theory and gender studies. Bliss Lim's *Translating Time: Cinema, the Fantastic, and Temporal Critique* juxtaposes Bergson's "corrective theory of time" with postcolonial scholarship to argue that Newtonian time, largely a Western construct, occludes the more deracinated, plural, crisscrossing forms of temporality that are on display in non-Western science fiction and fantasy film. I join Lim in reading Bergson's critique of the cinematograph not as a rejection of the medium as such but as an arrow directed at schools of thought that "regard time as a measurable quantity . . . the scientific and mathematical view of homogenous time . . . [from] the legacy of Newton's clockwork universe."[16] In *Time Travels: Feminism, Nature, Power*, Elizabeth Grosz offers an observation that I take as another embarkation point for this study: that the notion of the virtual, one of Bergson's signature if slippery concepts, is far richer and more complex than today's vocabulary suggests: it "has been with us a remarkably long time. It is a coherent and functional idea already in Plato's writings, where both Ideas and simulacra exist in some state of virtuality."[17] Jean Baudrillard suggests something similar when he complains that in its contemporary sense "the virtual stands opposed to the real. . . . We no longer have the good old philosophical sense of the term, where the virtual was what was destined to become actual, or where a dialectic was established between the two."[18]

Today the virtual has become practically synonymous with digital and computer-based technology and media. But this sense of the word, as we see in Garb's essay, emerged relatively late in the twentieth century. The 1960 edition of *Roget's Thesaurus* perhaps unwittingly captures the good old philosophical dialectic that Baudrillard refers to, and his plaint about its cleaving. In that volume the word *virtual* is indexed under the entry for "Nonexistence," along with the following synonyms: "unreal, potential, unsubstantial, chimerical, fabulous, ideal." But *virtual* is also indexed under another heading, "Intrinsicality." In this competing entry, synonyms include "immanent, inherent, incarnate, indwelling, indigenous, instinctive, natural."[19] These clashing entries suggest that virtuality, at the dawn of the information era, was an antilogy or a contranym: it simultaneously invoked existence and nonexistence, reality and unreality, fact and fable. Fifty years later, though, the immanent, incarnate, and indwelling have been submerged in favor of the ideal and the unsubstantial, which, in a Neo-Platonic turn, have likewise become synonyms for one another.

Meanings for the word *virtual* that have nothing to do with the simulacral or immaterial first appear in the English language in 1398. The word is descended from the medieval Latin *virtuālis*; its oldest definition is that which is "possessed of certain physical virtues or capacities; effective in respect of inherent natural qualities or powers; capable of exerting influence by means of such qualities."[20] This ancient virtuality was not opposed to the actual. It was deeply rooted in the present world, conducive to earthly actions and concerns, and infused with embodied, sensorial, time-bound experience. It has the whiff of what is conveyed by the still extant expression "I am virtually there." This phrase does not mean "I'm not there" nor "I appear to be there by simulated proxy, but in actuality I am somewhere else," but rather "I am nearly there, almost there, close enough to be practically indistinguishable from being there."

Scholars such as Gilles Deleuze, Pierre Lévy, Brian Massumi, Quentin Meillassoux, and Rob Shields have worked closely with this more grizzled sense of virtuality; their commentaries appear from time to time throughout this book. In *The Virtual*, Shields critiques the notion that the virtual is not "real" and outlines some of the dangers of the fantasy of pure abstraction. Like Deleuze, Grosz, and others, he invokes Proust, who wrote that memories are virtual in the sense that they are "real without being actual, ideal without being abstract."[21] In this Proustian formulation, the virtual is not a parallel, unreal world, separated by a chasm from the present world, but an interstice that connects the two and is the site of becoming or being-in-process. Lévy offers the following related formula: "The virtual . . . has little relationship to that which is false, illusory, or imaginary. [It] is by no means the opposite of the real. On the contrary, it is a fecund and powerful mode of being that expands the process of creation."[22] Massumi defines the virtual as "that which is maximally abstract yet real, whose reality is that of potential—pure relationality, the interval of change, the in-itself of transformation."[23] Hayles, in turn, calls for the recovery of "a sense of the virtual that fully recognizes the importance of the embodied processes constituting the lifeworld of human beings."[24]

These writers suggest that a virtual virtuality, more enabling and capacious than its successor, lies nascent within it, and that we might even seek to recover it in works of digital media. This is in part the undertaking of this book. The task does not require that we choose between the two terms in Baudrillard's dialectic, nor that we adopt the stance of an analog, materialist purist to recover what is lost, nor even that we privilege and isolate the sublimated moment of digital-analog synthesis. Rather it understands the virtual from another angle: as a new reality on the cusp of existence that emerges in an interval of present time that is rich with past and future images. The virtual, in this view, is a potential treasure chest full of images that perform and elicit memory, intuition, and speculation, all while retaining an underlying continuity with what is here in the present moment. The figures in this book deny the digital its divorce from the tangible and time-bound, implicitly critiquing the Cartesian dream of immateriality and countering transcendence with immanence. At the same time they reveal other, more genuinely progressive potentials that lie dormant in digital forms, in large part by the way they work with time and change.

:: :: ::

The chapters that follow elaborate these ideas primarily through Bergson's philosophical writings on time and the virtual, as they illuminate and are illuminated by contemporary, time-based works of art, film, and video. However, chapter 1, "Keys to Turing," provides a backstory to this argument, dialing back the clock to the life and work of Alan Turing. Turing is perhaps best known for his World War II military intelligence achievements at Bletchley Park in England, where he cracked the infamous German Enigma cipher. As part of this work, he designed a series of machines that served as prototypes for the modern computer. Turing was also a brilliant mathematician who conducted pioneering research in artificial intelligence. In the 1950s, though, he was arrested on gross indecency charges and, as an alternative to prison, was subjected to chemical castration treatments that may have driven him to suicide. The cause of death was ingestion of a poisoned apple, a possible reference to Disney's *Snow White,* which was Turing's favorite film and one from which he frequently quoted. According to an unproven rumor, the Apple Computer logo pays tribute to Turing.

Turing's life and work represent a queer drive in the development of the computer. Proceeding through close analysis of Turing's biography, writings, and texts that inspired him, I argue that his sexuality—or, more specifically, the way he endured the oppressive social burdens of homosexuality in his time—was not incidental to his mental genius and not simply a side note to his mathematical achievements. Rather his deep immersion in logic and machines can be read as part of a search for a transparent form of communication, one that would be free of the enigmas and opacity of everyday human interaction. Computer language offered a refuge, albeit one with its own limitations, from the kinds of cryptic channels through which gay men in World War II–era England were obliged to interact with one another. The quest for this refuge shaped and drove his research, until he reached a remarkable turning point and came to define intelligence itself as the ability to engage in casual, sociable, even illogical conversation: to simulate, in other words, the analog aspects of face-to-face interaction.

In chapter 2, "Christian Marclay's Two Clocks," I elaborate definitions of the analog, the digital, and the virtual in large part through Bergson's collected writings. The chapter begins with a meditation on Bergson's infamous critique of the cinematograph: his perplexing claim that the cinema is not a genuinely time-based medium and his use of it as a metaphor for static, synchronic ways of seeing and thinking that fail to apprehend life as movement and change. Gilles Deleuze, perhaps the most well-known heir to Bergson's thought, found this claim so peculiar that he devoted two whole books to its refutation—at least this would be one way to understand the impetus behind *Cinema 1: The Movement-Image* and *Cinema 2: The Time-Image.* By juxtaposing the cinematograph with a suite of other metaphors found throughout Bergson's writings, I attempt to account for his rejection of the cinema in greater detail.

I sort through these new ways to understand the digital, the analog, and the virtual through a work of visual art, Christian Marclay's *The Clock* (2010). This twenty-four-hour digital video is made entirely out of sampled found footage of images of clocks large and small, and it functions as an accurate timepiece. My reading of the video installation begins with a simple question: Is this a digital or an analog clock? The attempt to answer it unsolders these two terms from their medium-specific connotations and reveals them to be less fully opposed to one another than one might think.

Chapter 3, "Matter, Time, and the Digital: Agnès Varda's Videos," explores the connections between organic and inorganic matter and digital video aesthetics in Varda's documentaries *The Gleaners and I* (2000) and *The Beaches of Agnès* (2008), which use digital video as a way to depict earthly, embodied, and, importantly, mortal concerns. These films are expressly about aging, memory, and the urge to forestall as well as the aspiration to let go of passing time. *The Gleaners and I* is a film about salvaging and demonstrates a relatively early use of consumer-grade digital equipment to create cinema that is materialist, feminist, phenomenological, and political. *The Beaches of Agnès* is a film about memory that, contrary to the digital dream of permanence, total recall, and infinite storage, is underwritten by forgetting and displacement. Varda imagines a form of virtual memory that is involuntary, indirect, and noninstantaneous—a digital memory that is not modeled on the principles of computer storage and the database. These late films of Varda's are exquisitely attuned to the new and progressive in equal measure with decay and dissolution and to states of evolution and change that are inseparable from the visible signs of entropy toward which her camera often gravitates. My readings of the feature-length films are supplemented by observations about her video installation *The Widows of Noirmoutier* (2006), a work that is in dialogue with both of these films.

Chapter 4, "Beyond Repetition: Victor Burgin's Loops," focuses on two video installation pieces by the artist and writer Victor Burgin, *The Little House* (2005), which explores Rudolph Schindler's King's Road House in Los Angeles, and *A Place to Read* (2010), which includes a digital reconstruction of Sedad Hakkı Eldem's Taslik Khave coffeehouse in Istanbul. Both of these works are structured as loops. Taking inspiration from this form, I identify and describe modes of repetition that do not operate according to the logic of the death drive, of the Freudian repetition compulsion, nor of eternal return without difference. Burgin's video loops repeat, but they do so in a Bergsonian way, as four-dimensional spirals or cones that activate connections across multiple viewings, linking past images back to the present and vice versa, as well as opening out toward the future. The repetitions are more properly reprises, refrains, or rereadings, a distinction that I develop through Deleuze as well as through Bergson's writings on the phenomenon of déjà vu. They repeat both in their looped structure in the gallery installation setting and in terms of the way they engage with the diverse combinations of texts, histories, and visual materials that have inspired them. These disparate points are connected not as a linear chronology, nor simply by juxtaposing them in opposition to one another, but rather through a slow, digitally crafted looping, panning, and scrolling movement, a trope that cannot help but emphasize continuity over disconnection. In Deleuze's beautiful phrase, Burgin's videos supply "a story [*histoire*] that no longer has a place . . . for places that no longer have a history [*histoire*]."[25] In *A Place to Read*, this place is a digital reconstruction of a destroyed Turkish coffeehouse, which Burgin created using 3-D modeling software.

Chapter 5, "The Powers of the Virtual," takes up Deleuze's concept of the powers of the false, a notion that has, directly and indirectly, inspired a group of contemporary works of art, film, and video that fuse fact and imagination as well as documentary and fictional modes of storytelling. This power, I claim, is perhaps better understood as the power of the virtual. In *Cinema 2*, Deleuze makes clear that the powers of the false have less to do with the propagation of outright lies than with the capacity to forge or fabricate: not necessarily with the aim of deception but in the more general sense of making or inventing something new out of material that already exists. The four artists in this chapter engage in a chiasmatic gesture: they virtualize analog media, revealing its hidden potentials, and they unvirtualize digital media, reinserting it into worldly settings and relationships. Each of the four works I discuss remakes, reuses, or restages an "old," analog form of media in a new work that relies at least in part on digital technology. These works are Eric Baudelaire's *The Makes* (2009), a forged documentary video about Michelangelo Antonioni's supposed Japanese period; Ming Wong's *Persona Performa* (2011), a mixed-media installation restaging Ingmar Bergman's film and relocating it to Queens, New York; Erin Shirreff's *Roden Crater* (2009), a video about the astronomical earthwork by James Turrell created from a single photo grabbed from an online image search; and Matmos's recombinant electronic music album *For*

Alan Turing (2006), made in part from sampled, digitized sounds of a World War II–era Enigma machine. These new creations are not simply false copies of their analog source materials, nor do they aspire to replace or render them obsolete. Rather all four artists exercise the power of invention to create a virtual Antonioni film, a virtual earthwork, and so on, each of which is actual and substantive in its own right.

The book concludes with chapter 6, "Another World Is Virtual." I begin this chapter by invoking the familiar political slogan "Another world is possible," which expresses a thrilling sentiment. If we want to be absolutely precise, though, the other world invoked by its incantation is not "possible"; it is virtual. The chapter begins with a discussion of potentiality, juxtaposing Giorgio Agamben's account thereof with those of Bergson and Deleuze. Agamben's primary interlocutor is Aristotle, whereas Bergson and Deleuze follow Spinoza. But they share a philosophical goal, which is to separate the idea of the potential, which is radically open-ended, from the possible, which relates to a closed set of options that can be calculated and assigned a probability. The possible assumes that the future is already written, as a complete menu tree of more and less likely options if not as an absolutely certain outcome. It thus leaves no room for the exercise of radical free will or for the development of something utterly new, unpredictable, and other. I put these ideas into conversation with a final audio "medium" that is both old and radically new: the people's microphone, employed by the Occupy Wall Street movement in the autumn and winter of 2011. The people's microphone, in my account, is a special kind of speech-act, an actualization of the principles of collective democratic process *in viva voce*. It is truly potential, both a dramatization of political change and the means of its enactment. It is also truly virtual, a medium that is no mere simulation since it brings into being the change that it imagines.

CHAPTER 1

Keys to Turing

PEEB MYMJ NXLL BHHE LPLY CGAM XMYG HROW COPH PNCM VCHY ZKJF GZXQ FVTP QIXB WBBK IWUM QARW SZQV LJCA PBOY SXNQ TGIQ FPOA PZHO IIFZ IELM ZJYQ XQYB WZMN MXIN UAST EGDM MINE HCRC EIBA OJPB KU.

—PKTG GYOEYKII WHOBHB

Once upon a time computers were human. By and large they were women who worked in institutional laboratories.[1] Their labor involved performing simple mathematical calculations, delegated to them in order to free up the men for more complex thinking. Many such human computers were employed at code-breaking facilities during World War II. One of these was Bletchley Park in England, where, alongside their male colleagues, the female computers helped to crack some of the most notorious ciphers in history. This chapter does not directly concern these women, but it does tell a story—part Pinocchio, part Snow White—about a mathematical wizard named Alan Turing who tried to make the computer human again, and it attempts to show how his computational research was shaped at many key moments by fantasy, by a queer sensibility, and by a form of intelligence that has sometimes been labeled "feminine."

One of Turing's final projects was a computer-based, automated love-letter generator, which some have identified as the first known work of new media art.[2] It was programmed by Christopher Strachey in 1952 for the Manchester Mark I computer. As a professor at the University of

Manchester, Turing maintained this machine, which was fondly known as M.U.C., and generating love letters was but one among its many applications. It operated with a template similar to the game of Mad Libs, into which the computer would insert nouns and adjectives of endearment randomly selected from its database. By this means it wrote letters like one that Strachey published in the literary journal *Encounter*:

> Darling Sweetheart
>
> You are my avid fellow feeling. My affection curiously clings to your passionate wish. My liking yearns for your heart. You are my wistful sympathy: my tender liking.
>
> Yours beautifully
> M.U.C.[3]

As Noah Wardrip-Fruin has suggested, it is interesting that Turing and Strachey were both gay men and that their first literary collaboration for the computer imagined it as the author of a one-sided epistolary romance. The tangled mash-up of sentimentality bespeaks a twinge of longing beyond the one that already accompanies the genre; one can almost sense M.U.C.'s thirst, as if the computer were struggling to speak from the heart but discovered that its vocabulary had been arbitrarily limited to the language of clichés. Like the wooden puppet in search of the Blue Fairy, the computer longs to be human; like Snow White fleeing into the forest, it longs to be admitted into the company of those who are capable of care and affection.

I offer the story of M.U.C. as a prelude to this speculative biographical reading of the life and work of Alan Turing. This chapter is meant to provide a backstory to the remainder of the book: a queer history of the computer, in a manner of speaking, which lies dormant among histories of technology in the twentieth century. My aim is not simply to insist on the fact of Turing's identity as a gay man, as if this information would somehow provide a key to the riddle of his exceptionality. Rather I am interested in the way his research, his approach to mathematical and technical problems, and, as we see in M.U.C.'s love letters, his creative projects were tinted with a romantic, humanist sensibility, one both buoyed and thwarted by the stressors that he experienced in his daily life as a queer subject in the era of World War II and its aftermath. Turing the quixotic and persecuted lover, in other words, is not a minor character who emerges during the off-hours of Turing the great computer whiz. They are both operating at the same time, and they are inextricable.

TURING'S APPLE

Born in London on June 23, 1912, Alan Turing was educated at Sherborne School and King's College, Cambridge, where he read mathematics and attended lectures by Ludwig Wittgenstein. Legend has it that they clashed, largely due to Turing's insistence that mathematics must not remain a purely self-contained activity but should instead pursue practical, worldly applications, such as the designing of bridges and machines. In spite of these beliefs, Turing, at the tender age of twenty-five, dedicated his efforts to solving one of the most abstract, arcane mathematical riddles of his time: David Hilbert's notorious *Entscheidungsproblem*, which had perplexed such great minds as Gödel. In the course of solving this problem—thrown into the bargain, as it were—he invented a little mechanism, the Turing Machine, the idea for which formed one of the prototypes for the electronic computer. It was a hypothetical digital tool designed to perform basic operations of calculation and logic using simple if/then statements in binary code stamped on a two-way moving tape.

Turing's mathematical talents soon attracted the attention of the British government, and during World War II he was summoned from the university to serve at the top-secret military intelligence facility at Bletchley Park. Heading a team of elite cryptologists in Hut Eight—the highest level, most clandestine wing of the organization—Turing toiled away at the German Enigma code, a cipher that at the time was assumed to be unbreakable.[4] Building on the work of a group of Polish cryptologists, Turing eventually cracked the Enigma, revealing the locations of submerged U-boat fleets and helping to catalyze the end of the war in Europe. By some accounts this feat shortened the war's duration by at least three years and saved many thousands of lives. As part of his work in cryptology, Turing designed the Bombe, a room-size appliance studded with colored dials on its front and a spaghetti of tangled wires on its back. Like the Turing Machine before it, the Bombe, whose name cap-

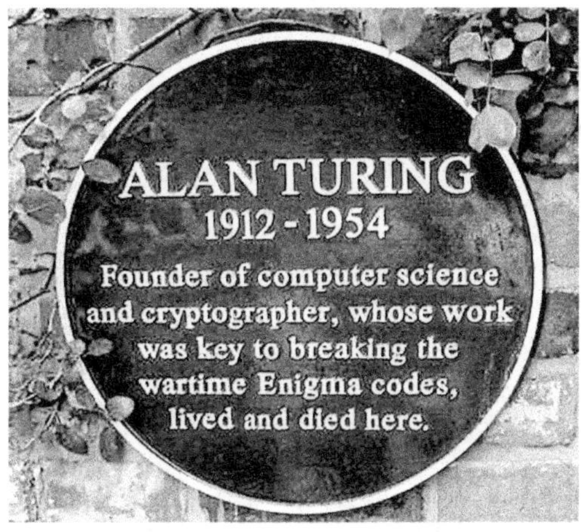

1.1. Plaque marking Alan Turing's former home in Wilmslow, Cheshire. Photo courtesy Joseph Birr-Pixton.

tures the loud ticking sound it emitted while operating, has been identified as a prototype for the modern computer.

In the postwar era, after Turing had departed Bletchley and returned to a quieter academic life at the University of Manchester, he conducted pioneering research in the field of artificial intelligence. Turing proposed a simple criterion for establishing whether a machine could be called intelligent or not: if a computer program could pass for human over a significant duration of time in a casual, open-topic conversation, conducted through a typed interface, its thinking could be said to be functionally indistinguishable from that of a human being. Just as we do not question the humanity of another person we engage in conversation, in spite of the fact that we can never know for certain whether or not that person is truly thinking, so, Turing proposed, we should not discriminate against the machine that can engage in the same style of interaction. In some of his writings Turing went so far as to compare this sort of discrimination to prejudices of race and disability, citing the example of Helen Keller, a person of great intelligence whose perceptual system and method of communication were nevertheless different from that of her contemporaries.[5] He does not mention homosexuality in this list, but its absence speaks the obvious. In a precociously poststructuralist, posthumanist, and queer gesture, Turing implied that the convincing performance of intelligence is what intelligence is. His sug-

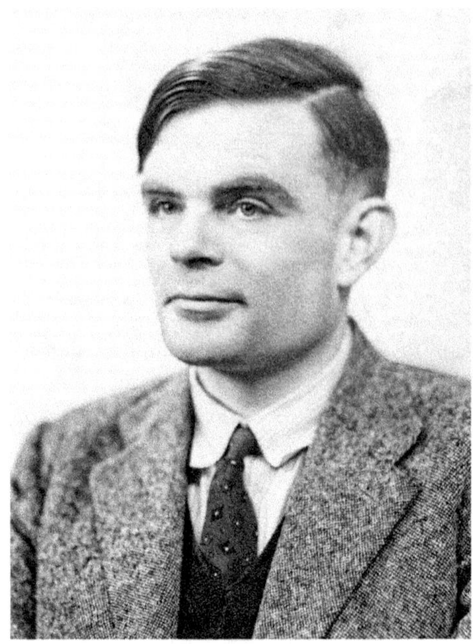

1.2. Alan Mathison Turing. Portrait taken on March 29, 1951, at the Elliott & Fry studio, at the time of his election to a Fellowship of the Royal Society. © National Portrait Gallery, London.

gestion moreover involves a somewhat perverse inversion of Cartesianism: since we cannot be sure of anything beyond what is verifiable by our own minds, it follows that we cannot logically deny the thinking capacity of any entity, organic or otherwise, that displays all the salient characteristics of thought.

The Turing Test remains a standard for assessing artificial intelligence today. It is used in the annual Loebner Prize competition, where the world's most convincing computer chatbots, mixed in with human decoys or "confederates," compete against one another to trick a panel of judges into mistaking them for real people.[6] Contrary to a prediction that Turing made, no computer program has yet managed to fool a judge for more than a handful of minutes within the space of the contest. Many humans, though, have been falsely identified as computers, and countless chatbots set loose in the wilds of the Internet have been mistaken for real people, sometimes for months at a stretch.[7] The 2011 debut of the Apple iPhone 5, the final project by Steve Jobs, brought Siri, an interactive voice-recognition program, into the world. While not attempting to "pass" as human per se, Siri attempts to understand and simulate colloquial human speech.

Neither Turing's class status nor his vast accomplishments did anything to win him special treatment when he had a disastrous run-in with the law in 1952, the same year that Strachey programmed the love-letter generator for the Mark I computer at the University of Manchester. Turing sometimes patronized the Union Tavern in Manchester, an early example of a milk bar in a neighborhood known for cruising. In that milieu he met a working-class man named Arnold Murray, with whom he had an affair. Shortly after having given Murray a set of keys to his house, Turing was robbed. When he reported the crime to the police—and divulged to them the nature of his relationship with the prime suspect—he was arrested on charges of gross indecency. In March 1952 he pled guilty in the case of *Regina v. Turing and Murray* and, as an alternative to prison, chose to undergo hormone treatments that rendered him impotent, caused him to grow breasts, and inflicted various other physical and psychical ailments on him. His meticulous biographer, John Hodges, conjectures that Turing "chose thinking and sacrificed feeling"; that is, that he opted for the course of action that allowed him to continue his work and research, knowing that this choice would temporarily obliterate his erotic life and bring with it other physical and social disabilities.[8] As an amateur biologist, Turing may have also incorrectly speculated that the effects of the hormones would be manageable and temporary. The conviction also resulted in the withdrawal of his military clearance, which, combined with the constraints of the Official Secrets Act, ensured that he never received recognition for his military intelligence work during his lifetime.[9] He did not receive a royal pardon for this conviction until 2014, sixty years after his death.

Two years after his arrest, after having suffered the brunt of chemical castration, Turing was found dead at home by his housekeeper. Although some speculate that he died by accident or may even have been murdered, the coroner ruled his death a suicide. The cause of death was ingestion of a poisoned apple, an apparent reference to Disney's *Snow White*, which was Turing's favorite film and one from which he frequently quoted. Although Turing was not chronically melancholic, he had written a letter to a friend in 1937, less than a year after having seen the Disney film, in which he confessed that he was feeling depressed and had thought of "a scheme for ending his life involving an apple and electrical wiring."[10] Turing's mother remained convinced that his death was an accident; she knew that her son often conducted science experiments in his kitchen, some of them involving toxic substances, and had warned him to exercise caution.[11] As Hodges suggests, it is possible that if Turing did indeed take his own life, he choreographed his death in such a way as to leave this possible interpretation open for her and others.

According to a persistent rumor, the Apple Computer logo is said to pay tribute to Turing. Steve Jobs and the logo's designer, Rob Janoff, denied the connection in interviews, explaining that the apple is not Turing's, but Newton's.[12] Jobs stated that the company's name was initially inspired by the All One Farm, an apple orchard where he spent time after dropping out of Reed College, and by his belief in the benefits of a fruitarian diet.[13] The apple in the computer company's best known logo has a bite taken out of it, suggesting an iconography not of Newton's falling fruit of rational enlightenment nor the pastoral purity of organic produce but rather the temptations of secret erotic knowledge: Eve's fall from grace, Snow White's fall into a sleeping death. As J. Halberstam writes, "We recognize the Apple computer symbol as a clever icon for the digitalization of the creation myth. . . . The bite now represents the *byte* of information." While Newton's apple suggests an enlightenment-style confidence in the capacity of human genius to solve and master the world's riddles, the more archaic apple casts knowledge as a seductive, treacherous, and poisonous thing. As Halberstam notes, Turing's apple is an amalgamation of the two that tells "a more complicated story . . . [suggesting] different configurations of culture and technology, science and myth, gender and discourse."[14]

These and similar pharmakon-like paradoxes, I claim, are operative throughout Turing's life story and intellectual pursuits. His choice of and approach to his research subjects wavers between investigation and fascination, the calculable and the dangerously unknown, the affectively detached and the emotionally, sexually charged. In this chapter I claim that Turing's scientific researches were influenced by erotic desire, specifically by an enmeshment in dynamics of concealed attraction, a perplexity over secrets, and a fascination with cryptic signs that might or might not indicate hidden intentions. Turing's sexuality—or, more precisely, the way he endured the oppressive social burdens of homosexuality in his time—is not fully separable from his work in mathematics,

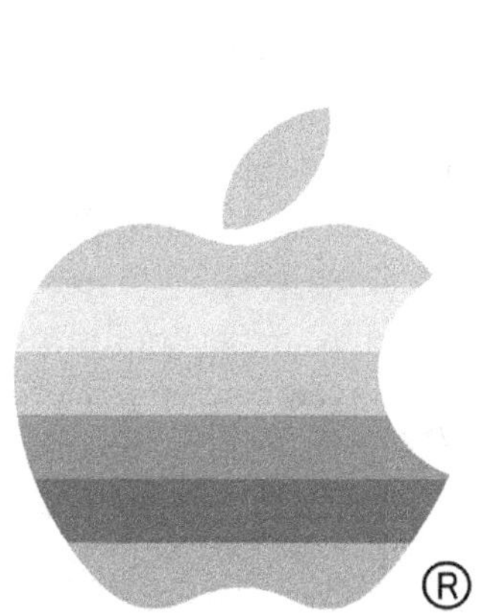

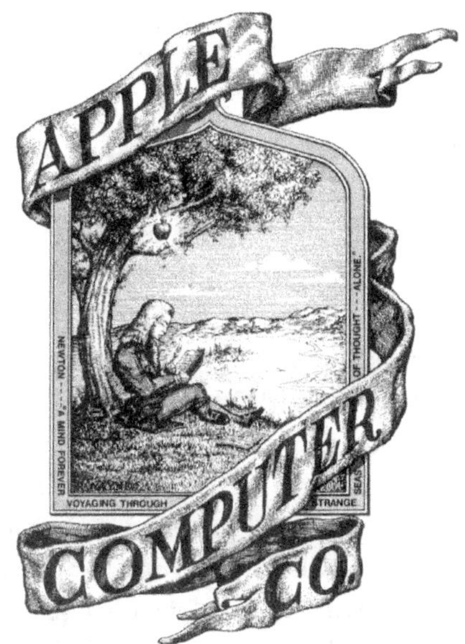

1.3. Apple Computer logo, designed by Rob Janoff, April 1, 1976.

1.4. First Apple Computer logo, pre-1976, drawn by Ronald Wayne. The text reads, "Newton—A mind forever voyaging through strange seas of thought—alone."

military intelligence, and digital computing. The history of twentieth-century computing is often understood to have been shaped by mythically ingenious, antisocial, deeply unrelational personalities, with Jobs as perhaps the most obvious example. My reading aims to tease out an alternative history of the computer, one immersed in a richly intersubjective dynamic and one that has less to do with solo genius than with de-individuation, anonymity, and impersonality.

There is a way to read Turing's abiding commitment to logic and machines as part of a quest, albeit a doomed one, for a fully transparent form of communication: a way of speaking with others that would be free of the enigmas, gaffes, and partial understandings that riddle everyday conversation. The clear-cut language of numbers and protocols offered a sanctuary for Turing, albeit one with its own limitations, of accuracy and intelligibility—a refuge from the at times confusing, at times playfully secretive strategies through which gay men in World War II–era and postwar England were obliged to connect with one another. Turing was known to be exceptionally literal-minded and frank; to the amazement of friends and colleagues, he was unflappably out in most of his relationships (those with his family constituting a notable exception). He propositioned male friends and acquaintances with a directness that bespoke unusual, even reckless trust. He also demonstrated equanimity on the occasions when his advances were rejected and remained cordial and even friendly with most of these men after the revelations.[15] While at Bletchley Park he developed a close but largely intellectual friendship with a woman named Joan Clarke, whose senior position as cryptanalyst, as opposed to human computer, gave her, in Hodges's words, "the status of honorary male"; their relationship was, in its own way, a somewhat queer one. Following the custom of many in his situation, Turing proposed marriage to her, only to retract the offer a few days later. Honest to a fault, he confessed that what he called his "homosexual tendencies" would likely destroy their partnership.[16] Fittingly, he quoted to her from Oscar Wilde in his breakup speech.[17]

Turing's computer-like lack of guile and literal-mindedness extended beyond his personal relationships. Hodges relates an anecdote in which military officers admonished him for failing to sign his government-issued identity card; by way of explanation, Turing replied that he had been told not to write anything on it.[18] More dramatically his decision to report his 1952 burglary to the police along with a vivid account of his relation to the suspect Murray demonstrated a commitment to fact (or perhaps an inflated sense of his own lack of precarity) that rose to the level of folly. As one of the arresting officers recalled, Turing proffered "a lovely statement, written in a flowing style, almost like prose, albeit beyond them in some of its phraseology." They were struck by his absence of shame: "He was a real convert. . . . He really believed he was doing the right thing."[19] The "right thing," in this case, seems to refer both to Turing's sexuality, which he bore with unrepentant candor, and his indignation at having been burgled. His elite class status provided a false security net; given his social standing, he seems to have taken for granted that his status as victim rather than criminal was assured.

While at times unvarnished to a self-sabotaging degree, Turing clearly also had an ear for more subtle uses of language when he liked, as the policeman's description of his flowing prose style attests. He had an affinity for double entendre and slightly bad puns—forms of wordplay that are also found in Polari, a cant dialect used among gay men in

London and Manchester that combines bits of Italian, rhyming slang, and backslang.[20] Hodges recounts that Turing took delight while on a boating excursion in remarking that he ought to be more careful of "the *buoys*"; he also quipped to a colleague that he might "find nice *pages* like that" in his books. Turing occasionally tried his hand at poetry and fiction. In the early 1950s he wrote a short story featuring a thinly masked alter ego named Alec Pryce in which he refers to the Turing Machine as "Pryce's buoy"—a designation that equates the computing system with an object of erotic desire. He also makes reference to finding a "gay man" with whom to consort. As Hodges notes, it is impossible to tell whether this is "plain-text or cipher-text"—explicitly or implicitly queer, an out work of gay fiction or a straight but merry lad—given that the term *gay* was in use in America at the time but not yet in England.[21] Having spent time abroad and with a circle of well-traveled acquaintances, Turing would certainly have known the American idiom. But like his other puns, the word's status as permanent quasi-code in this text leaves intact a quaver of undecidability, not so much about its meaning, which, whether literal or figurative, is unmistakably queer, but about whether its author is offering this meaning openly or with one hand held coyly behind his back. A third possibility presents itself: that Turing anticipated that both options would remain in play, that he knew that future readers might wonder about the intentions that motivated his choice of words, and that this captivating, fundamentally undecidable guessing game—the impossibility of ever knowing precisely what the other is thinking, or even whether or not the other is thinking or is capable of intelligent thought in the first place—was precisely the kind of playful interaction he wished to set in motion.

THE DECISION PROBLEM

In a 1936 paper modestly titled "On Computable Numbers with an Application to the Entscheidungsproblem," Turing provided a solution to Hilbert's legendary decision problem.[22] Hilbert had posed a logical challenge in the form of three questions: whether the system of mathematics was formally complete, consistent, and decidable. The Austrian scholar Kurt Gödel answered the first and second of these questions in his 1931 treatise "On Formally Undecidable Propositions of '*Principia*

Mathematica' and Related Systems." Gödel's solution involved encoding proofs as integers within the arithmetic itself, which allowed him to introduce self-reflexive statements into the math. One such assertion in effect said, "This statement is unprovable." The assertion could not be proven true within the logic of the system, which foundered on the rocks of such paradoxes; the system was therefore *incomplete* in Hilbert's sense. There were questions that could be posed in its terms that could not be answered within those terms.

Insofar as it exploited the flaws that self-reference tends to introduce into logical propositions, Gödel's solution resembled the move by which Bertrand Russell had discovered his famous paradox. Russell proposed that we imagine the set of all sets that do not contain themselves, and asked, Does this master set contain itself or not? The riddle has no solution. Russell's Paradox is perhaps more easily grasped through the following example. Consider a book that indexes all books that cite themselves within their own text—in other words, all self-referential books. Now imagine a counterpart book that catalogues all the books that do *not* cite or refer to themselves. Should that second book index itself? It should, but if it does, it shouldn't.[23] One is left to imagine the entry being inserted and deleted over and over again to infinity.

Turing's solution to Hilbert's Entscheidungsproblem involved a similar paradox. He answered Hilbert's question in the negative, proving that there exist mathematical problems that will remain perpetually unsolvable within mathematics' own terms. Turing proposed a hypothetical machine comprising a scanner and an infinite roll of tape divided into squares, which might be stamped with a one or a zero or left blank. Moving one box forward or backward at a time, the machine could erase an old value or enter a new one, and by this means execute algorithms. It could also be said to possess a primitive form of digital memory: numeric values could be calculated and retained in long strings of binary code. Some scripts would cause the machine to move forward, performing an ongoing series of calculations, eventually arriving at an answer. Others would arrest it in a loop, causing it to shuffle perpetually back and forth on the same squares of tape. Turing answered Hilbert's question by introducing a script for which it would be impossible to say for certain whether the machine would move forward or get trapped in a loop.[24] As the logician Richard Zach puts it, Turing proved that there is no "general mechanical procedure which, for any formal axiom system and any formula, can decide if the formula can be derived from the axioms in the logical calculus."[25]

In some ways Turing's interest in Hilbert's decision problem can be explained simply by virtue of the fact that it was a prominent challenge within formal logic and mathematics, one to which any talented young scholar would be drawn. But my capsule summary of Turing's work in this area—oversimplified from a mathematical perspective for current purposes—suggests that Turing's attraction to epistemological questions sprang from a deeper well than academic interest alone. Questions that center on the limits of knowledge—whether it is inevitable that certain unknowns will remain forever unknown—were of abiding interest throughout his work across a range of disciplines and projects. Turing was fascinated with the enigma of riddles as such, and this fascination infused both his research and his social and erotic life.

Moreover the two were not fully separate for him. Turing once said that he derived a sexual pleasure from mathematics.[26] As Adam Phillips notes in his book *On Flirtation*, "Lovers are notoriously frantic epistemologists, second only to paranoiacs and analysts as readers of signs and wonders." Phillips might have added mathematicians to this list, if not in their pursuit of ever more signs and possible interpretations of them, then in their interest in hermeneutics as such, the overarching systems by which such interpretations can be vouchsafed and proven true or false. Phillips, who wants to imagine ways that the lover might escape this obsessive form of rumination, proposes an alternative: "What would falling in love look like if knowledge of oneself or another was not the aim or result? . . . Another way of saying this might be to imagine a meeting or a relationship without answerable questions."[27]

In a sense Turing did precisely this. He imagined a machine that might endlessly ponder an unanswerable question, shuttling its ticker tape back and forth forever, stuck in a perpetual loop. The Entscheidungsproblem was settled. As in a game of "He loves me, he loves me not" played with a flower possessing a permanently indefinite number of petals, Turing had proven that there was no surefire protocol that could predict whether the final pluck would yield a one or a zero. This was cold comfort, but at least it offered the certainty that uncertainty could never be fully eradicated. During this phase of his career, Turing's

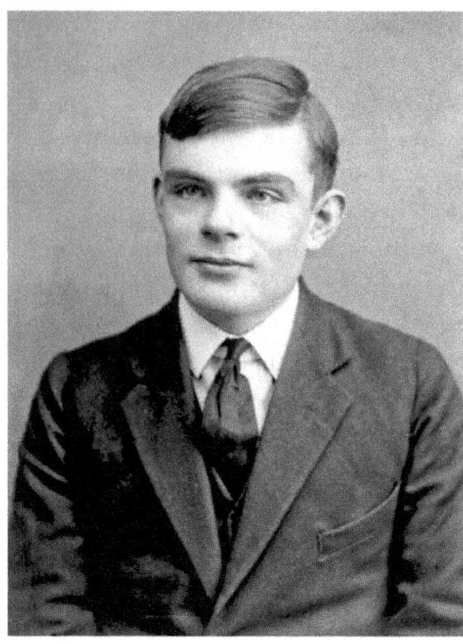

1.5. Alan Turing as a youth, age sixteen.

research involved a search for a method by which one might determine precisely where the knowable left off and the unknowable began.

Were one to perform a psychobiographical interpretation, one might find a point of origin for this quest in his relationship with Christopher Morcom, a childhood friend with whom Turing was intensely infatuated. The two boys exchanged letters sharing astronomical maps and tender accounts of midnight stargazing; in a sense their relationship was formed around the exchange of celestial hermeneutics. Turing spent a holiday with Morcom at his family home, the Clock House, and wrote an effusive note of thanks to Morcom's mother that described his sense of wonder at "the telescope, the goats, the Lab and everything."[28] The Clock House seems to have struck Turing as part fairy castle, part scientific observatory, a fusion of the magical and rational. After battling a long illness, though, Morcom passed away in 1930. In a letter to his mother dated February 16, just after hearing the news, Turing wrote, "I feel sure that I shall meet Morcom again somewhere and that there will be some work for us to do together as I believed there was for us to do here. Now that I am left to do it alone I must not let him down but put as much energy into it, if not as much interest, as if he were still here."[29] Turing here expressly dedicates his future work to his friend, making a commitment to sublimate the energy of the lost connection into his research. The phrase "if not as much interest" is telling since it makes clear that the young Turing's work in science and mathematics was stimulated by an affective spark, charged with added "interest" due to its association with his friend. Or was it the other way around? Perhaps Turing's interest in Morcom benefited from the passion that Turing already enjoyed for scientific inquiry and from their mutual curiosity about the workings of the universe. Either way, "interest" seems to apply both to their companionship and to their scholarly work in a reciprocally reinforcing way.

The young Turing, just in his eighteenth year, took this loss especially hard. Morcom's premature death left their fledgling romance permanently virtual, almost but not quite something more than a friendship. It meant that the question of whether or not Turing's feelings were requited would remain forever unresolved. It was a schoolboy-crush version of the Decision Problem that, like Hilbert's, had been answered in the negative: the only known was that he would never know whether his feelings were reciprocated, what Morcom would have been like as a grown man, how their friendship might have progressed had he lived, what great scientific discoveries they might have made together, and so on.

The ability to allow some questions to remain unanswered—in other words, to tolerate ambiguity and ambivalence—is one of the characteristics that separates humans from machines. Indeed the little indeterminacies that we perceive in others are part of what makes us perceive them *as* human: as bearers of some quality that escapes the clutches of tabulation. In his revisions to theories of psychoanalysis pioneered by Freud and Lacan, Jean Laplanche refers to something like these little incalculable qualities, which he calls "enigmatic signifiers": kernels of unintelligibility buried deep within the psyche that cannot be translated or undone.[30] In Laplanche's account of subjectivity, these kernels constitute the motive force for relations with others. They are buried relics from infancy, a time when every communication from an other was an enigma due to insufficiencies of language and comprehension. These messages, archived in memory but permanently indecipherable, are reactivated in future scenarios whenever one enters into a confusing exchange with another. On the one hand, enigmatic signifiers provoke anxiety and a potentially paranoid, even violent curiosity. On the other, this curiosity, and the impossibility of its ever being fully satisfied, is, for Laplanche, what compels us toward relations with others in the first place.

To insist on the other as absolute enigma is, in a sense, a gross refusal of recognition of that other's subjecthood. When the other is perceived as irremediably alien and mysterious, there can be no common ground, no affinity or sense of mutual responsibility. However, to disallow others the dignity of that little enigmatic kernel—to strip them of privacy, parcel them into quantifiable data, or insist that all their attributes and desires can be known, rendered as variables, quantified and calculated—is, according to Laplanchean logic, one possible definition of extreme antisociality or even psychosis. Prejudicial impulses and, at the extreme, genocidal impulses are underwritten by a certainty that the other is fully known and unchanging, so much so that this other's value or lack thereof is taken to be assessable by an algorithm in an actuarial column. On the eve of World War II a homosexual man in Europe might have had some inkling of the dangers of this way of thinking.

Computers are also antisocial, in their curious way, because they are not built to handle indeterminacy or ambivalence. It makes them hang, endlessly spin their pinwheels, and shuttle back and forth until they are rebooted. In the beginning stages of Turing's career, the stage in which he solved the Decision Problem, invented the Turing Machine, and wrote his dissertation, his intellectual work was dedicated to the elimination of ambiguity, at least in one small corner of the world. This aim resembles that of the psychotic mind bent on eradicating ambiguity. As a fantasy, though, it is an utterly logical reaction to the obstacles Turing met in his social and erotic life: taboos on the disclosure of homosexual desire and the resulting, maddening uncertainty of interpersonal interactions. The enigma of others was compounded by the fact that, in some ways, Turing was also an enigma to himself, if not with regard to his sexuality, about which he seems to have had little doubt, then in other ways. Turing spoke with a stutter and reportedly had difficulty reading his own handwriting; he frequently apologized to Morcom for his letters' illegibility. According to one of his teachers, his writing was "so bad that he lost marks frequently . . . sometimes because his misreading of his own writing led him into mistakes."[31] It was as if the very gesture of communication had to be bundled with a statement about communication's difficulty or even impossibility. The curious trait of not being able to decipher one's own writing provides a neat allegory for the condition of internal alterity, non-self-sameness, or a self unknowable to itself: a rift between the one who writes and the one who reads. Computational logic and numbers, however antisocial, offered a sanctuary for Turing, a pristine, clear space of thought and expression cleared of such thick fogs of bewilderment and the fatigue of attempting to navigate through them.

Later Turing would make an about-face of sorts. In his research into artificial intelligence, he would dream not of a human who would speak with the precision of a computer but of a computer endowed with sociability. He dreamed of a machine that would be capable of chitchat, humor, flirtation, and other nonutilitarian utterances: a computer that could engage in what the sociologist Georg Simmel calls "the lively exchange of talk as such. . . . the adequate fulfillment of a relation, which is, so to speak, nothing but relationship."[32] This change, perhaps surprisingly, came after Turing's code-breaking work during World War II.

MESSAGES FROM THE UNSEEN WORLD

During World War II military messages were sent the old-fashioned way, by radio waves and telephone cables. Like information sent over fiber optic cables or wireless Internet today, these transmissions could be intercepted and thus had to be heavily encrypted. The German Enigma machine encoded messages in a polyalphabetic cipher. In its least complex version, the machine had three rotors, each of which could be turned to one of twenty-six positions corresponding to the letters of the alphabet. The number of possible combinations on this machine was thus 26^3, or 17,576.[33] Later versions increased the number of rotors to five and six, raising the number of possible states to 26^5 and 26^6. The machines were also equipped with seven double-ended plugs, each of which could connect one letter to another manually, prior to the initial enciphering of the message. These substitutions, which were not decrypted by the receiving machine, were significant enough to thwart decryption efforts but minor enough not to distort the transmission

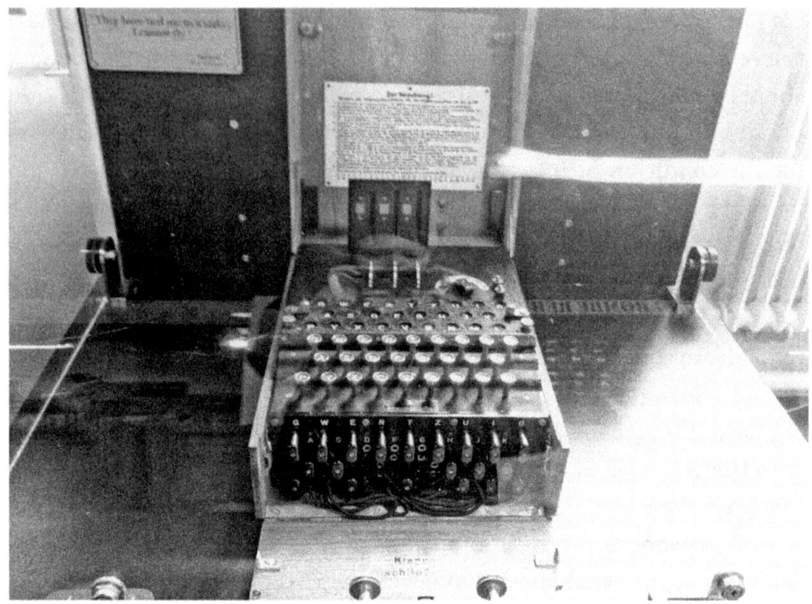

1.6. The Enigma machine. Collection of the Bletchley Park Trust. Photo by the author.

beyond legibility once the rest of the message had been correctly decoded; the reqder would still be qble to get the gist of the messqge, so to speqk. This process, called "steckering," added more than one trillion additional enciphering possibilities.[34] A key consisting of three, five, or six letters determined the initial position of the rotors. This key was reset daily, giving the code-breakers at Bletchley Park only twenty-four hours before their work would have to begin again from scratch.

The letters selected for the daily key were meant to be arbitrary, but the German operatives, convinced that their code was unbreakable, would occasionally slip and choose a meaningful key, such as the first few letters of a girlfriend's name or her initials. In addition certain words were of necessity transmitted with some frequency; for example, a daily report on climate conditions contained the word "WETTER" (WEATHER), with its helpful repetition of E-T-T-E. The code-breakers called these revealing combinations "cribs." In an act of extreme carelessness, one German military station sent the message "FEUER BRANNTEN WIE BEFOHLEN" (BEACONS LIT AS ORDERED) every evening at exactly the same time, yielding a daily crib, though unfortunately one that arrived rather late in the day.[35] Another code-cracking technique that the British military used involved planting a bomb in an unpopulated town with a highly distinctive, crib-like name, in hopes that the Germans would transmit a message containing the town's name shortly after it went off. They called this practice "gardening."

In his entry in the 1951 edition of the British *Who's Who* directory of notable persons, Turing listed "gardening, chess, and long-distance running" as his recreational activities.[36] Turing was indeed a strong distance runner and an expert chess player—he was interested in games in general, including Monopoly, for which he designed his own board to pass the time at Bletchley—but he was not in fact much of a gardener.[37] Perhaps "gardening" was another of Turing's double entendres, an inside joke that only those who had worked with him at Bletchley would be able to decode, given that this facility's existence remained classified until the 1970s.[38] The word *gardening* in the directory was itself an example of gardening, in this case a nonviolent one: an encoded message in a bottle sent out to an invisible readership. Like his references to "buoys" and "pages," these signals were part of the ongoing stream of semaphore by which Turing attempted to communicate, sometimes at great risk, with those in his community.

Encoding, whether of the sort done by the military or of the sort in which Turing engaged when he played with double meanings and homonyms, involves an act of substitution. In psychoanalytic theory this act goes by the name *displacement*: one term stands in for another, obscuring the original yet leaving it available for translation by those who crack the pattern. The things that gave away the German Enigma cipher were much like Freudian slips, parataxes, or symptoms, telling hints obtruding in a mass of gibberish. On the one hand, the work of breaking the code might proceed via computation, moving systematically through every possible substitution and ruling them out one by one; this is what the Bombe was designed to do. However, the sheer number of possibilities required that this work be accompanied by a process of intuition, otherwise known as the "probable word" method: a search for telling clues like the lover's initials, the obsessive talk about the weather, the daily lit beacon, or the name of a familiar town. Here the cryptanalyst takes on the role of the psychoanalyst, the lover-epistemologist, or per-

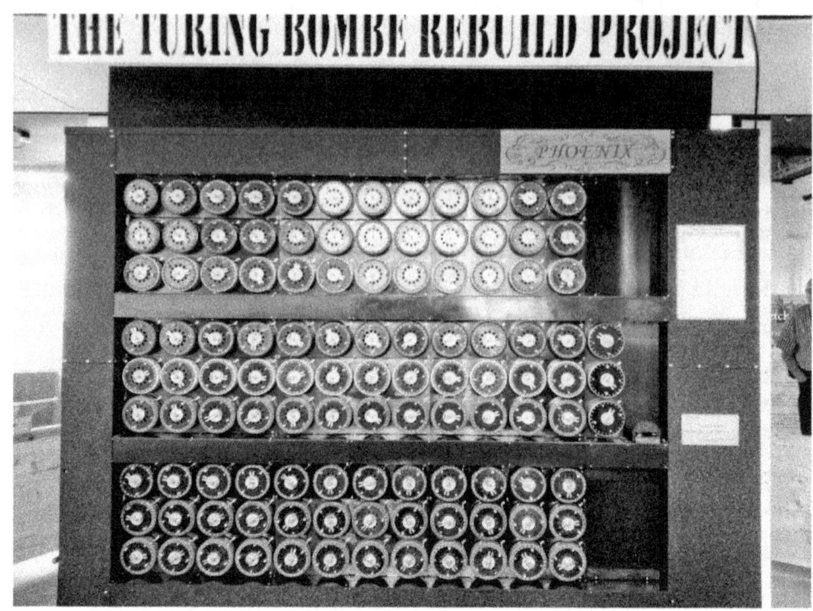

1.7. Replica of Alan Turing's Bombe computer at the museum at Bletchley Park. Photo by the author.

haps an adept poker player, scanning for obtrusions of desire, tells, and compulsive repetitions.[39]

Another way to describe this process would be to say that the digital method of code breaking must be accompanied by an analog method. In some ways a cipher is inherently digital; the word has roots in the French *chiffre* or "number," which in turn comes from the Arabic for "zero."[40] A cipher is digital not only in that its operations proceed numerically but also in that the entire text is given in advance, from the start, and the time and method by which it is decoded do not affect the underlying message in a qualitative way. To invoke a metaphor from Bergson, it is like a jigsaw puzzle. "The problem is to construct with the pieces . . . the design it is unwilling to show us," but this construction is in fact a "reconstruction."[41] The act of putting the pieces together does not add anything substantive; it is merely a matter of reconstituting a picture that has been determined in advance. It makes no difference how many hours or nanoseconds we take to decode a cipher, whether we work alone or in a team, with only our hands or employing some sort of tool. Like a photograph rendered in millions of colored pixels on a computer screen, the end result will always be the same if done correctly, regardless of the protocol we employ to render it. The underlying message is outside time; it does not change over the duration of its reconstruction.

Turing began work on the Enigma code using purely digital methods. To continue with Bergson's puzzle metaphor, the project was, in a sense, to design a machine that would solve the puzzle without making any assumptions about its final picture, using sheer computational speed to try each piece in each slot in a systematic fashion. Parallel to this pursuit, though, Turing began to insist on the value of the analog method, one predicated on a certain intuition or knack for seeing resemblances, analogies, and meaningful patterns, and through these resemblances keying into the enigmas of intersubjectivity, the little psychopathologies of everyday communication.

In his doctoral thesis Turing had written about the faculty of intuition, defining it as the capacity for "making spontaneous judgments which are not the result of conscious trains of reasoning."[42] Although from a standpoint of design and practical implementation, he gravitated toward computation, he was also compelled by intuition: by modes of thought that explored the interpretively open, diachronic aspects of language rather than operating in the closed, synchronic, predictable space of numerical calculation. This interest seems to have taken hold in the years directly following Morcom's death. During a 1932 stay at the Clock House, which Turing still visited and where he retained a relationship with Morcom's family, Turing wrote an essay entitled "Nature of Spirit." In this short meditation he comes to the conclusion that not everything in the universe can be predicted based on the laws of science: "It used to be supposed . . . that if everything was known about the universe at any particular moment then we can predict what it will be through all the future. . . . [However,] when we are dealing with atoms and electrons we are quite unable to know the exact state of them; our instruments being made of atoms and electrons themselves. The conception then of being able to know the exact state of the universe then really must break down. . . . The theory which held that as eclipses etc. were predestined so were all our actions breaks down too."[43]

:: :: ::

Intuition is the faculty that helps us to understand that which is not predestined and cannot be calculated or predicted in advance. It is also a privileged faculty for Bergson. His account of intuition attributes to it an open-endedness, almost a form of divination: speculation about the contents of a picture puzzle without yet knowing what it depicts. This capacity, in Bergson's vocabulary, is the opposite of "intellect," which also sometimes goes by the name of "intelligence" in his writings. For Bergson intellect is a problematic business: it is not reflective or contemplative; it apprehends the world in a utilitarian way in which perceptions are deemed valuable only insofar as they suggest possible actions of will upon the matter they reveal. Its way of viewing the world is "an *effective* one, limited to objects on which the being can act: it is a vision that is *canalized*." Intellectual vision proceeds via tunnel vision; it relegates unimportant things to the periphery. It is also most at home in the world of solid matter: the intellect "dislikes what is fluid, and solidifies everything it touches." It is like a sieve; that which is moving, liquid, or indeterminate tends to slip through it, leaving behind separate, static known quantities. "Of the discontinuous alone does the intellect form a clear idea," Bergson writes.[44]

Bergson also associates the intellect with plant and animal life. This somewhat surprising attribution makes clear that for Bergson intellection is not a superior faculty of the human mind. It is a faculty that is operative in even the most primitive life forms, even in unspecified biological matter. Bergson writes in *The Creative Mind*, "Every tissue of a living being generalizes, I mean classifies, since it knows how to gather, in the environment in which it lies, the parts or elements which can satisfy this or that one of its needs."[45] According to this view, the capacity for abstraction and categorical thinking—a capacity that in Bergson's view is directly related to the ability to use language, to think logically, and to engage in rational activity—is not a power unique to humanity but an ability that is utilized by even the most primitive cellular life forms every time they gravitate toward objects that fall under the heading of "nutrition" or avoid objects classified as "toxins." It is a basic prerequisite for biological persistence. Elizabeth Grosz suggests that one of Bergson's most striking hypotheses is that "the brain does not make humans more intelligent than animals; the brain is not the repository of ideas, mind, freedom, or creativity."[46] Practical action of any sort, whether on the part of a cell differentiating one kind of molecule from another or a team of scientists building a computer, relies on the faculties of abstraction, generalization, and classification. Otherwise it would be as if the cell were encountering a completely novel, unidentifiable substance each time another bit of matter came into contact with its membrane. It is this simple faculty that Bergson calls by the name "intellect."

Without intellect, life might never have gotten off the ground. But there are consequences to the intellect's way of seeing and understanding the world. Through the work of the intellect, Bergson writes in *Creative Evolution*, matter is entirely subordinated to purposeful action: it is "made to appear to our thought as an immense piece of cloth in which we can cut out what we will and sew it together again as we please." This way of thinking, a hangover from the days of monocellular life, ultimately leads us to "treat the living like the lifeless."[47] While the intellect is absolutely necessary to ensure that basic vital functions are met, it is not attuned to moving, durational, living, breathing reality. It is attuned to outlines and categories, to space rather than time. It must freeze-frame matter in order to apprehend or manipulate it.

For Bergson the universe is not a finite collection of enumerable particles. It is in a state of continuous "creative evolution" in which changes of state are part of an indivisible movement, fully saturated with durational time, and in which we cannot saw the particles off into separate entities and then analyze them as if they were distinct from the whole. Bergson uses the term *evolution* in ways that can be perplexing at times; he associates it with the biological but also with artistic creativity, invention, movements of thought, and, implicitly, political change. But Bergsonian evolution is non-Darwinist, at least not in the way Darwin is commonly misconstrued; it is not about "survival of the fittest," competition, natural selection, or the liberal notion of teleological progress toward ever-greater excellence and robustness.[48] Rather it has to do with the possibility for deviation from what already exists. Evolution means change, not progress or victory, and it includes entropic change.

In a related point, for Bergson "negation" itself is a form of creation or affirmation, not a destruction or elimination.[49]

As Bergson matter-of-factly puts it, the intellect "is characterized by a natural inability to comprehend life." He would probably have concluded that digital computers too cannot really comprehend life. Like monocellular organisms, they may have intellectual intelligence, but they lack intuitive intelligence. In *Creative Evolution*, Bergson characterizes intuition as a kind of "sympathy."[50] He offers his most detailed account of it in a late text, *The Two Sources of Morality and Religion*, where, interestingly, he embeds it in a discussion about the emotions. He suggests that there are two kinds of emotion. One is "the consequence of an idea, or of a mental picture . . . the result of an intellectual state"; this type is "self-sufficient" and is stirred as a direct, even reflexive reaction to a perception. This kind of emotion is associated with the intellect. The second type of emotion, by contrast, has to do with intuition; it is "a cause and not an effect," and it is "pregnant with representations, not one of which is actually formed." Bergson suggests that this second kind of emotion "can alone be productive of ideas." It produces something "which seemed to baffle expression, and yet which *had* to express itself." He notes that this second type of emotion has been "unfairly maligned as 'feminine.'"[51]

In the context of code breaking, the intuitive method might involve just such a "feminine" or emotional approach to language. It might require that the analyst decode social cues embedded in gendered grammar ("das Wetter") and hierarchized modes of address ("wie befohlen"). One can imagine a computer program that would index all these grammatical structures, akin to contemporary automated translation services like Google Translate, but even today these automated programs lack the ability to adjust their approach to the text to account for the idiosyncrasies of styles of utterance, to differentiate colloquial speech from grammatically perfect speech, and of course for tone and context. Like Bergson's picture puzzle, the computer decoder, at least when left to its own devices, operates as if its text were outside time and outside relationships, emanating from an unchanging system of grammar and a finite dictionary stocked with static definitions. It is a purely linguistic system rather than a fully semiotic one. The intuitive or "analog" method, by contrast, requires the ability to think in time, to extrapolate

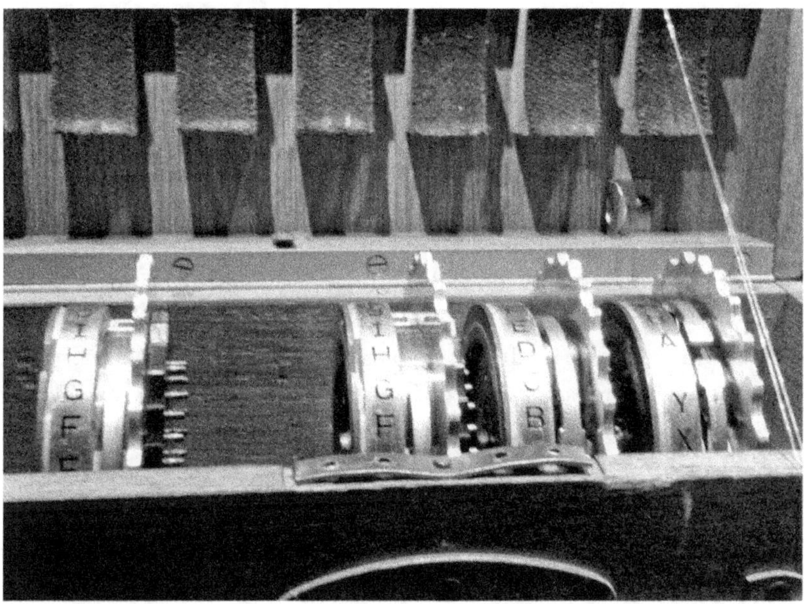

1.8. Enigma machine rotors on display at the museum at Bletchley Park. Photo by the author.

forward and backward, and to think relationally, attuning to the parataxes of desire.

Turing is still perhaps best known for his work in cryptology, specifically for cracking the Enigma. This achievement has at times been understood as purely computational. But the capacities to think when confronted with indeterminacy, to abide the undecidable, and to relinquish the fiction of a fully transparent semiotic also played significant roles in the breaking of the Enigma cipher: the ability to think intuitively and to exist in a world in which not every switch is unquestionably in either an "on" or an "off" position. These abilities are also, I would like to suggest, queer, in the sense that they are nonbinary and thrive in spaces and times of communicative complexity. What might qualify as one of the greatest victories in the history of military intelligence curiously required a "feminine," queer style of thought, characterized by a gift for creating and decoding doubly and triply couched meanings, a rock-like ability to bear the burden of secrets as if one's very life depended on it, and antennae finely tuned to unintended signals of affect and relation.

The Turk was a late eighteenth-century automaton that could play a winning game of chess against a skilled opponent. However, the Turk was in fact not a machine but a hookah-smoking puppet on a mirror-encased chamber within which a diminutive human grandmaster was ensconced. Walter Benjamin famously saw a political allegory in this contraption.[52] In light of Turing's education and training, one might imagine his vision of an "intelligent machine" to be modeled after something like the Turk: a chess whiz. But his landmark 1950 essay, "Computing Machinery and Intelligence," proposes a very different definition. In this text Turing provides what Hodges calls "an operational definition of 'thinking' or 'intelligence' or 'consciousness'" for machines that is in many ways the opposite of Benjamin's chess-playing automaton.[53] Turing's definition of intelligence is much closer to intuition than intellect in Bergson's senses of those words; it involves the ability to produce creative thought in real time, or at least the convincing impression of it.

Turing modeled his test for intelligence after a parlor game in which an interlocutor would attempt to guess the genders of two test subjects, who would remain hidden and communicate via typewriter or an interlocutor. Turing called it the "imitation game," and he described the rules thus:

> It is played with three people, a man (A), a woman (B), and an interrogator (C) who may be of either sex. The interrogator stays in a room apart from the other two. The object of the game is for the interrogator to determine which of the other two is the man and which is the woman. He knows them by labels x and y, and at the end of the game he says either "X is A and Y is B" or "X is B and Y is A." The interrogator is allowed to put questions to A and B thus:
>
> C: Will X please tell me the length of his or her hair?
>
> Now suppose X is actually A [the man], then A must answer. It is A's object in the game to try and cause C to make the wrong identification. His answer might therefore be: "My hair is shingled, and the longest strands are about nine inches long . . ." The object of the game for the third player (B) is to help the interrogator. The best strategy for her is probably to give truthful answers. She can add such things

as "I am the woman, don't listen to him!" to her answers, but it will avail nothing as the man can make similar remarks.[54]

Turing proposes a version of the game in which A and B would be replaced by a machine and a human being, and in which C's object would be to unmask the machine. Interestingly, he puts the machine in the place of the man, and the human in the place of the woman. Scholars have noted that the Turing Test is a test of passing and that it is related by virtue of Turing's example to the performativity of gender identity.[55] As Ian Bogost points out, there is a sense in which all computers are engaged in this style of performance: "A computer, it turns out, is just a particular kind of machine that works by pretending to be another machine. . . . They pretend to be calculators, ledgers, typewriters, film splicers, telephones, vintage cameras and so much more."[56] In many cases the performance is tied to skeuomorphic design principles, an iconic resemblance between the digital version of a tool and its analog forbear. In the case of the Turing Test, though, the computer pretends to be a human interlocutor without necessarily simulating a human appearance or voice. The illusion is based on the style of dynamic interaction, not on an iconic similarity to a human figure.

According to the Test's logic, intelligence is measured by the capacity for live, spontaneous interaction in verbal language. This form of interaction could go by a much simpler name: conversation. Simmel, perhaps the preeminent theorist of conversation (as opposed to dialogue, where Plato reigns), suggests that it is "the most general vehicle for all that men have in common." For Simmel conversation is not about imparting information or even exchanging ideas or feelings. Unlike in Socratic dialogue, there need not be an aim of disabusing one's interlocutors of false notions or arriving via dialectical processes at a greater truth. In its purest form, conversation involves "talk for the sake of talking" that "becomes its own purpose."[57] Simmel uses the German reflexive verb *sich unterhalten*, a synonym for "to converse" that can also mean "to entertain or amuse," "to maintain," "to stay or support," or literally "to hold (oneself) under"; perhaps the closest equivalent in English is the phrase "to carry on (with others)." There is a sense of durational activity in this phrase: conversation passes the time, and it also implies the continuation of a movement already in progress.

Conversation involves some of the same features that Giorgio Agamben associates with gesture, a type of a movement that is not executed in the service of a goal ("marching as a means of moving the body from point A to point B"), nor even movement as "an end in itself" (as in dance). Rather gesture in Agamben's sense is a movement that makes "*a means visible as such* . . . the communication of a communicability."[58] It is the communication of a potential for communication. What matters is not precisely the aim, persuasive or otherwise, nor the content or information exchanged. Even form, if it is construed as an "end," is irrelevant for Agamben. While gesture does not map perfectly onto Simmel's definition of conversation—he stresses the importance of conversational form and calls it an "art"—it reveals an important dimension of it, that the display and modeling of a shared capacity for interaction is its distilled essence. As Leo Bersani puts it, Simmelian sociability mobilizes "the pleasure of the associative process itself, of a pure relationality which, beyond or before the satisfaction of particular needs or interests, may be at once the ground, the motive, and the goal of all relations."[59]

In his writings on sociability, Simmel initially stresses the binary aspects of conversation, noting that it "presupposes two parties." "It is two-way," he continues, adding that "among all sociological phenomena whatever, with the possible exception of looking at one another, talk is the purest and most sublimated form of two-wayness." He enlists coquetry as a subset of this dyadic relation, writing that its aim is "to play up, alternately, allusive promises and allusive withdrawals . . . [to] swing back and forth between 'yes' and 'no' without stopping at either." The relation is binary, and its possible outcomes are two in number. But this connection's survival, at least in this form, is predicated on the parties' lasting refusal to foreclose either possibility. Simmel notes that coquetry involves a "freedom from all gravity of immutable contents and permanent realities," which gives it "the character of suspension."[60] His description aligns coquetry with some of the same dynamics that characterize Turing's solution to the Decision Problem, which likewise hinges on a perpetually suspended answer to a question. It also captures the quality of permanent indeterminacy that characterized his relationship with Morcom, fated never to be actualized but preserved virtually in amber as something that always might have been. The suspension to which Simmel refers also recalls the indeterminacy that supports and maintains the Turing Test, where the game, much like a coquettish flirtation, remains active until the question of whether one's interlocutors are human or machine is finally called.

The "freedom from all gravity of immutable contents and permanent realities" of which Simmel speaks—reminiscent of the "overcoming of gravity" that Vivian Sobchack associates with the computer age—might initially strike us as a denial of commitment or a failure to act decisively, one that would seem contrary to an attitude of co-responsibility for the other and the shared social world. However, Simmel situates ethics in its pure form not in the space of "immutable contents and permanent realities" but in the more mutable space of sociability, which he calls "the play-form for the ethical forces of concrete society."[61] This is because Simmel's ethics is ultimately, as might be expected, a social ethics: one that requires more than two people and requires that relations persist buoyantly over time, beyond the completion of a given goal or finding the answer to a given question. In his sociological writings, the dyad soon expands into a collective. In one particularly compelling formulation, he states that conversation is nothing more nor less than "a means for liveliness, harmony, and common consciousness . . . a content in which all can participate alike; it also is a particular individual's gift to the group—but a gift behind which its giver becomes invisible: the subtlest and best-told stories are those from which the narrator's personality has completely vanished."[62] Simmel refers to this aspect of invisibility or anonymous vanishing into the group again in his standalone essay on sociability, where he writes that "man, as a social creature . . . has removed all the objective qualities of the personality and entered into the structure of sociability with nothing but the capacities, attractions, and interests of his pure humanity."[63] Conversation, in this sense, is not about getting to know one another; on the contrary, it requires a certain distance. In addition the pursuit of determinate goals or contractual outcomes in effect signals the game is over; as Simmel notes elsewhere, the "rhythmic exchange" in which participants are "spellbound" reaches "a caesura in the moment of its fulfillment."[64] The ethical and political forces that emerge from this rhythmic exchange require the subordination of the personality and the person not to an overarching structure or system but to an open-ended play of dynamics unfolding in time: of "capacities, attractions, and interests" that may develop and take root without specified agents or demands.

The impersonal in the Simmelian sense is thus related both to the computer and to queer subjectivity. The imitation game is a form of extended foreplay, even a perpetual deferral that refuses to binarize, to genderize, to heteronormativize, in effect, to declare that "X is A and Y is B." The secret of the Turing Test is that it doesn't really work. Like Hilbert's mathematical problem, it is undecidable. At the very moment that the question is called, its operating definition of intelligence is no longer applicable: either C has been fooled or C has outwitted the opponent. The conversation is over; the rhythmic exchange reaches a caesura. Even if the computer passes the test, the question will always remain: Could it have passed for a longer amount of time? Would it have failed eventually? There can be no ontology of intelligence, according to Turing's definition. Like desire, it is always provisional, an open-ended question, always in motion. There is no such thing as knowing or not knowing in truth or falsehood, in perpetuity. There is only knowing or not knowing in durational time, and for the present moment.

The key to Turing's life and work is not that he was gay or homosexual. Such a literal explanation does an injustice not only to the man and his genius but to all the complex, variegated, and incalculable or even infinite forms that queer subjectivity might take. The mode of thinking that would posit an identity category, fixed in its attributes over time and over a range of members, and then attempt to interpret a life's work according to that list of attributes, is utterly antithetical to the social, intuitive, analog mode of thought that I have attempted to argue quietly drove the majority of Turing's research. Some understand Turing as the genius who invented the computer and, relevant to the remainder of this study, as a co-creator of the first work of digital art. What secret, what psychological makeup, drove his inventive brilliance? Sexual identity is not the answer to the riddle, nor is antisocial scientific genius. But the keys to Turing have been hiding in plain view all along, like the key to the gemstone mine that the dwarf Dopey hangs on a hook next to the very door that it opens in Disney's *Snow White*. The answer is the same as the riddle itself: it is curiosity about all that does not compute and a fascination with the rhythmic signaling of all that communicates without being fully seen or known in advance.

CHAPTER 2

Christian Marclay's Two Clocks

In order to advance with the moving reality, you must re-place yourself within it. Install yourself within change.
—Henri Bergson, *Creative Evolution*

Bergson famously associated the cinema—or, in his preferred term, the cinematograph—with immobility. This characterization might strike some as surprising, given that cinema's very innovation was, presumably, to replicate a lifelike moving image. From its earliest attempts at narrative, cinema was also telling stories that suspended the logic of linear time through ellipsis, dream imagery, and eventually crosscutting, flashbacks, and other temporally complex techniques. The idea that film is static and unchanging goes against common sense; for many of us it is the first art form that comes to mind when we think of time-based media. As I remark in the introduction to this book, Gilles Deleuze, perhaps Bergson's most well-known philosophical heir, found this claim so peculiar that he devoted two entire books to its refutation. This is obviously an overstatement, but it would be one way of understanding the question to which *Cinema 1: The Movement-Image* and *Cinema 2: The Time-Image* provide the answer.

Deleuze begins *Cinema 1* with an exploration of Bergson's theory of movement. He notes that "it is strange that Bergson should give the oldest illusion such a modern and recent name ('cinematographic')," given that the attempt to reconstitute movement out of static frames or instants dates back at least to Zeno's paradox.[1] In fact there is a passage in *Creative Evolution* in which Bergson himself acknowledges that the "illusion of movement" in cinema is not strictly speaking an illusion. He conceded that there *is* real movement in cinema but suggested that it is "in the apparatus" rather than in the image itself. Bergson describes the projector's movement as "abstract and simple, *movement in general*, so to speak."[2] Creating the impression of motion by running a reel of still frames through a machine, in other words, is like adding tap water to dried vegetables. The apparatus may be turning, but the images on the still frames will not truly be set in motion, any more than the vegetables will be restored to a freshly picked state.

What Bergson seems to object to most about cinema, though, is not its infamous tendency to create an impression of movement out of what are in reality only still fragments. He is no Platonist, and no moralist about the phoniness of sensory appearances. His famous definition of matter as an "aggregate of images" in *Matter and Memory* says as much.[3] Rather he objects to cinema's determinism: the fact that the entire film is already there on the reel, already engraved in a fixed number of frames. Barring some disaster with the projector, it will not reveal any genuinely new images when it is played. Cinematic movement may be false, but the trick is a problem only to the extent that it dupes us into thinking that *all* movement and all temporality is modeled after that of the film apparatus. Bergson's critique of the cinematograph falls only gently on its fragmentary state and not at all on its cave-of-shadows illusionism. His primary devil is the deterministic way of thinking: the idea that matter and movement could be unfastened from the weathering influence of time. Cinema is immobile not because its images stand still but because once they have been printed onto the celluloid, the story will be told the same old way every time the film is shown.

THE PUZZLE AND THE MELODY

We can comprehend Bergson's issues with cinema more fully by turning to two similar metaphors he invokes throughout his collected writings: the jigsaw puzzle and the mosaic.[4] As described in chapter 1, a jigsaw puzzle is made up of fragments of a larger image whose creation predates the act of putting the pieces together. Its picture is available all at once, often on the box in which the pieces are contained. It does not add up to more than the sum of its parts. The whole picture is already there, in schematic form, before we begin to work on it. If the pieces are put together properly, nothing wildly unforeseen will emerge. The duration of time that we spend on it will not qualitatively affect the result. We can put it together in an hour or over the course of a whole year, in a single sitting or in ten-minute sessions. We can start with the edges or from the center; none of these choices will affect the final image. The activity of solving a puzzle is purely mechanical. The image is not really created by the one who puts it together; it is, as Bergson puts it, "reconstructed."[5] It has been fabricated in a separate time and place from the time and place in which we assemble it. This separate time and place corresponds to an unearthly, quasi-theological realm, as well as to the deterministic, eternalistic modes of thought to which Bergson is so allergic.

Bergson's picture puzzle is a metaphor, before its time, for the digital. Like jigsaw puzzles, digital images are made up of pixel pieces that have been coded elsewhere. If the program runs properly, they will display a picture that has already been composed in advance. Like someone who assembles a puzzle, the computer that displays the image on a screen or monitor does not really create this image; it reconstructs or "renders" it. It can render it using a different suite of software programs, different hardware, on screens of dimensions large and small, but none of these is meant to alter the resulting picture beyond recognition unless a glitch or error is introduced.

In his discussion of a similar form, the mosaic, Bergson notes that in order to reproduce a painting accurately with fragments of tile, one would require "an infinity of elements infinitely small, presenting an infinity of shades."[6] In one sense his assessment is hyperbolic; modern computer users know that mere millions of pixels (not an infinite number) suffice to produce a remarkably lush digital copy of a painting to the naked eye. But in another sense Bergson's remark is still instructive: the digital image will always fail to reproduce the *whole* of the painting, even if it offers a completely identical facsimile of it. The computer cannot reproduce the *durational* aspects of the painting: the three-dimensional layers of paint that have accrued, dried, cracked, and faded over time (even if these are visible in the reproduction), or a line drawn over a shorter amount of time by the hand of a painter in a continuous gesture (even if the line appears unbroken in the copy). As Bergson notes, a picture made up of discrete points, however numerous they are, is based on the same fallacy of divisibility that plagues Zeno's paradox: on the abstract geometrical principles that claim that any whole can be endlessly divided, broken into parts, and reassembled without fundamentally altering it. The grout, cuts, and frame lines between the pieces, however micro thin, will always be there.

For Bergson the cinema too is "digital" in this sense. In *Creative Evolution*, the cinematograph is the primary culprit in promoting what he sees as a widespread misunderstanding of how new things and events are rolled out into the world. He takes cinema as an emblem for a way of seeing in which the world is "cut up into little bits . . . substituting for movement immobilities put together." We all, Bergson claims, have set going a kind of cinematograph inside us that slices up reality into discreet units of useful data, easy to instrumentalize but artificially removed from the stream of time. This operation introduces three kinds of falsifications. First, it presents essentially freeze-framed versions of objects, matter, and phenomena that are in reality always changing and in motion, however miniscule those changes and movements may be. Second, it attempts to reassemble a whole out of these instants: twenty-four static frames per second or similar "partial views put end to end," as Bergson calls them.[7] The frames, strung together like beads on a string, are taken to represent a continuous duration of time: twenty-four beads might be equivalent to one second, sixty beads might equal one minute, or whatever ratio we assign. But in reality the beads are not distinct from one another: time is more like one whole, continuous bead. Third, as with the jigsaw puzzle, all of the data are determined in advance, ready to unroll, and nothing that has not been recorded will spontaneously appear. In life, though, the utterly unexpected does appear from time to time: the pieces, beads, and still frames are not all in the box when we start.

The cinema is a symbol, albeit only a symbol, of the deterministic view of history in which everything that will ever happen has already been programmed in advance by the proverbial deity as clock maker. The clock metaphor originates in theological thought, but Bergson associates the cinematograph largely with Newtonian time: secular, scientific, statistical ways of thinking. These ways of thinking also claim for themselves a muted omniscience or modest ability to predict the future when they place confidence in the rules of probability and chance. For Bergson, though, probability is smoke and mirrors; it "works" only due to an empirical fallacy that brackets the radically unforeseen from its calculations.

Bergson provides a group of metaphors for the opposite of the cinematograph: a kind of thought that in his view is more accurately grounded in durational time. These metaphors for what some call "process-based" thought are strewn throughout his writing, and they include an inflating rubber balloon, drawing, dancing, walking through a town seen for the first time, and a melody. He turns most often to music for this purpose. In *Matter and Memory*, he analogizes true temporal continuity to a musical piece played by heart.[8] Whereas a line of grout separates the tiles of a mosaic, musical notes can liaise with one another. He suggests that in music, future notes are already somehow present in or anticipated by past and current notes, while remaining in no way predetermined by what has come before. In *The Creative Mind*, he describes this movement from the other end: just as the future is virtually anticipated in the present, so too the echoes of past notes resonate in new notes. Bergson describes this phenomenon as "the indivisible and indestructible continuity of a melody where the past enters into the present and forms with it an undivided whole." He contrasts this live musical continuity with its bead-like representation on paper, in which "we line up, one after the other, states which have become distinct."[9]

In his *Theory of Film*, Béla Balász turns to Bergson's writings on melody in order to elaborate his concept of polyphony. Balász writes that although a melody is composed of single notes in a sequence, it "has no dimension in time. . . . The last note, which may not be played for some time, is yet already present in the first. . . . The melody is not born gradually in the course of time but is already in existence as a complete entity as soon as the first note is played."[10] This passage might seem perplexing since music is Bergson's metaphor for that which is genuinely time-based, not that which exists all at once in advance. But the contradiction is only apparent. The key is that for both Balász and Bergson, the melody is an indivisible whole, not a collection of parts that can be separated, rearranged, and thrown back together without altering the music in a qualitative way. It exists "all at once" not because we might just as well play all the notes in the score as a single chord but because it is not isomorphic with itself. Unlike, say, a crystal, we cannot break off a chunk of a melody and have the resulting segments retain the identity and structure of the other connected parts. So it is, Bergson says, with time and matter as a whole.

Bergson's metaphors are refreshingly concrete, particularly the ones that are found in texts other than *Matter and Memory*, which is perhaps his most oft-read work among English speakers. They allow us to picture something as abstract as the difference between durational time and its corrupted successors in vivid detail. These metaphors, though, are still only metaphors; they are most helpful when we refrain from transposing them onto their corresponding aesthetic forms and media and onto the matter that allows them to exist in space and time. His metaphors for immanent, durational forms—music, drawing, dance—emphasize the time-based process of creating, performing, and observing these forms over and against any static objects that might result from them (the gesture of drawing a line rather than a framed drawing; the movement of walking as opposed to a map of the walk). Similarly his metaphors for deterministic forms—the cinema, the jigsaw puzzle, the mosaic—tend to bracket the time of production and reception in favor of certain physical characteristics of their assembly (the canned reel of still frames as opposed to the experience of watching a film). There are time-based works of art that behave as if they were immune to the effects of time, or that can be broken into segments without necessarily affecting our core interpretation of them. There are also stationary works of art that solicit an awareness of time passing, that "change" depending on how long we look at them, or that are designed to decay and alter their shape over the years. We may find that a wildly kinetic film operates as if it were isomorphic with itself and predictable from the start, or we may discover an experience of felt duration in a monochromatic, still image. Some works, like the one I will introduce in the following section, might even do both at the same time.

Imagine a clock that marks each second with an abrupt tick or flick of ordinal numbers. This type of clock is digital, figuratively speaking. It is cinematographic in the Bergsonian sense. Each second appears to be immobile and complete in itself, demarcated by a metaphorical line of grout between one instant and the next. By a fiction of division, each artificial unit of time appears separate. In the commonsense understanding of how time works, it is either 11:00 or 11:01, and both cannot be true at the same time, even though a moment's reflection confirms that even according to the clock's own logic, it is only "exactly" one or the other one second out of sixty. Now imagine a clock with hands that move smoothly and continuously around in a circle, or with numbers that fade into one another. This clock is analog, according to the Bergsonian definition we are now in the midst of working out. Each minute "melts" gradually into the next without abruptly articulated outlines. Although it is still only a metaphor for time, and one that suffers the flaw of depicting it spatially, it more closely imparts a felt sense of Bergsonian duration.

Christian Marclay's breathtakingly meticulous *The Clock* (2010) is a work that helps us better comprehend and appreciate the differences between these two modes. A twenty-four-hour digital video installation, *The Clock* is assembled entirely of found footage from film and television history, most of which contains images of timepieces or references to the time conveyed through dialogue. Marclay edited the footage such that the minutes unspool in order, with the timeframe that the film encompasses in a one-to-one ratio with its run time. Under the screening conditions that Marclay stipulates for the work, the video is synched to the time zone in which it is shown. It functions as an accurate timekeeper. With images collected largely from commercial Hollywood and British film, the work is a tour de force of sampling and astonishing in its precision.

Is Marclay's clock analog or digital? Its source material, celluloid film and VHS tape, suggests the former, whereas its installation as a digital video suggests the latter. But these answers take the question too literally. Instead we might ask whether the work operates according to digitalic principles (those that Bergson associates with the cinematograph and the jigsaw puzzle) or analogic principles (those that he associates with the melody), keeping in mind that such principles are not endemic to the matter out of which the works are composed. The answer to the second question requires fewer contortions of taxonomical thinking but is also less obvious.

In an initial reading, we might be tempted to label *The Clock* the ultimate example of Deleuze's time-image, a film composed entirely of images of time. The work takes time itself as its subject matter and content. We see image after image of clocks and watches of every conceivable brand, size, and shape; there are sundials, sand timers, gorgeous pocket watches, and a seemingly omnipresent Big Ben. The fact that the work screens only as a synched twenty-four-hour loop would seem further to qualify it as a durational experience, perhaps a cousin of contemporary slow film, long-form musical experiments of the 1960s, or "drag-time cinema," as Parker Tyler dubbed it, à la Warhol's *Empire* (1964).[11] All of these features would seem to situate *The Clock* conceptually on the side of the analog, as a work in which time matters: a work that makes us heavily conscious of the passage of time.

2.1. Christian Marclay, *The Clock* (2010), installation view. © Christian Marclay. Courtesy of Paula Cooper Gallery, New York, and White Cube, London. Photo by Todd-White Photography.

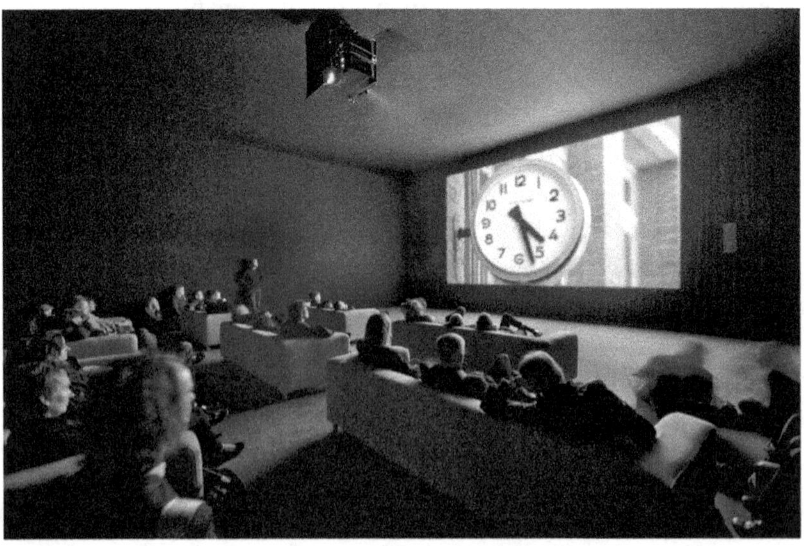

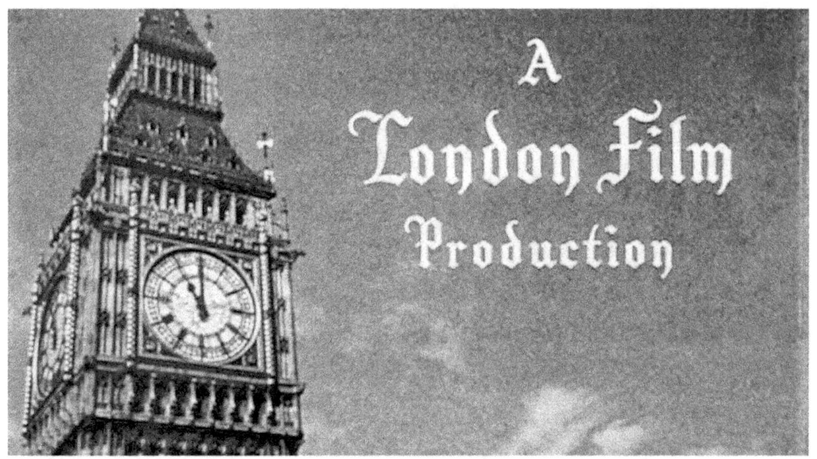

2.2. Big Ben, from the opening titles of *The Third Man*, directed by Carol Reed (1949).

And yet several critics have noted that the experience of *The Clock* is surprisingly less one of tedium or palpable endurance than piqued anticipation. A. O. Scott notes that *The Clock* "generates a peculiar kind of suspense."[12] Roberta Smith writes that while *The Clock* "is accurately parsing real time, movie time goes nuts, rushing past in an exhilarating, surprisingly addictive flood."[13] For a work that we approach by preparing ourselves for an endurance test or perhaps hoping for a meditative, contemplative state, we instead encounter the quick tempo of an action film. Much of the praise that Marclay has accrued relates to the achievement of a work of epic duration that is nevertheless intensely, even compulsively absorbing.

The suspense or captivation that *The Clock* solicits is due almost entirely to its use of classical continuity editing. Cut by cut, with the accuracy of a Swiss timepiece, it deploys the techniques of suture explained by film theorists of the 1970s. It rarely violates the syntactical conventions of continuity, rarely breaks the spell of primary identification with the look of the camera and secondary identification with the looks of characters. The transitions are for the most part straight cuts: eyeline matches and movement, direction, and position matches that carefully obey the 180-degree rule. The majority of these are also "false" matches, as film scholars sometimes call them. At 2:52 p.m., for example, there is

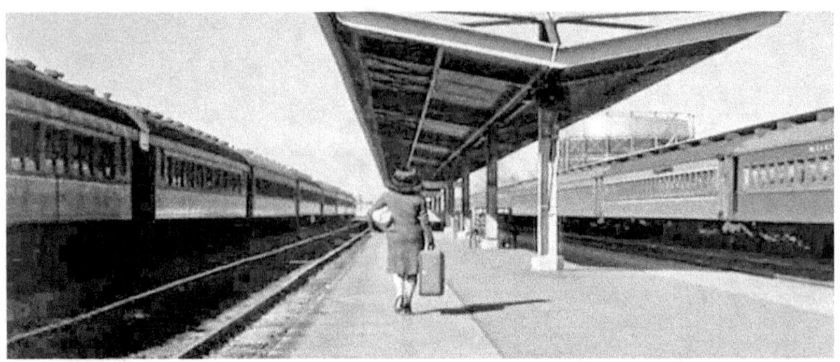

2.3. Tippi Hedren in the opening sequence of *Marnie*, directed by Alfred Hitchcock (1964).

a shot of a black-clad group driving in a van on a dusty road; the driver glances into the rearview mirror. The next shot, which, according to the rules of continuity, should reveal what this character sees in his mirror, is from a different film, as becomes clear in its reverse shot, which now reveals Nicholas Cage looking into his rearview mirror in *Raising Arizona* (1987). A similar cut brings us from an image of a character peering through binoculars to a masked point-of-view shot from another film. The movement of characters between rooms and through doors also provides ample material for false continuity cutting. A character knocks at the door of a house at 3:41 p.m., but two shots later Orson Welles replaces this figure at a different door in *Mr. Arkadin* (1955), filmed from a similar angle and distance, for a kind of cinematic knock-knock joke.

Many of Marclay's edits are less precise in their spatial geometry but still well within the parameters of narrative continuity. In these cases the rough edges are smoothed over with a skilled use of sound bridges, unsurprising for an artist who has worked extensively in audio. At 2:43 p.m. we hear the sound of a train in the distance. A cut brings us to a shot of a train platform, followed by another shot of a different train platform. A dark-haired woman with a yellow handbag walks away from us. It is the opening shot of Hitchcock's *Marnie* (1964), which, in the original film, is silent but for the sound of Tippi Hedren's shoes ticking down the platform. In *The Clock*, though, the sound of the train persists and helps us to forget that we are in fact watching a sequence strung together out of different train stations, film stocks, and so on.

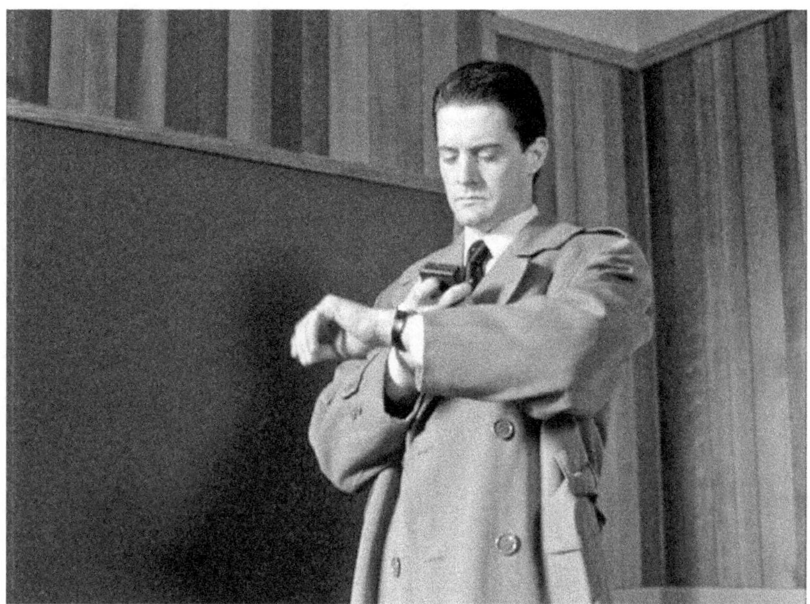

2.4. Kyle MacLachlan as Special Agent Dale Cooper, checking his watch in an episode of *Twin Peaks* (ABC, 1990).

At times Marclay uses dialogue to shift from one clip to the next, for example when a question posed in one film is answered by a character in another. Given the fact that much of the dialogue concerns the time—Kyle MacLachlan, microcassette recorder at the ready, tells Diane that it's 12:27 p.m.; Gael García Bernal speculates about the 3:10 train to Yuma—these transitions work almost effortlessly. Echoing Marclay's *Telephones* (1995), an earlier found footage work, phone calls placed in one diegesis spread into several others. At 4:10 p.m. a pan on an old-fashioned spiral phone cord continues across a cut to a distressed Mia Farrow, who now picks up the receiver. Graphic matches, particularly in close-up, likewise provide a kind of automated continuity: shots of clock faces, watches, and portable electronic devices showing the time cut easily to similar shots from other films.

While time is in large part *The Clock*'s subject matter and topic, and while the march of minutes provides a kind of coatrack on which its clips are hung, *The Clock*'s primary principle of cohesion is not time, but space. It is a work about clocks and the ways that they metaphor-

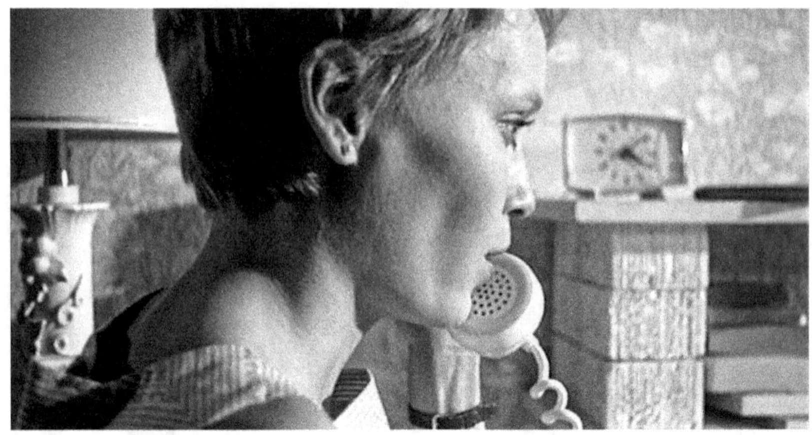

2.5. Mia Farrow on the telephone at 4:10 p.m. in *Rosemary's Baby*, directed by Roman Polanski (1968).

ize time rather than a work about duration. The work adheres strongly and expertly to the editing conventions of classical Hollywood, which, as Stephen Heath and others have explained, were inherited from Quattrocento-era principles of perspectival painting designed to provide the viewer with a naturalized perception of space that was in fact man-made.[14] These conventions operate to promote a sense of space as contiguous and mappable, even when that space does not exist in the real world, perhaps having been cobbled together out of various half-built studio sets and painted backdrops. As Marclay puts it, in *The Clock* "you become aware of how film is constructed—of these devices and tropes they constantly use. . . . An actor looks down at his watch and, suddenly, you have a close-up of the watch. But, if the first clip is in black-and-white and the next is in color, you know you've been fooled."[15]

In this way, as Marclay acknowledges in the same interview, *The Clock* owes a debt to Bruce Conner's *A MOVIE* of 1958, often credited as the first found footage film or, more precisely, with pioneering the technique of creating continuity out of diverse archival material. Marclay's description suggests that *The Clock* operates didactically, teaching a lesson about cinema's illusionism by showing how the techniques it uses to maintain the fiction of continuity can be deceptive. Of course, Conner already taught this lesson, and one could argue that cinema has been teaching it in various ways since its inception, by wittingly or unwittingly revealing its own sleights of hand.[16] The glue that holds Conner's and Marclay's disparate clips together is the same glue used in conventional narrative film: our minds piece together a Euclidean geometry of space as long as the camera does not cross the 180-degree line, as long as there is a sound bridge in place to give us the impression that we are still within earshot of the previous shot, and so on. If we are still fooled by this illusion, shame on us.

I will soon be suggesting that *The Clock* actually has more to offer than its creator attributes to it in this short, somewhat decontextualized quotation. What is clear, though, is that due to its heavy reliance on the conventions of spatial representation, *The Clock* is as much a movement-image as it is a time-image. In spite of its long duration, it formally has more in common with classical Hollywood than with *Empire* and its slow-film kin. One might call it a digital clock masquerading as an analog clock: a work whose face appears to be a valentine or eulogy to an archaic form of cinema but whose underlying mechanisms are digital in the Bergsonian sense I have described. Its pleasures are largely those of suspense. Like the second hand that ticks abruptly from one line to the next rather than gliding smoothly through them, the shots tend to be articulated with straight cuts. The cuts are rapid, as if we were zapping a remote to access scenes from around the world and across decades. Time does not wash over us; we must remain hyperalert to keep up with the work's rapid pace. *The Clock*'s underlying structure is thus cinematographic in Bergson's sense and narrative in Heath's sense: it chops up the flow of time into separate instants, and the flow of space into gridded segments. It thereby exposes the "digital" aspects of classical continuity editing in general, even when used on analog, celluloid film.

According to this reading, *The Clock* offers *not* Deleuzian or Bergsonian time-images in all their complexity but rather a database of sliced-up minutes that exist synchronically, all-at-once, and that only happen to have been arranged in a way that implies diachronic duration. The work is also at least somewhat isomorphic with itself: while not absolutely excerptable or divisible, its argument does not develop gradually over the course of its full running time; audiences seem to find that they get the structure of the work within only a few minutes. Like the jigsaw puzzle whose completed picture is visible on its box, we already know,

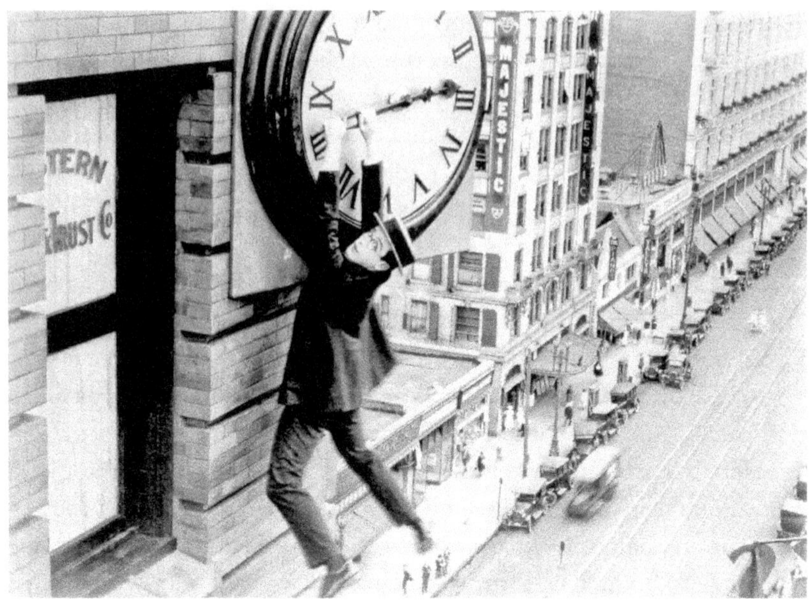

2.6. Harold Lloyd hangs from a clock in *Safety Last!*, directed by Lloyd (1923).

in a way, where *The Clock* is going and how long it will take to get there. At many points we could substitute a close-up of a different clock from a different film without significantly altering our experience or interpretation of the work.

There is an additional "digital" aspect of this clock, one that the work invites but that is to some extent at the discretion of the viewer. This is the game of trying to identify the source footage, treating *The Clock* like a long round of pub trivia. As A. O. Scott writes, "You can't help but engage . . . in a game of visual Name That Tune. This is both stimulating and somewhat enervating." Some of the most satisfying shots in *The Clock* are ones gleaned from familiar, canonical films: Harold Lloyd hanging precariously from a clock tower in *Safety Last!* (1923); the shrill scream in *The Tin Drum* (1979) that shatters the glass of a grandfather clock; Orson Welles in *The Third Man* (1949) bellowing the line "In Switzerland, they had brotherly love, they had five hundred years of democracy and peace, and what did that produce? The cuckoo clock." These clips' omission from the work's pantheon would somehow be wrong, and their appearance induces the pleasure of recognition for the avid cinephile.

The activity of identifying the footage, though, takes us out of the durational experience of the work into a scattered, deracinated encyclopedia, treating it like a massive digital database of clips. Indeed that was its genesis: Marclay hired assistants to cull through over ten thousand clips of digitized found footage and sort them into folders, one for each minute.[17] The work, when viewed this way, becomes a static archive that we match up with names and dates from our memory files (or from our smartphones). This is not necessarily a bad thing, but it is not conducive to an experience of durational time, except insofar as it compels us to speed up our note taking.

THE ANALOG

This reading of Marclay's *The Clock* as digital rather than analog and as movement-image rather than time-image is only a first step. This clock has two faces, and the second face is exquisitely attuned to durational time. In order to see it, the viewer must partly let go of both the Name That Film game, which keeps us stuck in the logic of the database, and the riveting suture of the montage, which keeps us locked in the geometry of space. When we do so there are moments when time almost seems to deviate from the metronome. For example, 3:00 p.m. seems to last an awfully long time. Bells go off as students are released from school, Little Miss Sunshine shows up late for a talent show, Big Ben pops up yet again, and we check in on a man gagged and bound in a basement who has been there since at least 2:40. We hear children singing and counting in German; it is the opening sequence of *M* (1931), which enters first as a sound bridge over a shot of a man counting on his fingers in close-up. The high-angle shot of Lang's children playing their counting game in a circle resembles the shape and movement of a clock. Here the payoff lies not simply in knowing that the image is from *M* but in the unexpected graphic match and the "reading" of this image as a clock—perhaps even as a reminder of how little time remains for the child about to be kidnapped. By 3:05 p.m. we have jumped to an image of the Palantine campaign headquarters in *Taxi Driver* (1976). Like *M*, this film is in part about child predation, and we have just seen a series of images of children being released from school; there is thus a dramatic irony superimposed on the connections demanded by conti-

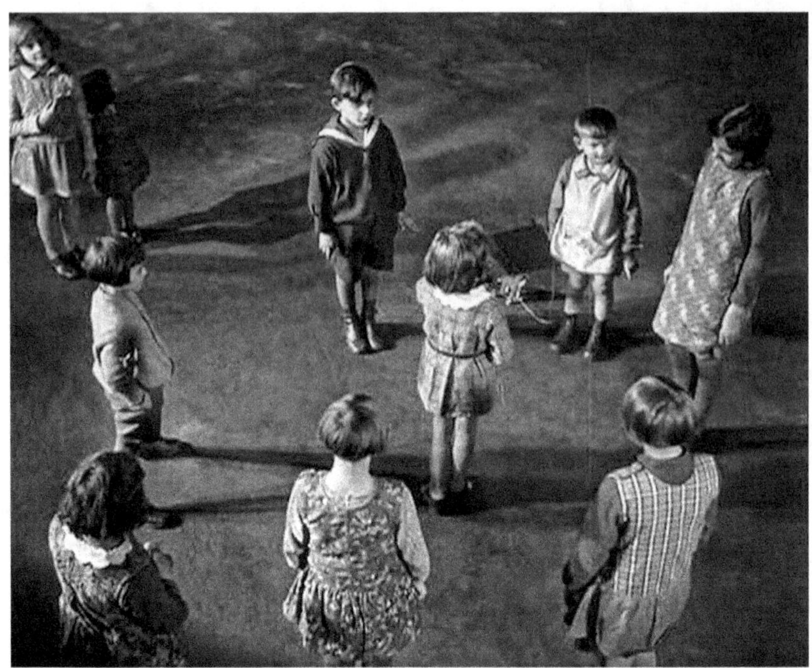

2.7. Children in a high-angle shot from *M*, directed by Fritz Lang (1931), make for an unexpected graphic match with the shape and movement of a clock.

nuity editing. At 4:18 p.m. Marclay cuts from Maggie Smith to Maggie Cheung, as if establishing continuity on two Maggies. Here the work's movement seems more playful, more "creative" in Bergson's sense, less like the outline-matching operations of the cinematograph. The duration of these sequences also feels different, like something other than the few minutes of screen time or the hundred-odd years of film history we traverse.

There is a second mode of sequencing in *The Clock* that likewise functions analogically, so to speak. Several segments concern characters who are waiting or who have been made to wait: the man bound to a column in a basement; Joan Crawford's beleaguered daughter sitting at the dining table after being served her "rare not raw" steak and refusing to eat it. Often the source films elide the full span of these characters' waiting periods because they too have abided by narrative continuity rules that allow for ellipsis and an uneven ratio of screen time to die-

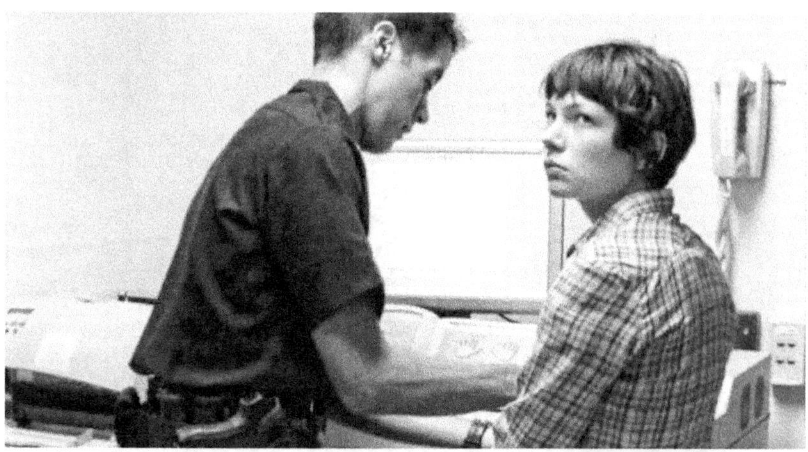

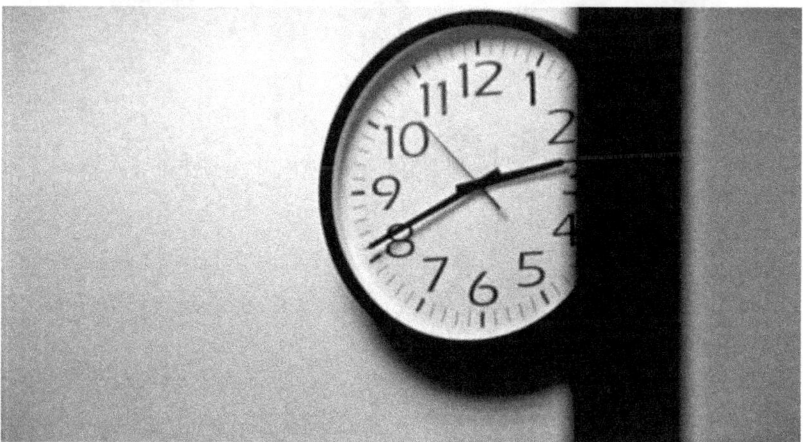

2.8. Michelle Williams is fingerprinted in *Wendy and Lucy*, directed by Kelly Reichardt (2008).

2.9. The police station clock in *Wendy and Lucy*.

getic time. As *The Clock* is a twenty-four-hour work, though, Marclay is able to install these scenes in their proper places on the timeline. In a scene sampled from *Wendy and Lucy* (2008), a ragged Michelle Williams is fingerprinted in a police station, with an institutional round, white clock visible on the wall. More than two hours later we see her again, in the same room, still waiting to be fingerprinted. In Reichardt's original film, the machine has malfunctioned and Wendy has been detained

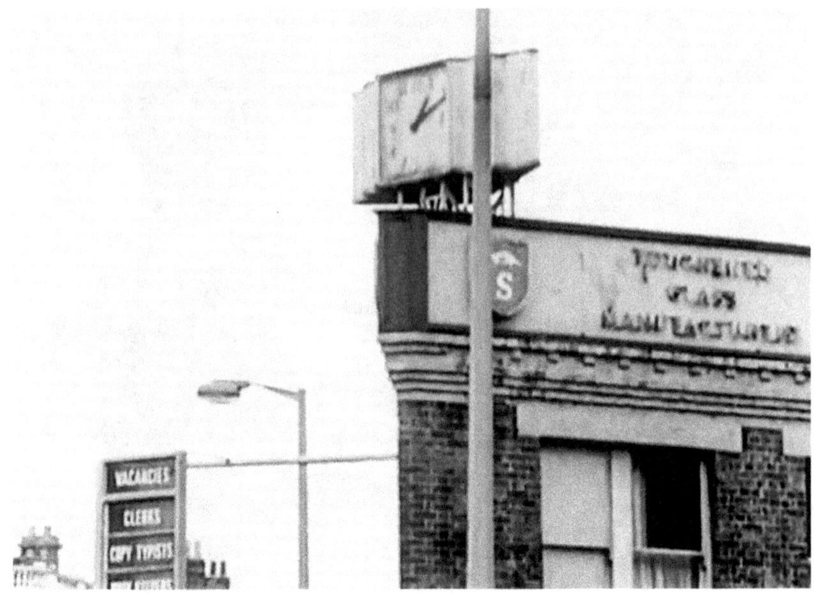

2.10. The clock atop Steele's in *The Girl Chewing Gum*, directed by John Smith (1976).

there during the interim, but we are spared the waiting time by the magic of ellipsis. Marclay's viewer, by contrast, comes to appreciate the length of the interval that has elapsed.

There is a third type of transgression *The Clock* makes against digital logic, one that often coincides with the sense that there is a particular consciousness behind the selections, a predilection or fondness for certain films that earns them a disproportionate amount of screen time. One of these is a longish sequence devoted to a portion of John Smith's *The Girl Chewing Gum* (1976), an experimental film that, like Conner's *A MOVIE*, seems to serve as a touchstone for Marclay. The original work, like *The Clock*, relies on a trick played with cinematic conventions, in this case the use of a post-dubbed voice-over to create the impression that the film is being directed from the sidelines while we watch what is, in fact, documentary footage. At 1:10 p.m. the camera tilts up to reveal a clock face, then zooms unsteadily into a close-up on it. Just prior to this point in Smith's original film, the narrator gives the order "Now, I want everything to sink slowly down as the five boys come by. Hold it.

. . . And now I want the clock to move jerkily towards me." Smith's original voice-over continues, "Now, I want the long hand to move at the rate of one revolution every hour, and I want the short hand to move at the rate of one revolution every twelve hours." As if by magic, the world obeys his commands.

The conceit of *The Girl Chewing Gum* is cinematographic: the narrator can pretend to control what appears in the frame because it was in fact already there on the reel. The pedestrians' movements, the clock's rate of revolution, even the tilting of the horizon are, in one of Bergson's metaphors, like opening a fan to reveal, presto, an embroidered image that was actually already there, prefigured on the silk.[18] The comedy of Smith's film arises from this mock omnipotence. In Marclay's repurposing, we, like the narrator, can pretend to a degree of omniscience: we all already know what time the clock atop the Steele's building will display. Those of us who have seen Smith's film also know that soon the girl chewing gum will walk by. In the footage that he samples for *The Clock*, though, Marclay removes Smith's voice-over, thereby eliminating the separate off-screen space from which the film is faux-enunciated. He retains some of the original diegetic sound, the ringing of an alarm bell, and overlays and harmonizes it with cello music.

In his book on the painter Francis Bacon, Deleuze offers an account of digitality and analogy that, while not expressly drawing on Bergson, is in keeping with his philosophy. Deleuze begins this discussion with the somewhat Peircean proposition that the digital operates "through code, convention, and combinations of conventional units"—units taken to be discreet from one another, like the tiles of a mosaic. The analog, by contrast, "proceeds by resemblance." Not content with this formula, Deleuze suggests that digital language too contains aspects of "similitude or analogy . . . analogy by produced resemblance." He makes a version of the reverse claim too: that even painting, which he calls "the analogical art par excellence," at times participates in codes. Abstract painting, in Deleuze's view, involves a process of codification, albeit one that at its best does not apply an external code (red = blood, green = nature, and so on) but rather elaborates its own codes internally. "It is thus a paradoxical code since instead of being opposed to analogy, it takes analogy as its object; it is the digital expression of the analogical as such." In a long paragraph about musical synthesizers, he suggests that it is finally the notion of "modulation (and not similitude)" that conceptually distinguishes the analog from the digital.[19]

The faculty of modulation, the ability to respond to variations of volume, tone, and quality as they occur in time, brings us back to music. In *The Clock*, the soundtrack always has at least one foot in the analog. Its sound bridges finesse the editing, but they also sustain affect, memory, and a different kind of movement across clips whose relations to one another are otherwise primarily geometric. By removing its theological voice-over and substituting a musical score, Marclay in a sense "modulates" *The Girl Chewing Gum*, restoring to it the feeling that something immanent, something that has not been scripted by an off-screen deity, might occur. In other words, Marclay undoes the cinematographic aspects of Smith's film, restoring to it a sense of virtuality.

This sense, like the "pure duration" of Bergson's melody, is foreign to what I have been calling "digitality"—with a reminder of the caveat that digital media do not always obey digitalic logics. Still, computers execute commands that are issued in advance, from the outside, by an enunciator who is off-screen and extradiegetic, so to speak, be it a programmer or a user. They also excel at sorting through and manipulating data: possibilities, variables, things that can be systematized and rendered numerically. It is difficult to deny that the computer appears to be the culmination of Bergson's "cinematographic thought," in a way a much more apt metaphor for this way of thinking than the cinema, the jigsaw puzzle, or the other art forms that Bergson deploys as figures in his writing.

As any proper cinephile can attest, what Bergson calls cinematographic thought is not the only kind of thought in which film can engage. Deleuze's cinema books are, among other things, an extended proof of this very idea. Similarly, digitalic works of art, music, literature, and so on are not the only kind that can be produced with a computer. In his *Parables for the Virtual*, Brian Massumi notes that digital technologies have "a remarkably weak connection to the virtual, by virtue of the enormous power of systematization"; he adds, however, that they may one day enjoy a "privileged connection" to the virtual, perhaps one "far stronger than that of any preceding phylum." At the same time, he affirms the argument against medium specificity: "If all emergent form brings its fringe of virtuality with it, then no particular medium of expression has a monopoly on the virtual."[20] All types of media, in other words, can tap into its source.

THE VIRTUAL

What is this virtuality, this fringe that surrounds all media of expression? Bergson offers one of his more focused explications of it in "Memory of the Present and False Recognition," one of the key texts collected in *Mind-Energy*. It is immediately clear that the virtual has to do with time. Bergson begins by linking the virtual to the past and memory, analogizing it to a long tape of images generated simultaneously with our present experience, as if reflected in a moving mirror running constantly alongside us. "Our actual existence," he writes, "whilst it is unrolled in time, duplicates itself all along with a virtual existence, a mirror-image. Every moment of our life presents two aspects, it is actual and virtual, perception on the one side and memory on the other."[21] The virtual, according to this metaphor, is the stream of images that duplicates and accompanies our perception at any given moment. It is a live broadcast of sensory experience that is being reflected and duplicated at every sentient moment and that constitutes memory. In *Matter and Memory*, in the same passage in which Bergson defines matter as "an aggregate of images," he clarifies that by "image" he means "a certain existence which is more than that which the idealist calls a *representation*, but less than that which the realist calls a *thing*."[22] Importantly these virtual "mirror-images" are of this type: they are more than representations, less than things. They are of the world, not simply of our minds.

For Bergson the virtual includes both this mirroring of the present in the form of the past and projections into the future, which form another jet in the stream. He calls the second stream a "pantomime": sketches of possible courses of action in response to perceptions of matter in the world. As Bergson puts it, "Thought is directed toward action, and when it does not end in a real action, it sketches out one or several virtual, simply possible, actions."[23] These thoughts may take the form of plans, one or more of which may be actualized after an interval of time, or of fantasies, hypothetical scenarios, wishes, or experiments. In *Matter and Memory*, Bergson describes these activities as forms of "foreshadowing": a draft or blocking out of possible movements as they might be "acted or played out in space."[24]

Bergson also places a whole set of present-tense perceptions in the category of the virtual, those that remain occluded from consciousness at any given moment. Perceptions that remain on the fringes, either because the conscious mind must block them out in order not to be overloaded by an insupportable amount of stimulation or because the typical frames and lenses, or "canals," through which we allow perceptions to enter are too restrictive to allow reality its full girth and complexity, are virtual in this way. With this third sense of the virtual, Bergson tiptoes toward but stops short of equating it with what other philosophers have called the real. It includes everything in the world that we have missed seeing and experiencing because at the time we encountered it, our attention was directed elsewhere—focused on things that were more relevant to our interests, things that we have recognized in a "habitual" way.[25] These habits are the canals or grooves through which perceptions get sorted, filtered, and reshaped. They are what manifests to the intellect rather than what becomes visible with intuition.

Bergson references Leibniz when he describes this third sense of the virtual: "Each monad, and therefore *a fortiori* each of those monads that he calls minds, carries in it the totality of the real. I should not go so far; but I think that we perceive virtually many more things than we perceive actually."[26] In another text he puts it the following way: there are mechanisms or canals in our minds that are "designed to screen from perception objects which by their nature are beyond the reach of action. [But] if these mechanisms get out of order, the door which they kept shut opens a little way: there enters in something of a 'without' which may be a 'beyond.'"[27]

The virtual is this "beyond." It is always available, but it is usually screened out. In order to access it, there must be a coalescence among memory images from the past, hypothetical images directed toward the future, and present-tense images that tend to fall under the radar of everyday awareness. The *kind* of time that allows for access to something beyond and for the emergence of the virtual is not just ordinary, everyday time. It is what Bergson called *la durée*, duration. The virtual emerges through an encounter with durational time. It goes into hiding when time is experienced as abstract, enumerable, and computable, as if it could be rendered as a long roll, yearbook, or timeline of calendrical units superimposed on the universe. The virtual surfaces when time is perceived as a continuous stream of images that forks, loops, and doubles back on itself, beyond any computational or instrumental framework that we might be tempted to impress upon it.

That said, the virtual is not merely what we see when we extrapolate forward or backward in time. It requires more than a capacity to picture the future or recollect the past. To experience the virtual, we must connect past and future images to the now, maintaining their continuity and metonymic proximity with the present moment and the world, but without collapsing the distinctions among these temporalities. As Deleuze puts it, there is "coalescence" between the actual and the virtual; they are "mutual" images where an "exchange is carried out."[28] We must neither inhabit a perpetual present tense nor get lost in a reminiscence or daydream.

In his essay on dreams, Bergson describes how even in sleep, present-tense perceptions are not fully blocked out: "The eyes, when closed, still distinguish light from shade, and even, to a certain extent, different lights from one another. These sensations of light, emanating from without, are at the bottom of many of our dreams."[29] Even when we lower the blinds, shut our eyes, and stop up our ears, indeed even when we are unconscious, small changes and stimuli emanating from the here and now are always present and available. But they do not usually claim the bulk of our awareness. A surprising amount of our attention goes elsewhere: preoccupied with the past or the future, ruminating over or becoming nostalgic for yesterday's events; planning, dreading, or fantasizing about tomorrow's; dreaming, daydreaming, catastrophizing; sometimes shuttling rapidly among all of these without any awareness that our attention has wandered at all. As anyone who has attempted to meditate silently on the present moment can attest, the past and future (at least the most engrossing parts of them) do not exactly require an engraved invitation to grace our conscious minds. To the contrary, it can be incredibly difficult to maintain a concentrated focus on the things and sensations that are here in the present, even for just a few moments.

The doorway to the virtual—that little "'without' which may be a 'beyond'"—opens when we become aware of the continuity of time.

It requires that we connect to the present in ways that busy habits of mind normally preclude. But it also requires that we not separate the present moment from all the others, as if the universe were beginning again with a blank slate at each passing instant, as if nothing had ever existed prior to this moment and nothing will follow it—a fiction that computers cannot help but subscribe to, at least at this point in their development.

The virtual is also connected to matter, but it is not determined by it. In precisely the same way, the virtual connects to the analog and the digital but is in no way predetermined by them. It is a mode that does not inhere in any particular type of matter or organization thereof. It is not tied to medium specificity: the minerals, substances, and particles that store and release an image or sound cannot be analyzed for their virtual properties. It is radically open-ended without being unspecified or abstract. As Deleuze states, "The virtual corresponds in all respects to the formula by which Proust defined his states of experience: 'real without being actual, ideal without being abstract.'"[30] The virtual, it is true, brushes up against the Ideal; although it is always immanent within matter and the world, it includes more than what Bergson's realists might call mute or brute matter, bodies and concrete objects still stuck in a Cartesian dualist paradigm. For all this, the virtual is still very real, and it cannot exist without a connection to matter of some kind. It relies on matter not simply because materialism and embodiment are good things that sustain living beings and a precarious planet but also because it requires a continued existence over time.

Durational time requires matter. It cannot be simplified into a two-dimensional line, abstracted into units, or laid out before us like a blueprint on a table without being stripped of this powerful quality of virtuality. We cannot grasp it all at once. Nor can we disconnect entirely from the "at once." The virtual requires the mutual enfolding of here and elsewhere, and now and then.

CHAPTER 3

Matter, Time, and the Digital

Agnès Varda's Videos

Everything is time—stone, tree, mountain, ocean; thoughts, doubts, clouds—we are time.
—Trinh T. Minh-ha, *The Digital Film Event*

Walter Benjamin offered a critique of Henri Bergson's philosophy: he wrote that "death is eliminated from Bergson's *durée*." The passage continues, "The *durée* from which death has been eliminated has the miserable endlessness of a scroll. . . . It is the quintessence of a passing moment that struts about in the borrowed garb of experience."[1] Benjamin is correct that Bergson's philosophy lacks a strong account of mortality. It is unapologetically vitalistic, focused on the new, the emergent, and the movements of change and becoming. In one way it is strange that Bergson does not approach the death drive in a systematic way in his philosophy, since his interest in time and organic matter would suggest it and since, as a reader of Freud, he had undoubtedly given thought to these ideas. There is an additional biographical detail that makes the omission strange: Bergson suffered from degenerative rheumatism that left him half-paralyzed in his later years.

Bergson uses the word *death* only infrequently in his oeuvre, and when he does, the reference is often incidental. In *Mind-Energy*, he mentions death in the context of a discussion about unusual mental phenomena, citing the example of seeing one's life flash before one's eyes just prior to the moment of dying. It is clear in this case that he is more interested in the perceptual anomaly—a long, vivid parade of images spanning many years that rush by in an instant—than in death itself. In another example from that volume, he discusses Alfred Maury's dream of being guillotined as a reaction to the sensation of his bed frame falling onto his neck in the middle of the night, which Freud also analyzes in *The Interpretation of Dreams*.[2] Here again it is not the apprehension of death that concerns Bergson; it is the temporal anomaly by which Maury's mind, in the split second between the headboard falling on his neck and his jolting awake from the blow, created a detailed story about the events leading up to his execution, which he retroactively experienced as a long, narratively intricate dream.

In chapter 3 of *Creative Evolution*, Bergson directly addresses the concept of entropy, although without using this word. He describes a kind of gravity that afflicts all matter in the world: "The vision we have of the material world is that of a weight which falls." He suggests that the counterforce to this downward pull is life, an energy in living creatures that has a tendency "to accumulate in a reservoir . . . something that would have otherwise flowed away. It is like an effort to raise the weight which falls."[3] Matter and life are locked in a kind of struggle, the one pulling downward, the other swimming vigorously toward the surface.

Bergson notes that this gravity cannot be fully overcome. Life succeeds only in slowing down its work: "Incapable of *stopping* the course of material changes downwards, it succeeds in *retarding* it."[4] The result is an interval of duration, the span of a life, during which their forces are in balance. Matter, for Bergson, is not simply a raw building block out of which life crafts itself; it is what stops life from getting out of bounds. It is the barrier to immortality, which would be the destruction of durational time, and the barrier to total disembodiment, which would be the achievement of the Cartesian dream. Thus, to return to Benjamin's critique, it is not so much that he ignores or eliminates death from his account of durational time; rather it takes an unexpected form. He separates it from life and situates it in gravity-bound matter. In a way he undoes the categorical distinction between inorganic and organic matter. All matter is inorganic and pulls downward; all of it is "dead." But all of it has the potential to be "alive," and in this state, for a brief time, it gets diverted from its downward spiral. It is given a lifespan and infused with duration.

Creative evolution and decompositional entropy require one another.

Eliminate the latter, and we do indeed end up with something like what Benjamin describes in his critique of Bergson. Without entropy and the halting, delaying power of matter, time has this quality of "miserable endlessness." But without life, matter is but a string of passing moments; it is disconnected from the past and from its own continuity of existence over time. Both are necessary. Life is like a spark that flares for a brief moment through the tinder of matter; as Bergson puts it in a beautiful sentence, one of the few in which he uses the word that falls at its conclusion, it is "the fiery path torn by the last rocket of a fireworks display through the black cinders of the spent rockets that are falling dead."[5]

DIGITALITY AND MATTER

Agnès Varda's *The Gleaners and I* (2000) is a digital video film about salvaging. It is a film made in an ultracontemporary medium that, as I discussed in previous chapters, at times seems to aspire to immortality and immateriality. This film, though, is expressly concerned with the expired and out of date. Varda introduces us to all manner of people who gather the world's decaying leftovers for reasons of survival, ethics, or simply pleasure. We meet homeless laborers, a chef who collects his own herbs, artists who sculpt from recycled materials, a literacy instructor who lives off discarded produce at the outdoor market. Varda's subjects pick and collect a trove of objects that only seem to have reached the ends of their lifespan: unharvested wheat and figs, lost buttons, broken dolls, day-old loaves of bread, broken refrigerators, and oddly shaped fruits and vegetables. Varda in turn counts herself among these gleaners, but what she collects are images, not things, using her digital camera as a receptacle. Like a *flâneuse* with a portable camera, the *glâneuse* navigates through the world's glitter and rubble.

The Gleaners and I is a profoundly materialist film, one that uses digital video in a manner contrary to digitalic principles. D. N. Rodowick has noted that the digital arts have come to be associated with the "abstract," the "ephemeral," and the "desubstantialized."[6] Lev Manovich likewise lists "numerical representation" and "mathematical manipulability" as the primary defining elements of new media.[7] Digital images aspire to be matter-free in several ways. First, at the level of recording, they lack the photograph's indexical tie to their referents, as celebrated by André Bazin and Roland Barthes. As is by now familiar, Bazin called the photographic image "a kind of decal or transfer" of its object, and Barthes famously suggested that "the photograph is literally an emanation of the referent."[8] At the level of media storage the two media also differ: digital images are stored numerically as data in binary code. Unlike a photograph they do not exist in material form, even a negative form, until generated in hard copy. The digital could thus in many ways be said to realize the dream of a disembodied, timeless, and transcendent form of representation.

The Gleaners and I, however, is a film that denies the digital this divorce from the tangible and time-bound. It offers an implicit critique of the Cartesian dream of immateriality, the fantasy of freedom from the body, from the gravity of earthly constraints, and from the suspicion of the senses. Varda's film counters transcendence with immanence, insisting on matter, body, and duration, despite being made in a medium that is the logical outgrowth of the desire to overcome these things. With *The Gleaners and I*, Varda crafts a digital cinema that is materialist, feminist, phenomenological, and political. A materialist cinema: Varda is concerned about the fate of material objects, and she practices what Siegfried Kracauer names "the redemption of physical reality."[9] A feminist cinema: at the start of her film, Varda reminds us that once upon a time there were only female *glâneuses*, not male *glâneurs*, because gathering society's leftovers was considered women's labor—but this is a type of labor with which Varda proudly identifies her own filmmaking. A phenomenological cinema: the film is about the world of concrete, everyday things experienced through the senses, not a timeless world of abstract Platonic ideals. A political cinema: Varda and her gleaners are enmeshed in what Arendt calls "the web of human relations," networks of individuals who help each other to think, create, and survive and who are in fact defined by these reciprocal acts.[10] All of these things, we will come to see, are also related to the entropic forces that inhere in matter and their inseparability from what is new, an insight that is revealed in part through Varda's attention to her own aging body.

The images that make up *The Gleaners and I* may be based in numerical digits: numbers, the system of transcendent universalism. But on screen we see not equations, but other types of digits: hands and fingers. We see the dirt-caked hands of Claude, a former truck driver who

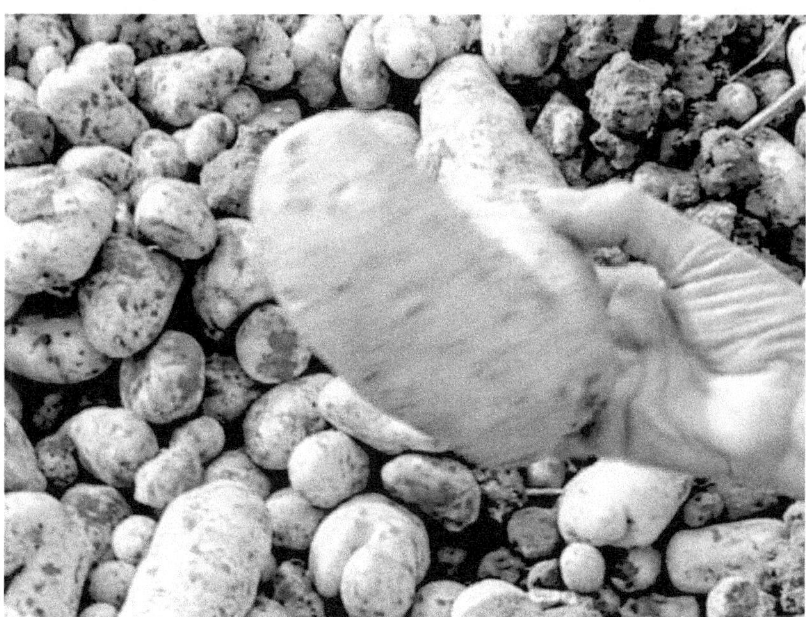

3.1. Agnès Varda's hand gleans a heart-shaped potato as her other hand films in *The Gleaners and I* (2000).

lives in a trailer park; we see the clean-scrubbed hands of schoolchildren making decorations from yogurt containers; we see rows of blue rubber gloves hanging in a shack near oyster beds at seaside. The filmmaker's own hands also appear more often in this film than is customary. Varda's hand appears not only as authoring agent but also as subject matter. The hand is both container and content: it picks potatoes and sorts postcards while offering itself up for a portrait. Varda's hand frequently appears against the earth, engaged in what she calls the "modest gesture of the gleaner," a twist on the expression "the majestic gesture of the sower." When Varda stoops down to gather, her hand becomes an agent of linking, a connector to things of the earth. Emphasizing the hands and body of the filmmaker, *The Gleaners and I* challenges not only the logic of digitality but also the conventions of documentary. As Anne Rutherford rightly comments, the film explores "embodied thought" and "embodied affect" and questions their exclusion from traditional documentary modes.[11]

In his book on Francis Bacon, Deleuze distinguishes among four "values of the hand": the digital, the tactile, the manual proper, and the haptic. He offers these values as a taxonomy of permutations in the relationship between hand and eye. The digital completely subordinates the hand to the eye; the tactile still relies on an optical structuring of space but reaches toward touchable referents within that space; the manual inverts this relation to subordinate the optical completely to touch; and the haptic eliminates the hierarchy altogether, putting in its place a kind of seeing and touching that are inseparable from one another (in the haptic mode, "painters paint with their eyes, but only insofar as they touch with their eyes"). In the digital mode, the hand is "reduced to the finger" that points and "chooses units," it relies on an "ideal" conception of space, and it grasps forms "through an optical code."[12]

In *The Gleaners and I*, more than any of the films she shot previously with a conventional cinema camera, Varda's hands and eyes enjoy a relationship that moves among the last three terms in Deleuze's taxonomy. At no point is the sense of touch completely absent from her camerawork, and at times it seems to take precedence over the visual register. The digital-optic mode subscribes to the silicon dream, the Cartesian dream of disembodiment; it aims to eliminate the fleshy, dirty hands and cloudy eyes and put in their place sleek cursors that click icons remotely, almost touchlessly. In Deleuze's other three modes, by contrast, something of the tactile, and therefore the matter of the body, remains operative. Deleuze's "manual" mode, in which the optical is completely subordinated to the tactile, is not usually accessed in film, given its strong emphasis on the visual register. But there are scenes in *The Gleaners and I* that come very close to this mode—the shaky hand-held camera that descends with Varda as she stoops to scoop up a potato, Varda's lens cap swinging against the ground, filmed by accident—scenes in which Varda appears to be more interested in what she is touching than what her camera is seeing.

Heart-shaped potatoes, dumped in a field because they have been deemed unmarketable by grocery standards, are the first items we see Varda's hand glean. In a sequel to *The Gleaners and I* entitled *Two Years Later*, she tells us that the potatoes have become the film's trademark, and her trademark as well. The potato is a rhizome, a root with underground circuits and radial offshoots. The rhizome suggests a constant source rather than an end product, and a solid foundation rather than an ethereal superstructure. It is thus a supreme emblem of the earthbound. Deleuze and Guattari proposed this symbol in *A Thousand Plateaus* in 1987, as a way of describing nonlinear, horizontal, and decentered structures.[13] They offer the rhizome as an alternative to the taprooted tree, for whose generational seeds and offspring it substitutes associative sprouts. The rhizome has also been adopted as a symbol of new media, most notably by Rhizome.org, founded in 1996, for whose collaborators the term describes the formal properties of the electronic arts as well as their grassroots, open-access, and collaborative potentials. A rhizomatic structure suggests interactivity and a dispersal of the individual across a wide field. This multiple significance of the rhizome suggests that electronic media need not be antithetical to materialist or earthly politics. The electronic image is not always a flash of ones and zeros; sometimes it is a root spreading in the ground.[14]

I have been describing some of the ways that Varda uses digital images against their tendency toward dematerialization. There is one sense in which the digital arts, broadly conceived, already implicitly contain a critique of what Rodowick calls the old Cartesian dream and what Yaakov Garb calls the silicon dream. In *The Language of New Media*, Manovich reveals another, unexpected way that the digital arts return us to the tangible, when he says that "the manual construction of images in digital cinema represents a return to the pro-cinematic practices of the nineteenth century, when images were hand-painted and hand-animated." Consequently, Manovich continues, "cinema can no longer be clearly distinguished from animation. It is no longer an indexical media technology but, rather, a subgenre of painting."[15] Thomas Elsaesser and Kay Hoffman make a similar observation in their preface to *Cinema Futures: Cain, Abel, or Cable? The Screen Arts in the Digital Age*, when they call attention to the digital arts' "curious melding of the very old and the brand-new" that occurs when "skills of draftsmanship and modeling dating back a century or more are 'rediscovered.'"[16]

Of course this is not literally the case in *The Gleaners*; Varda does not draw robots into her image, as George Lucas does. On only a few occasions does she manipulate individual frames with computer software; in one notable departure from her realist aesthetic, she experiments with composite images of pixilated mirrors and paintings, which she calls "stroboscopic" and "hyper-realistic." Even if she does not "paint" this film, the idea of manual creation is clearly thematized. Paintings, sculptures, and other artworks made by hand are on view, and they are discretely analogized to her own filmmaking. The gesture of the filmmaker is modestly analogized to the grand gesture of the painter. Varda's use of the hand-held camera—a style of filming that is tactile, manual, and haptic in addition to optical—at times evokes the swipe of a painter's brush stroke. This camera movement ceases to be a marker of liveness or urgency, the way it commonly signifies, for example, in television news footage. The little digital camera becomes like a brush or marker, an implement of what Varda calls "cinécriture," her portmanteau word for cinematic writing.

We see Varda's hand near the ground gleaning heart-shaped potatoes that have been discarded as worthless. We also see her hand framed against the sky, gleaning trucks, which, for all we know, may be transporting perfectly oval-shaped potatoes from the very same fields. During segments of the film shot on the road, Varda clasps her fingers around the images of trucks passing along the highway. Ernest Callenbach has noted that "the trucks are in fact a key element of the hugely wasteful system to which gleaning is a response."[17] Indeed trucks, unlike electronic modes of transport, waste quantities of fuel moving objects that could be produced and consumed in the same place. Here Varda shows us real commodities inside a real truck grasped by a real hand, all of which are stored in a virtual container: the digital camera. But they are no less tangible for so being, and this is a key trope of Varda's film. Moreover she tells us that she gleans them not to preserve that which passes but in order "to play."

DIGITALITY AND DURATION

This leads to another key element of Varda's cinema: the kind of temporality it expresses, an insistence on the time-bound. That which is bound to time has duration, but not the endless duration of an infinite scroll. It has a past, a present, and a future, but this future, importantly, is not known. It is pulled down to earth by an expiration date embedded somewhere in its matter, but this date cannot be calculated in advance with absolute certainty. There is both evolution (change, deviation, becoming) and entropy (gravity, immobility, sameness).

Varda makes note of both facets of this temporal movement, sometimes in the same image, and treats both its streams with equal parts gravity and levity. She often makes explicit reference to the time of her own film. She tells us that she started it at the turn of the century, on New Year's Day 2000, and that she completed filming on May 1. In so doing, she dates her film, grounding it in a specific historical era; this is a Varda trademark of sorts, a gesture she also makes in *One Sings, the Other Doesn't* (1977). *The Gleaners and I* reminds us of the time in many ways; it is full of clocks and schedules. The artist Hervé uses a trash collection schedule to plan his salvaging expeditions. The oyster gatherers use a tide table to plan the optimal harvest time. There are less obvious kinds of clocks as well. There are outdoor farms and orchards that reveal the time of year through foliage, weather, and quality of light. There are guests at the Musée d'Orsay who parade before Millet's *Gleaners* in time-lapse photography. And there are potatoes in Varda's home, displayed in varying stages of rot, thus letting us know how much time has passed since her visit to the potato field.

We know that the numeric coding of digital film allows for a nonlinear approach to time, both at the editing or postproduction stage and at the stage of viewing or reception. With nonlinear editing, an image can quickly be taken out of sequence and placed elsewhere, and everything else in the chain bumped forward or backward to accommodate it. Unlike with the old deck-to-deck systems, we do not have to start editing all over again from the point at which the image is inserted. We can also access images randomly: we are not constrained to a fixed sequence; we may jump instantly to past or future images without having to wait for the tape to spool through the intervening scenes in rewind or fast-forward. On the one hand, these features are part of what align the digital text with the urge to overcome the given material and temporal constraints of the phenomenal world. But these features are, of course, not unique to digital media, and they do not group well under the headings "analog" and "digital." Magnetic tape, celluloid film on reels, and texts in scroll form require that we move through them in ways that obey their own continuity: we can move in fast-forward or slow motion, forward or backward, but unless we cut them with scissors, we cannot access them at random. Digital texts and videos, vinyl records, and books in codex form, on the other hand, all allow for random access.

Nonlinearity is related to the cinematographic mode insofar as it chops up time into discreet units and imagines that they can be moved around without affecting the whole. But this feature is not ultimately what makes a text "digital" in either the technological sense or the conceptual sense that I have been elaborating. Durational time is also nonlinear: it includes layers and sheets of time that superimpose on one another, the coalescence of the past, present, and future. In her works shot on digital video, Varda shows that digital media can embrace many types of time. These media can take flight from durational continuity, then touch back down into it. A digital database of images may indeed exist all at once, as a paradigm without an obligatory sequence. But each separate encounter with it participates in some kind of temporal order or syntagma.

In her essay "Designing a Database Cinema," Marsha Kinder helps to further undo the binary opposition between "database" and "narrative," noting that they may in fact be understood as compatible and coexisting in various kinds of texts. We have come to understand the database as atemporal, synchronic or existing all at once, in opposition to narrative, which we understand as diachronic, existing in time and in a particular order. But databases surely invite us to construct chains of segments and narratives from their contents; in turn, all narratives are to some extent constructed, as Kinder notes, "by selecting items from databases (that usually remain hidden) and then combining these items to create a particular story." Kinder provides examples of database-narrative cinema ranging from Luis Buñuel and the French New Wave to contemporary films like *Run Lola Run* and *Y tu Mamá También*. She counts *The Gleaners and I* among this set: "Varda proves to be the most accomplished gleaner of all, especially as she recycles techniques and issues that have preoccupied her from *La Pointe courte* (1954) to *Vagabond* (1985)."[18]

The linked episodes in *The Gleaners and I* may or may not have taken place in chronological order. It doesn't matter, for we know the basic interval during which they were filmed. As in *Cléo from 5 to 7* (1962), a film about an actress's waiting for the results of a medical test, we are situated in a precise interval of time, and we experience a felt sense of the film's duration. And as in *Cinévardaphoto* (2004), a trio of essay films about still photographs, Varda is attentive to history without relying on teleological time (*Cinévardaphoto*'s three pieces unspool in reverse chronological order). In Varda's cinema, we also see conflicts and collaborations between generations of human beings. Witness the scene in *The Gleaners* of a group of teenagers who argue with a supermarket proprietor about stealing from his dumpster, or the episode showing the alliance of an elderly Vietnamese immigrant with his young African roommate. The film accommodates all of these indices of time, these ways of acknowledging its structuring effects.

The Gleaners and I may be set during the resolutely linear, teleological progression of the twentieth century toward its finale, but it shows us other kinds of time as well: the midnight ritual of dumpster-diving, the cyclical intervals of the tides, the too-late timing of overripe fruit, the meandering time of a vagabond's walk through fields, and the anticipatory time of a painting's unveiling. We move from one scene to the next not through the techniques of continuity editing, whether spatial or temporal, but almost exclusively with associative matches. As in *One Hundred and One Nights*, Varda often uses a visual rhyme, metonymic link, or verbal pun as her means of connecting one segment to the next. From the "crazy dance" of a lens cap, we cut to a town called La Folie; from a legal lesson on gleaning in a cabbage field, we cut to Varda filming purple cabbages and other lacey vegetables. We could call this technique "rhizomatic editing," and it suggests a connectivity of spectacularly vast potential. As Deleuze and Guattari put it, "A rhizome ceaselessly establishes connections between semiotic chains, organizations of power, and circumstances relative to the arts, sciences, and social struggles."[19]

The French word for "digital" is *numérique*, as in *horloge numérique*, a digital clock. On a nighttime trash-collecting expedition, Varda gleans a Lucite clock with no hands, which she takes home and installs on her mantle. She says that this handless clock will help her to forget the passage of time, to paper it over, and forget her increasing age. Perhaps it will. At the same time one could argue that it is the functional clock with its ticking of hands and digits that distracts from the raw experience of durational time. Indeed Varda probably knows as much, since her handless clock recalls the one that appears in a dream sequence from Bergman's *Wild Strawberries* (1957), another film that uses this symbol to convey a sensory, affectively charged experience of temporal dura-

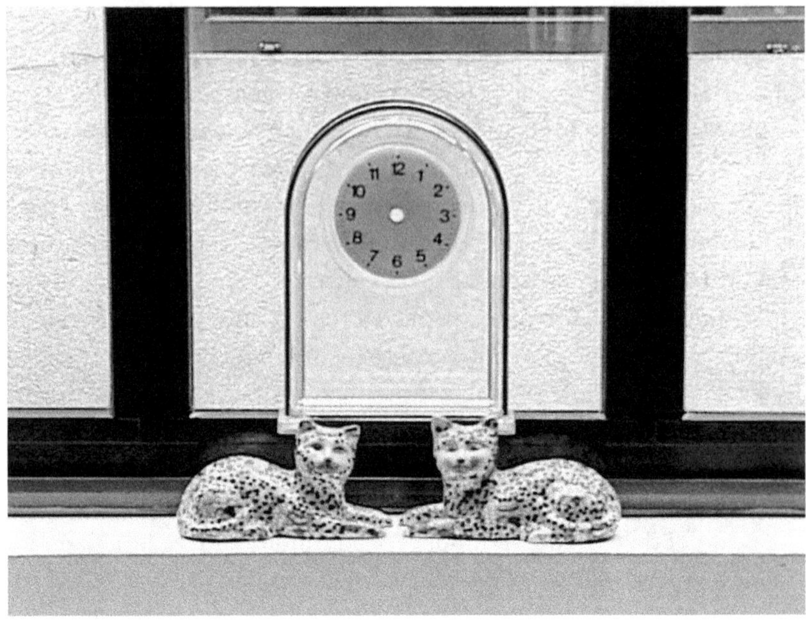

3.2. The handless Lucite clock in *The Gleaners and I*.

tion and an acute awareness of aging. In an unexpectedly Bergsonian insight, Jean Baudrillard observes in *The System of Objects* that the clock "makes us feel safe when it substantializes time and cuts it into slices like an object of consumption."[20] Clock hands, like their digital equivalent, numbers, may indeed make us aware of time's passing, but they also create the illusion that we know how much time we have left, that we can quantify, tame, and control it as if it were a natural resource. The handless clock, according to this way of thinking, is a more radical reminder of time, whether evolutionary or entropic, because it lacks the means of measuring and manipulating it. Just as when we are lost and wandering in a foreign city, it becomes possible for a less tightly canalized awareness of space to emerge, so it happens that when we *don't* know what time it is, we may experience time's passing in a more durationally rooted, intuitive fashion. Varda's clear, handless clock is in some ways the opposite of Christian Marclay's, at least in the "digital" reading of it.

In one sequence, returning home after a trip to Japan, Varda notices the growth of familiar mold stains on her ceiling: signs of the entropic

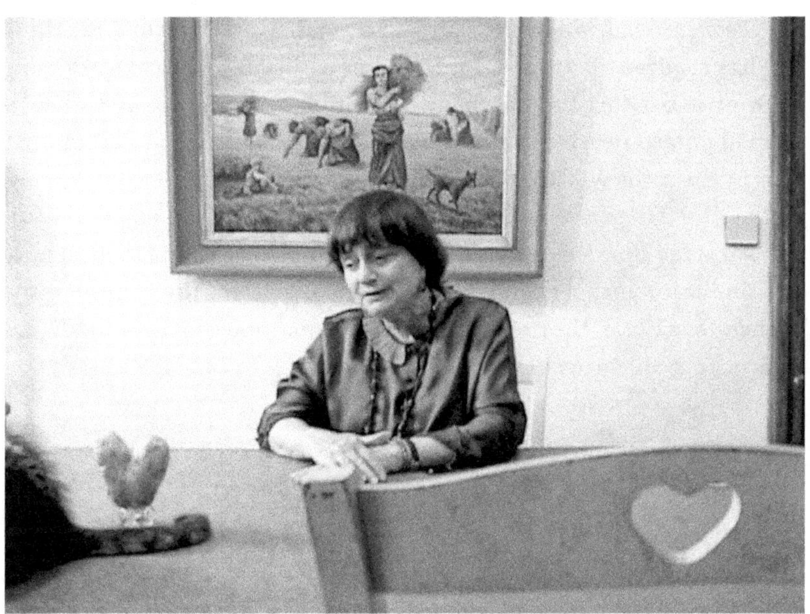

3.3. Agnès Varda in *The Gleaners and I: Two Years Later* (2002).

movements that have occurred during her absence. And once again we see hands: she shows us her aging fingers in close-up. This scene forms one of the film's hearts or centers. Varda films as she unpacks her souvenirs and pauses with some postcards of a Rembrandt self-portrait that she found on the top floor of a department store in Tokyo. Here the souvenir becomes an occasion for self-reflection in the present moment. Varda's self-portrait comes to her from afar, by way of both the seventeenth-century Netherlands of Rembrandt and contemporary Japan. The ethics of gleaning, this scene helps us to understand, is not limited to ecology and environmentalism, although these are obviously important aspects. Gleaning is not simply about saving objects (or ourselves) from the onslaught of time. Neither is it a straightforward preservation of beauty for history or posterity. Varda and her gleaners recover, save, and collect things not in order to embalm them but to use them, in the sense of putting them into practice and circulation—be they comestibles, tools, or pictures. Gleaning involves a recognition of transience, not a denial of it.

The penultimate scene of *Two Years Later*, Varda's follow-up piece to

The Gleaners and I, is a confession scene, where Varda tells us something she has realized about a scene from her earlier film. Seated at a table in front of the thrift store gleaners painting, with her cat and a heart-shaped potato nearby, she tells us that she has filmed her hands and hair in the same way that she filmed her late husband, Jacques Demy, in the film *Jacquôt de Nantes*, a tribute to him that she made in 1991. But she adds that she forgot the scene from *Jacquôt* and failed to note the similarity until a friend drew it to her attention. The history of the French New Wave, the present tense of cinema, and the future of digital imagery are all encapsulated in this image.

THE "NEW" IN NEW MEDIA

These scenes where Varda reflects on her old age, the waning century, loss, and the ephemerality of objects, are important aspects of this late film in her career. But it would be a mistake to let their melancholic aspects distract us from an equally important note the film sounds, which has to do with beginnings, becoming, and the possibility of the new. The opening sequence of *The Gleaners and I* emblematizes the faculty of initiation and the emergence of new, unexpected things in the world—things that were nevertheless contained as virtual, latent possibilities in what already existed there and without which they might never have been actualized. The film begins with a dictionary definition of the word *glâneuse*; Varda's dictionary is an illustrated one, with nineteenth-century pictures of gleaners by Millet and Jules Breton. Soon we cut to an image of Varda in front of the original Breton painting in the Musée d'Arras, where she poses cheekily with a bale of wheat over her shoulder, then drops it to pick up her digital camera. In so doing she aligns herself with both Breton and his proud gleaner. But she does so with a new, twenty-first-century twist: her digital camera, which has emerged in the place of both wheat and paintbrush. Her pose, though, does not so much declare a triumph of the sign over the object, or the digital over the analog, as simply remark upon the fact of change.

The ending of the film brings us full circle, with Varda making a pilgrimage to view yet another painting of gleaners, Hédouin's *Gleaners Fleeing the Storm*. The painting's canvas buckles in the wind as Varda films it propped against a wall after it is removed from storage. In stor-

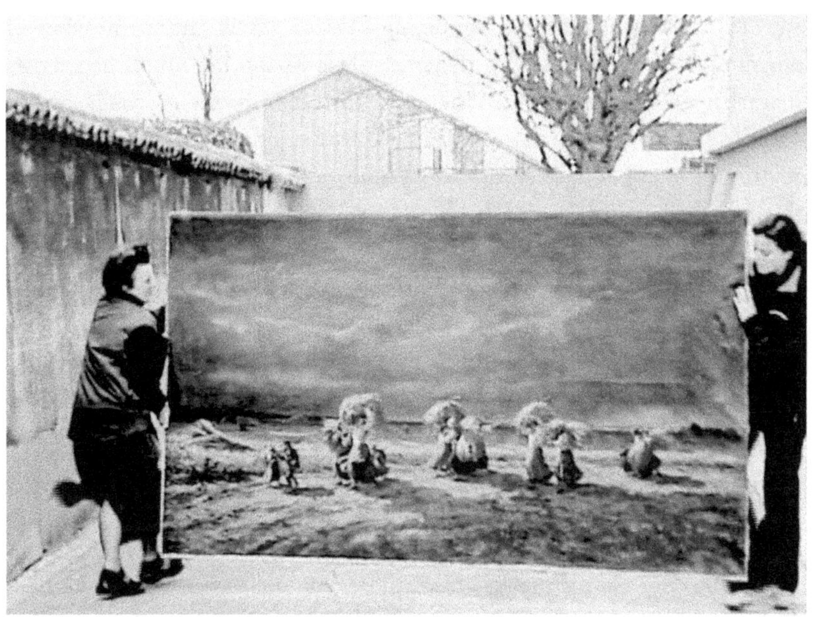

3.4. Hédouin's *Gleaners Fleeing the Storm* is removed from storage in the wind in *The Gleaners and I.*

age the painting is preserved from damage, sheltered from literal and figurative storms. In this sense storage is opposed to waste; it would seem to be an ecologically sound strategy. And yet an object in storage remains invisible, untouched and out of circulation. Taking an image out of storage is a way of putting it back into circulation—of making the virtual actual. Hence Varda's glee at seeing this valuable painting exposed to the elements, for its emergence from the warehouse represents a reentry into the present world. A degree of decay and weathering is a necessary prerequisite to the painting's forward movement in time.

In his treatise on new media, Manovich lists several principles that are hallmarks of this form. The one that is most important for my purpose is the principle of variability. Literally this refers to the use of variables in mathematical equations, but more generally it refers to the notion that the digital text allows for a play of substitutions in a series. Variability expresses the possibility of endless permutation and transformation, where there is never a final or definitive version of the text. It offers a remedy for what Hollis Frampton has called "the new stone age" of the visual arts: the tendency toward stasis and an illusion of permanence.[21] Of course the idea of endless variability might be seen as fostering an illusion of permanence or immortality in another way, insofar as it strives toward the infinite. But the concept of variability also invites us to appreciate transitional objects in their own right: mutable things, test versions, tentative beta forms in the process of becoming.

Varda also follows through on the promise of progressive movements and new variations with her sequel, *Two Years Later.* It contains footage shot at an antifascist march, which took place in Paris on May 1, 2000, the day the original film was completed. We also get a segment showing the response to the first film: the many prizes and awards it garnered, the massive amount of fan mail it generated, letters containing gleaned gifts written on recycled paper, including one sent inside a train ticket envelope. But the circuit of exchange does not stop there, for Varda packs up her camera and goes to visit the senders of this letter. The remainder of *Two Years Later* consists of episodes with gleaners old and new: follow-up conversations with some of the original characters, plus more interviews with people whom she has met through channels opened by the first film. This is an extraordinarily generative structure, one that mimics the prolific quality of certain electronic modes of communication. The response to the film becomes a springboard for further imagistic gleaning. In fact we might even go as far as to say that Varda's 2004 *Ydessa, the Bears, and etc.*—the first of the three shorts in *Cinévardaphoto*—comprises yet another variation on the theme, as this documentary's subject is also a gleaner of sorts: a collector of World War II–era photographs featuring teddy bears.

One of the characters Varda revisits in *Two Years Later* is the late psychoanalyst Jean Laplanche. He is featured in the first film not as an analyst but as a winemaker and grower of grapes. A trained master vintner, Laplanche took over his father's estate in Pommard and now resides there with his wife, Nadine. Varda, presenting herself as unaware of Laplanche's renown as an analyst and theorist, gives him the same treatment she does the other figures in the film. She asks him and Nadine about their winemaking methods and whether anyone has come to pick the leftover grapes. Affable and obliging, Laplanche answers her, and even quotes from a poem by Du Bellay: "We would see the gleaner,

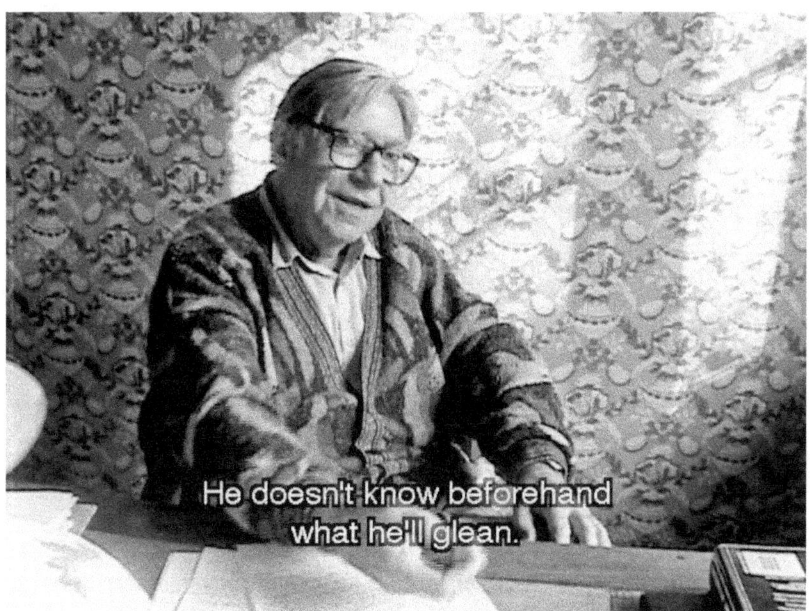

3.5. Jean Laplanche in *The Gleaners and I: Two Years Later.*

tramping along, gathering the relics/Of that which is falling/Behind the reaper."

In the second film, both filmmaker and interviewee note that they have made an omission in failing to note that Laplanche is a famous psychoanalyst and that psychoanalysis too involves a form of gleaning. As Laplanche puts it, analysts "pay attention to things that no one else does . . . to what falls from discourse, what is dropped." Like the filmmaker's look, the analyst's listening is a kind of gleaning, an attunement to the underremarked and to what at first glance seems insignificant or without value. It can in turn be a way to help the analysand reclaim words that he or she has disowned, to pluck unharvested fruit, or to venture in search of an unexplored field. Like a juicy bunch of grapes hanging just out of reach, the topic of psychoanalysis had itself gone unnoticed in the first film; Varda returns with her camera to pick it the second time around.

As mentioned in chapter 1, Laplanche is known in part for his theory of the enigmatic signifier. He offers a clear description of this concept in his Kent Seminar of May 1990, where he explains that enigmatic signifiers are messages that are clearly addressed to us but that we cannot understand and cannot decode.[22] In Laplanche's account, the enigmatic signifier becomes traumatic, and hence eroticized, a Sphinxian riddle without answer. Enigmatic signifiers are like psychical junk, unintelligible messages that are tossed like garbage into the unconscious, where they may fester and continue to cry out for us to decode them. On the one hand, Laplanche tells us, these messages are by definition irrecoverable and beyond decipherment, opaque "alike to sender and recipient."[23] On the other hand, they are a potentially infinite source of transformation and interpretation. In this way enigmatic signifiers are like digital base objects from which multiple versions of text may sprout. They are like templates that prompt a never-ending series of sequels, signs that may be recycled many times without ever being "used up."

Laplanche's enigmatic signifier may be a catalyst for new variations; it participates in the logic of variability that Manovich has attributed to new media. This concept thus serves as a helpful reminder that a feature like variability is not an innovation of digital media. It is instead a basic element of signification—a representational and aesthetic possibility that artists have relied on in textual forms ranging from baroque music to narrative cinema. In this way variability is akin to another catchword of new media, interactivity, which Kinder notes "did not begin in cyberspace" but can be found in forms ranging from eighteenth-century novels to *The Rocky Horror Picture Show*.[24] While these features are nothing new in themselves, their aesthetic principles seem to be facilitated or encouraged anew by the digital format. New forms of image making are not definitive breaks with the old, nor are they simply its filial offspring. They are the gleaned revivals of what was already contained there as virtual possibility and the extension of these possibilities into new and unexpected terrain.

VIRTUAL MEMORY

The title of Varda's film *The Beaches of Agnès* (2008) might be understood in two senses: as a possessive, suggesting beaches that belong to Agnès Varda, and in an almost opposite sense, suggesting that Varda is herself made up of beaches. The filmmaker expands on the latter of these mean-

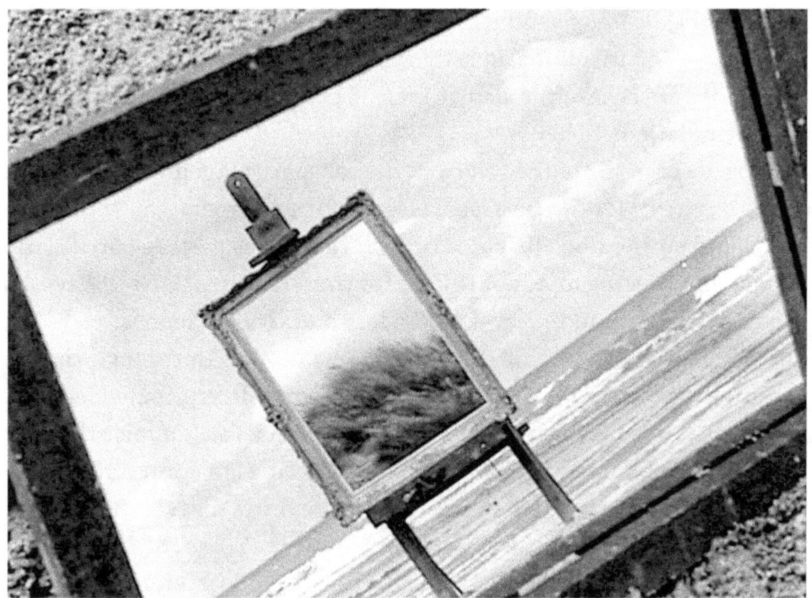

3.6. Mirrors at the seashore in Agnès Varda's *The Beaches of Agnès* (2008).

ings in the film's opening sequence. Walking backward along a stretch of French Mediterranean coastline, Varda speaks to the camera, explaining that although the film will take the form of her life story, it is really about others. "If one opened people up, one would find landscapes," she says. "If one opened me up, one would find beaches."[25] This sentence recalls a famous statement by Cézanne: "The landscape thinks itself in me, and I am its consciousness."[26] Maurice Merleau-Ponty quotes this statement in "Cézanne's Doubt," as does Kaja Silverman in her book *World Spectators*. Silverman glosses Cézanne, whom she takes to be saying, "I am not the painter of my paintings. I am, rather, the medium through which the things of the world paint themselves."[27] Like Cézanne, Varda sees herself more as a medium or conduit than the originator of her films; she subordinates her agency to that of the places, objects, and people that have moved and inspired her. This authorial divestiture is illustrated through a sequence of shots in which she and her crew place many mirrors along the sandy shore, allowing them to reflect not only human beings but also the landscape and each other. As the wind blows her scarf over her face, Varda jokes that this is how her self-portrait should appear. This opening sequence makes clear that Varda's autobiography will consist not primarily of images of herself—although there are plenty of these—but also of images of the external world that intrigue and fascinate her.

This decentering of the self from the self-portrait genre is not new in Varda's oeuvre: *The Gleaners and I* also performs autobiography through the found stories and objects of others. Nor is this gesture particularly unique in other examples of this genre from the French New Wave; as Silverman has noted, Jean-Luc Godard's *JLG/JLG* defines authorial subjectivity less through the activity of creation than through that of reception.[28] But in *The Beaches of Agnès*, Varda decenters herself in a different way, one that has further implications for feminist thought and feminist filmmaking. Key to this decentering is a surprisingly complex theory of memory that emerges through the film's structure and editing choices, one of the components of which is the idea that memory is not the source of artistic inspiration, or at least not in the ways commonly assumed. As Varda remarked in an interview shortly after the film's release, "Forgetting is a form of freedom; loss of memory is a subtext throughout *Beaches*."[29] *Beaches* begins with a reflection on the self as defined by its dispersal throughout the various landscapes that this self has inhabited; it ends with what seems like an emphatic declaration of Varda's will to survive and keep alive the memory of those she has lost. "As long as I live, I remember," she insists in the film's final image. But this pronouncement is not borne out by the rest of the film. Woven throughout *Beaches* are reminders of memory's instability and the simultaneous horror and pleasure of its evaporation.

Taking a cue from conventional autobiography form, *The Beaches of Agnès* proceeds in chronological fashion. Near the beginning of the film are a series of scenes in which Varda reflects on her childhood, speaking to the camera: "Everyone says childhood is a foundation, provides a structure. I don't know why. I don't feel a strong link to my childhood. It's not a reference in my thought process. It's not an inspiration." Looking through photographs of herself as a child on the beach, Varda refers to herself in the third person, saying that she would love to see "this little girl in the striped bathing suit, and also this one in the one with the big straps." The film cuts to a shot of Varda with two girls, costumed in 1930s-style bathing suits, playing with colorful paper flowers in the sand. Varda remarks, "I don't know what it means to re-create a scene like this. Do we relive the moment? For me, it's cinema, it's a game."

Varda actively rejects a psychobiographical account of artistic creation, dismissing as nonsense the notion that the artist's childhood biography functions in covert, symptomatically diagnosable ways as the explanation for the works she produces later in life. The next shots, though, speculate about how her childhood beachcombing might have influenced current projects; they show Varda decorating the grave of her cat Zgougou with colorful scallop shells. This connection is offered up more as a free association than a causal or explanatory link. If there is a correspondence between the seashell installation and the shores of her youth, Varda seems to say, it is an aesthetic and affective one and largely unconscious—revealed only retroactively—rather than the result of a conscious attempt to restore or preserve a moment from childhood. It is also more about the ongoing gesture of beachcombing than about a particular shell, beach, or seminal incident that happened with that object or at that place. She adds to this montage a clip from *The Gleaners and I* in which she holds a seashell-framed hand mirror up to her face, another link in the chain of seashell associations; it is as if this clip were the found footage equivalent of picking up a shell from the sand.

The next sequence expands on the notion that the self, like matter, is but an aggregate of images, ones that become grouped together in part by chance. Varda recounts that she has received a telegram from a doctor who now lives in her childhood home and has invited her to visit. Upon arriving with her camera, she notes that it looks the same but that she feels no emotion. She vividly recalls some of the objects and forms in the house—a pear-shaped decorative pond in the garden, a ceramic tile backsplash—but there are no memories of playing or crying, no affect associated with them. She asks the actor Yolande Moreau to read a text describing how Varda and her sisters used to prime the soil in the garden with butter knives, but as with the scene of the girls on the beach, the restaging does not provide a royal road to memory. Varda speaks of wanting to see the bedrooms where her sisters used to sleep, but instead of showing them, she digresses into a relatively lengthy sequence in which the home's current owner proudly shows off his miniature train collection. The brightly painted cars seem to capture her imagination more fully than do the home's walls and rooms. In the end Varda calls the trip "a bust."

This series of images suggests that it is only through chance encounter with a new, current and present sensory association that the past returns in vivid sensory fullness. One can only reencounter the past by displacing away from it; if we go looking for it in the spaces where we expect it to be, we may, as Varda did, come up empty-handed. Here Varda modestly revisits Proust's famous formula for involuntary memory, while putting the accent on the differences between the contemporary encounter with the madeleine and tea and the scene of the original memory, rather than on their similarity. It is the newly found seashells and toy trains that animate sleeping memory, not the walls and rooms of her childhood house. According to the theory of memory that Varda implicitly offers in *The Beaches of Agnès*, it is not simply that a chance encounter with a long-lost sensory experience provokes a rich, involuntary return to the past; it is also necessary that the object that elicits the new sensory experience not be identical with the original object.

Domietta Torlasco writes that in *The Gleaners and I*, Varda's house functions as a "heretical archive." The space serves not as "a monumental, official residence—the 'fortress' of Alain Resnais' *All the Memory of the World*, the French national library, of Freud's house-museum," but rather as a "fragile and yet enduring shelter, a domicile with porous walls, rhizomatically linked to the other odd depositories she encounters during her travels."[30] Torlasco calls attention to the feminist, nonfilial, nonhierarchical aspects of this style of archive, and notes that the film itself is a similar kind of depository. We can contrast Varda's "new" home in *The Gleaners and I* with her childhood home in *The Beaches of Agnès*: whereas the former archive evokes a seemingly endless tapestry of stories, many of which pay no heed to temporal chronology, going directly to the source in the latter yields nothing. The toy trains that Varda enjoys there, though, linked together, metaphorize the associative connections and forward motion by which memory proceeds in the second film. It is through the introduction of new objects and forms that the home ceases to be a mausoleum of her past and enters into a wider, more porous, more rhizomatic chain of displacements: into the present.

There is one figure in Varda's canon for whom the rule of displacement and nonidenticality does not seem to apply: her husband, Jacques Demy. Varda offers up one of the film's most enigmatic and startling revelations, that Demy was HIV positive and dying of complications from the AIDS virus, as if as a casual aside. In voice-over she says, "Jacques was dying, he knew he was dying. He knew AIDS was incurable, he knew it could only get worse. We all knew it. Nobody talked about it. It was a kind of affectionate silence, totally respectful of Jacques, who didn't talk about it." Her daughter Rosalie joins the voice-over in agreement: "We accepted this silence because it was Jacques's silence." And her son Mathieu adds, "It was his choice to remain silent, and so we did. In 1989, AIDS was considered a shameful disease." Varda concurs: "It was taboo." Varda's monologue begins with her speaking directly to the camera; after this there is a montage of images of Jacques: as an older man in a black-and-white still photograph, as a youth portrayed by an actor in clips from *Jacquôt de Nantes*, and again as an adult in documentary footage taken during the shooting of that film.

The enigma of how Demy acquired AIDS remains undisclosed to the film's spectators, and the voice-over segment leaves open the possibility that the family members also lacked this information. The idea that the couple had in some respects gone their separate ways is hinted at only indirectly, in a segment of the film describing their time in Los Angeles: Varda shows a clip from her film *Documenteur* (1981) in which, by chance, she filmed a couple in the midst of an argument, and her camera lingers on them for a long time, as if drawn to an unspoken analogy. This biographical revelation might threaten to undermine a significant if not defining feature of Varda's accumulated efforts at self-portraiture, that is, her emphasis on her passionate love for Demy: an identity defined by her status as his widow and a devotion, loyalty, and commitment to him that is assumed in these works to be reciprocal. One begins to wonder whether the emphasis in the film on forgetting might be not simply an attempt to subvert the traditional retrospective, biographical gaze but the result of an active forgetting or a desire not to know in the first place. There is also a sense in which allowing Demy this silence, this final enigma, comes across as the ultimate act of fidelity to his memory on the part of his widow and children.

There is a complicated sort of intersubjectivity at work in these sequences and the transactions they describe, particularly as they relate to gender and heterosexuality. If viewed as the loyal widow of a possibly unfaithful husband, Varda might strike some as the antithesis of the politicized feminist we see in the scenes of the film in which she protests for women's rights and participates in a pro-choice action with a group called the 343 Salopes. *Le Bonheur* (1965), a brightly lit, deceptively cheerful film in which a husband suddenly leaves his wife for another woman who seamlessly comes to occupy the place of the wife, might read differently for critics of the biographical persuasion in light of such information. But there is also a reversal of classic gender roles here. It is a truism of psychoanalytic film theory that women are classically portrayed as objects of desire, while men tend to occupy the role of desiring subjects. But there is an unavoidable sense, perhaps most evident in *Jacquôt de Nantes* and *The Universe of Jacques Demy* (1995), that Demy is Varda's muse, not the other way around. She unabashedly assumes the role of desiring subject in relation to him: he is her obscure object of desire, and her desire is only strengthened by the fact that he is available to her only in fragments. Indeed in all of Varda's work, there is a sense in which she is the subject of an active, curious, and desiring look. It is equally evident in those films and video works that feature female protagonists: *Cléo from 5 to 7*, *Vagabond*, and *Jane B. par Agnès V.* (1988). In Varda's films, vision is largely a metaphor for desire. While she often appears in her films on the spectacle side of the camera, she is rarely present strictly as the object of the gaze: she either looks directly at the camera or appears in the guise of someone who looks and films. If there is one consistent feature of her work, it is that she films things that she loves—"les choses qui me plaîsent," as she says in *The Gleaners and I*—hence the overwhelmingly optimistic and pleasurable quality of her images even when she turns her lens to darker subject matter.

WALKING BACKWARD

Varda confronts the subject of loss and mortality squarely in the face in her 2006 video installation piece, *The Widows of Noirmoutier*. A multiscreen work, the piece consists of fourteen small video monitors, each of which features a different widow from the seaside town of Noirmoutier. Fourteen chairs are arranged in the same formation as the

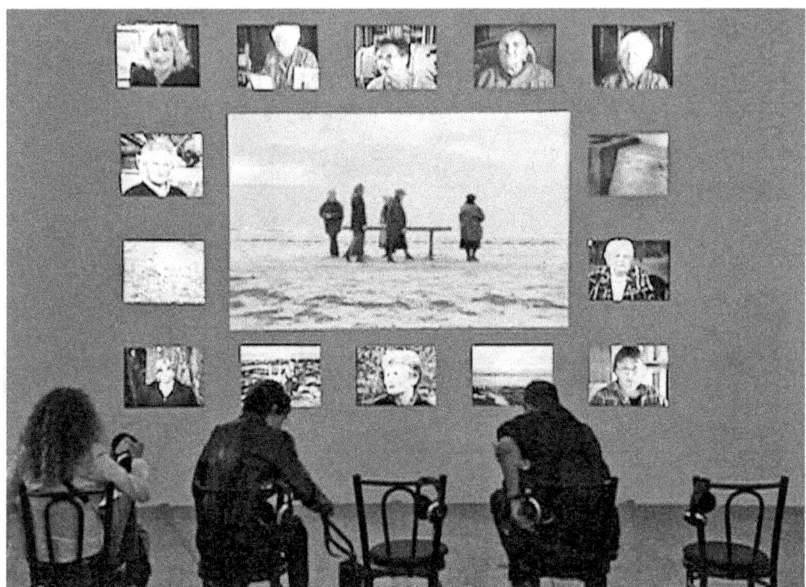

3.7. Varda's *The Widows of Noirmoutier* (2006) is shown in an installation shot during a sequence from *The Beaches of Agnès*.

monitors, each of which holds a set of headphones to hear the corresponding widow's monologue. In the center of the video monitors a larger screen features an image of the widows dressed in black, plodding silently on a beach. In Varda's description, the format "evokes old paintings—polyptychs or pictures edged by a predella."[31] There is an elegiac quality to the piece. Its true subjects, though, are not the men who lost their lives but the women who mourn them. Like much of Varda's oeuvre, the work is a tribute to women who assume the precarious role of desiring subjects. As in *The Gleaners and I*, Varda counts herself among the subjects of her film. She too is a widow of Noirmoutier, the island where Demy camped as a child and where the couple owned property.

This island is rife with associations for Varda. In a sequence from *Beaches*, she cuts wildly from an abandoned mill there to an oyster farm, an image of blue rubber gloves, bounties of oysters and potatoes, waves, and finally the French New Wave in the form of Chris Marker, who appears as the giant orange cartoon cat Guillaume with a synthesized voice and asks her to tell of her involvement in this historic film movement. A collage appears, one of many in this film, featuring photos of

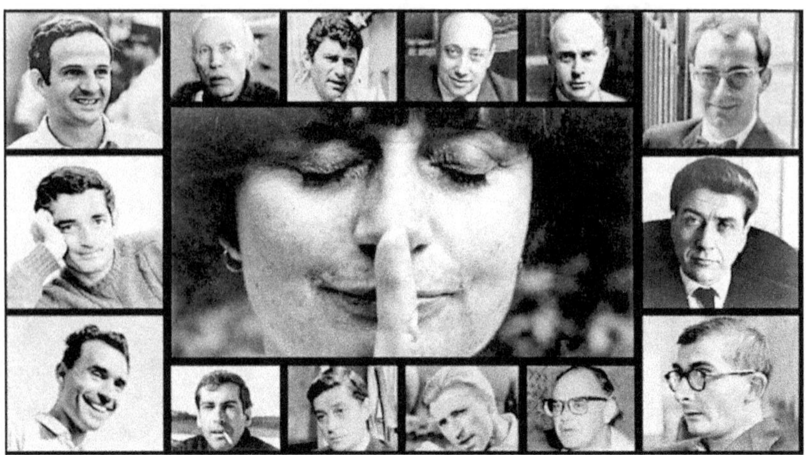

3.8. Filmmakers of the French New Wave appear in the same arrangement as the widows of Noirmoutier in Varda's *The Beaches of Agnès* (2008).

New Wave directors arranged in the same formation as the widows in the *Noirmoutier* piece. The formal correspondences further testify to the analogy between filmmaking and desire. Filmmakers, this image seems to say, are not only desiring subjects; they are subjects who desire lost objects, things that are in the process of disappearing and that may finally be impossible to capture on film.

Along with Varda's 1982 film *Ulysse*, one of three shorts included in her triptych *Cinévardaphoto*, *The Beaches of Agnès* and *The Widows of Noirmoutier* offer an implicit feminist reinterpretation of Homer's *Odyssey*. It is not Odysseus the cunning navigator who is the true desiring subject; rather it is Penelope, who waits on the shore, weaves and unweaves her text, and gazes over the water hoping for the desired image to appear. However, Varda does not remain fixated on her primary lost figure. Rather she opens her eyes to the entire sea of virtual images that could surface in that place in the meantime, some of which end up in her films. In this respect Penelope and her surrogates are also like Varda's gleaners, whom she celebrates not for their success in discovering a single golden object of desire but for their openness to any number of possible finds.

This analogy is carried through in the sequence in *The Beaches of Agnès* that directly follows the revelation about the cause of Demy's death. Varda describes her efforts to portray Demy's youth in *Jacquôt de Nantes*: "I didn't know how he viewed the reenactments of the scenes from his childhood, how we reinvented what he'd experienced or said. . . . He said, 'Oh yes, it's just right, I'm there!' His words encouraged me to continue." These words represent a vicarious fulfillment of the promise of involuntary memory. In *The Beaches of Agnès*, Varda's reenactments of her own childhood do not produce the desired coincidence of memory and affect. Varda continues her voice-over, noting that her filmic relationship with Demy took three forms at this time. First, there was the narrative biography of his childhood years from ages nine to nineteen that she was producing for *Jacquôt de Nantes*. Second, she engaged in a more intellectual sort of exercise—a "master's thesis," she calls it—in which she attempted to find analogues for scenes in Demy's films in his past and restage them in a more naturalistic style. She shows an example from *The Umbrellas of Cherbourg* (1964), a scene in which a young auto mechanic delivers a car to his customer with a song, juxtaposed with her reshot version of the scene, a black-and-white, realist counterpart to Demy's Eastman-color high artifice. Finally, Varda says, there was a third filming mode in which she simply felt compelled to document Demy for as long as she could, as closely as possible. She shows an extreme close-up of his gray hair, which she describes as being "like a landscape"; this is the same shot that she mentions at the end of *Two Years Later*, where she says that she had not made the connection between this image and the ones in *The Gleaners* in which she films her own graying hair and aging skin until the similarity was brought to her attention.

These three filming modes correspond to the three registers of the cinematic image that Barthes describes in "The Third Meaning." This 1970 essay proposes three levels of meaning: first, the informational, which pertains to communication; second, the "symbolic," which has to do with intellectually signified connotations; and third, the "obtuse," which is supplementary, "incomplete," and has to do with affect. As Barthes puts it, the third meaning "is an emotion which simply designates what one loves, what one wants to defend."[32] Barthes indicates that all three categories may be operative for any image; however, there is a sense in which Varda's three filming modes from *Jacquôt* invite these three types of engagement separately. Her attempt to provide an accu-

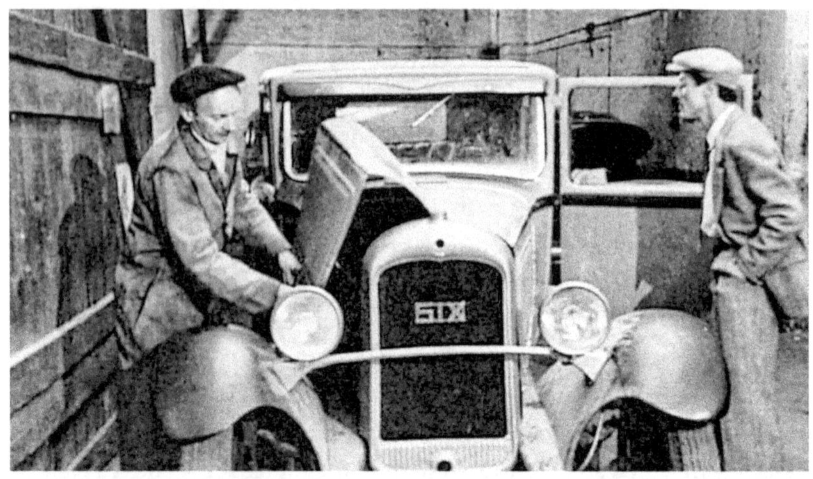

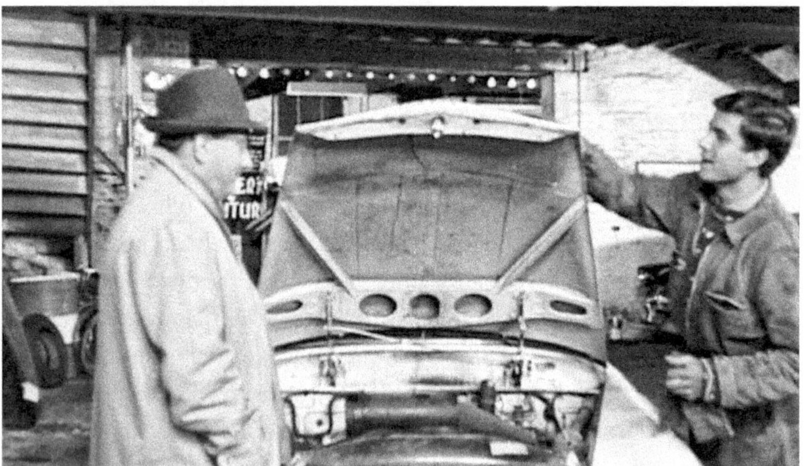

3.9. A scene from Varda's *Jacquôt de Nantes* (1991), re-created from Jacques Démy's *The Umbrellas of Cherbourg* (1964) in *The Beaches of Agnès.*

3.10. A still from a scene in Démy's *The Umbrellas of Cherbourg* that Varda re-created in her film *Jacquôt de Nantes*, shown in her film *The Beaches of Agnès.*

rately restaged depiction of Demy's early biography represents the informational register; in this case the film image aims to match a memory image from a real past. The symbolic register comes into play in the thesis-like restaging of Demy's film sequences. Here the past as such is no longer in play; the associative link occurs strictly between two "virtual" images, that is, between one film image and another. Finally, the landscape of Demy's skin and hair is rich with third meanings. This type of image is obtuse, blunt: there is no invisible source scene in the past to which it corresponds. Instead it corresponds with the image of Varda's own gray hair from *The Gleaners and I* and with any number of similarly evocative moments supplied by the psyches of the films' spectators. The childhood seashells that link Zgougou's grave to the seashell-encrusted hand mirror are also obtuse types of images. They are the ones that are most ripe for association and hence for forking paths into repositories of associated virtual memories.

When Varda says that she is an artist who films what she loves, she effectively says that she is searching for obtuse meanings to register on film. There is a vulnerability to this method, as well as a kind of radical openness. A certain ceding of control is necessary to make it happen: unlike the reenacted scenes in *Jacquôt de Nantes* there is no way to tell if such an image is "successful" or not at the level of accuracy, verisimilitude, and so on. And as the examples of the hair and seashells attest, the affective connections that make such images compelling are not under the filmmaker's conscious control. They may emerge only in retrospect, as in these cases, or not at all; as Varda notes, the trip to her childhood home was "a bust" in this respect. This seemingly most private and elusive type of image is also paradoxically the type that is most generative of wayward displacements. Toward the end of *The Beaches of Agnès*, Varda takes a series of still portraits in which she photographs her children against the same background as anonymous strangers. Her family, she says, is the sum of her happiness. However, she adds, "I don't know if I know them, each one, or if I understand them. I just go toward them. . . . Family is a somewhat compact concept. We mentally group everyone together and imagine them as a peaceful island." Her statement and the series of portraits that accompany it implicitly propose a more inclusive definition of family—not as a neat mental group, nor as an island, but as a finite yet vast shore that, if one is willing to walk down it backward, without knowing what one will encounter, may gradually expand the contours of what one loves and desires.

CHAPTER 4

Beyond Repetition

Victor Burgin's Loops

Memory is not the opposite of forgetting, but rather its lining.

—Chris Marker, *Sans Soleil*

In the 1980s and 1990s Victor Burgin made a trilogy of visual works that invoke Hitchcock's 1958 film *Vertigo*. These works—*The Bridge* (1984), *Venise* (1993), and *Another Case History* (1999)—enter *Vertigo*'s universe through references to San Francisco, through female figures who loosely resemble Kim Novak as Madeleine/Judy, and, perhaps most significantly, through sustained exploration of circular movements and forms. Several of Burgin's recent gallery works continue this exploration in their use of looped video and computer-simulated 360-degree panoramas. These video loops, though, do not repeat the circular theme compulsively; they forge a path beyond the automatism of the merry-go-round view of history. In Burgin's hands, the video loop provides a refreshing critique of infinitely recursive forms and the stagnation that accompanies them. In place of a future that is met with eager anticipation only when it offers an exact replica of what has already been, Burgin's loops seem to say that desire need not be a one-way ticket to an irrecoverable lost object. As if in answer to the question posed by the forms of self-enclosed, obsessive repetition so carefully rendered by Hitchcock, Freud, and others, Burgin offers another kind of spiral: a four-dimensional one, open at both ends, designed not to return to zero but to swirl up an ever-expanding range of interconnected times, spaces, people, and texts. We might think of them as continuous revolutions instead of eternal recurrences. Burgin's video loops allow us to see time not as a slice of petrified wood—even when that slice contains the majesty of a centuries-old *Sequoia sempervirens*—but as a still living tree.

REPRISE, REFRAIN

Burgin has used the word *reprise* to describe his video loops. This term suggests not so much an obsessive identicality as, in Burgin's description, a *ritornello* or "a *da capo* in music, where the reprised refrain sounds different the second time since it is shadowed by our recollection of the first."[1] The echo exists in close communion with its prior hearings, but each ring takes on its own character, informed and enriched by the others and rendered curiously both more familiar and less so. Another way to describe this type of repetition is with the notion of reseeing or rereading. In "Diderot, Barthes, *Vertigo*," Burgin describes how his multiple viewings of *Vertigo* allowed it to expand for him into an ever-wider spiral: "I find that my re-entry into the text of the film is by a different route—one destined to take me through a different sequence of images, until I have traversed the text again. . . . I find that the trajectory of associations has become attracted into [another] orbit."[2] The loop that Burgin builds into many of his gallery video works solicits from the viewer not so much a sense of uncanny déjà vu as a feeling similar to that of rereading a favorite novel and discovering things in it that one had not noticed before.

This process presumably occurs with any moderately complex text that one sees, reads, or hears again with an open mind. But Burgin's videos expressly invite it, both through their looped formats and due to their dense layering. The works are heavily intertextual, rife with more references than can be absorbed in a single viewing. To borrow a metaphor from Peter Wollen, their "apertures" are flung wide open to words and images from the outside.[3] Works like *Watergate* (2000), *The Little House* (2005), *Voyage to Italy* (2006), *Fogliazzi* (2007), *Solito Posto* (2008), and *A Place to Read* (2010) deploy the looped pan-like movement in a way that builds the opportunity for reviewing into their own structures. Our successive encounters with their images form strata, allowing us to sift through the sheaths of citations within the works. As Burgin puts it, the ideal viewer of his work is one "who accumulates her or his knowledge of the work, as it were, in 'layers'—much as a painting is created."[4] In this way Burgin's gallery videos are less cinematic than lectographic. With no obvious beginnings or endings, they lack the linearity of narrative film. Each seeming recurrence of the same—the same woman, room, gesture, or phrase of text—is shadowed by a stream of prior and future images that are connected to it but that do not depend on chronological ordering in order to operate in this way.

As I explained in chapter 2, Bergson had a name for this stream of prior and future images accompanying those of the present moment: he called it the virtual. The virtual is the intertwining of the past and memory, the future and imagination, and present-tense perceptions that drop out of our viewfinders because we have channeled our attention elsewhere. This way of understanding virtuality holds great value for rethinking repetition. In Bergson's view, what persists in and accompanies every fresh act of perception is not simply the repressed, censored, or traumatic material that populates the unconscious, as in a conventional psychoanalytic understanding. Rather it is the virtual in all of the senses described above: memory images that belong to the past, potential images that are thrown toward the future, fringe images that surround us in the present moment, and, most important, the cushion or interval of duration that invites these images in. This is why seeing something twice is not, as it would be for a computer, merely redundant but rather has the potential to reveal a vast new group of interconnected impressions.

A similar rethinking of repetition and its relation to visual perception and time is in play in Chris Marker's *Sans Soleil* (1983). This film revisits his 1962 *La Jetée* in its exploration of motifs of recurrence.[5] Toward the end of *Sans Soleil*, Marker makes pilgrimages to the sites where Hitchcock filmed *Vertigo*, a film that he confesses he has seen at least nineteen times. Marker replicates Scottie's movements through the steep streets of San Francisco to the forest canopy of Muir Woods and the stucco arches of Mission San Juan Bautista. In doing so he retraces the steps of *Vertigo*'s loop as an encounter with something unknown yet intimately familiar. These places activate in him a form of remembering "which is not the opposite of forgetting but rather its lining," as the

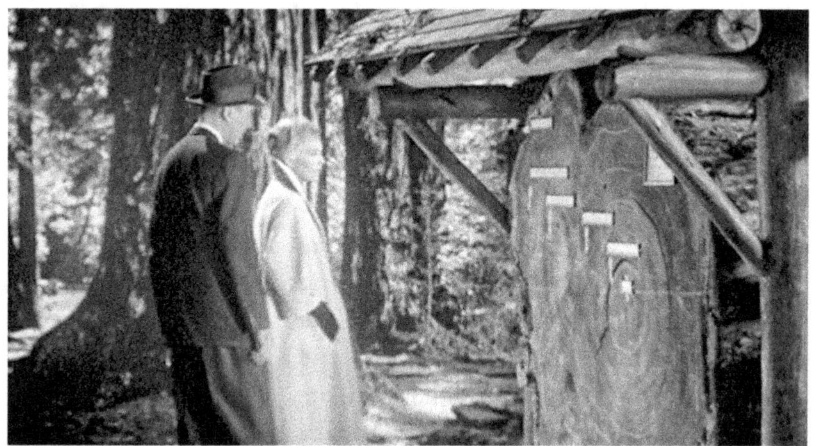

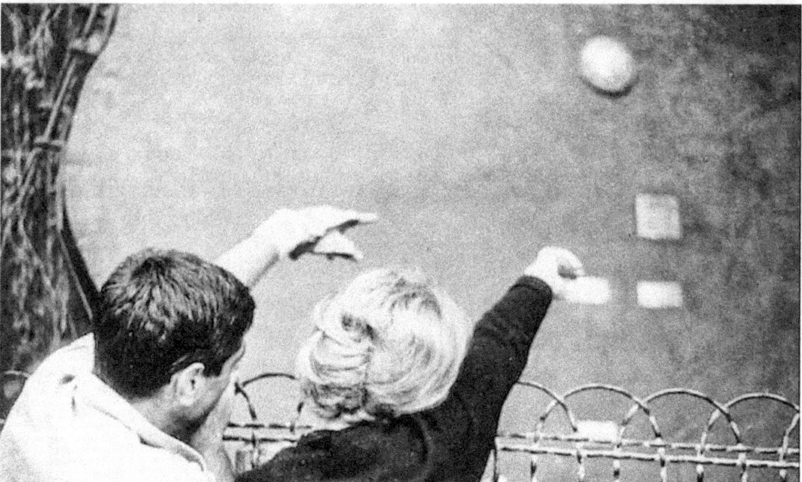

4.1. *Sequoia sempervirens* in *Vertigo*, directed by Alfred Hitchcock (1958).

4.2. *Sequoia sempervirens* in *La Jetée* by Chris Marker (1962).

narrator says. According to this evocative metaphor, memory and forgetting are not opposed to one another; they are folds of the same cloth.

Throughout *Sans Soleil* images repeat. Certain people, sites, gestures, and objects appear and reappear in cyclical rhythms: three children in Iceland, a temple for cats in Japan, a woman in Guinea Bissau who meets the camera's gaze, a pile of broken dolls ceremonially burned. Sometimes they are processed in bright, electronically generated colors. These repetitions, though, are more properly reprises—or perhaps rehearsals or recitals. Far from a notion of history in which we are fated to repeat the past mechanically or in which everything we see is force-fit into the frames of things we have seen before, these images assert the *impossibility* of an image ever fully coinciding with its predecessors or future versions. They simultaneously insist on these images' continuity and connectedness, not only with their own obvious doubles but also with the whole, far-flung group that is contained in the film.

In a sense this is the same conclusion that Scottie comes to (and suffers from) in his frustration with actual Judy's partial resemblance to virtual Madeleine in *Vertigo*. As long as we are bound to the flow of time, no image can ever absolutely replicate a previous one. No new object of affection will ever be exactly like an old one, even, curiously, when she is technically the same person. This is a fortunate situation since the alternative is a world populated by statues, locked in freeze-frame while time continues to whirl around them. Freud exploited a similar feature in the analytic situation by allowing for and then interpreting his patients' transferential reenactments, as in the case of the elderly woman who "repeatedly fled from her house and her husband in a twilight state . . . without ever having become conscious of her motive for decamping in this way."[6] Within a week of seeking treatment, she predictably decamped from Freud too. Had she remained, she might eventually have realized that Freud was not a replica of her husband, the analytic scenario not an encore of her marriage, and, possibly, her marriage not an encore of whatever prior scenario had driven her to flight in the first place.

For Bergson, Marker, and, as the remainder of this chapter explores, Burgin, the relationship between the virtual and the actual is less redundant. The therapeutic benefit of ensuring their absolute separation is not taken as given, nor is the fatalistic notion that the psyche longs primarily for their absolute identicality. For these thinkers, past and present, virtual and actual, enjoy both gaps and concurrences. They layer over and spiral through one another. Bergson describes a similar phenomenon in his essay on dreams: "Sensation longs for a form into which to solidify its fluidity; memory longs for matter to fill it, to ballast it, in short, to realize it. They are drawn toward each other."[7] There is a striving on the part of virtual images—be they memories, speculations, or peripheral phenomena—to connect with what is here in the present moment, and a striving on the part of present perception to be enriched by this throng of images. But the magnets pull them closer without one time frame ever fully eclipsing the others. Bergson might have called this the longing of time for its durational continuity to be restored to it.

SITE READING: *THE LITTLE HOUSE*

The Little House (2005) begins with a signature Burgin visual trope: a slow, scrolling movement from left to right over a still, panoramic image of a landscape. We see the corner of a concrete building and a patch of green lawn enclosed by a tall hedge, then another side of the building, paneled with rectangular windows framed in natural wood, revealing the structure's distinctly California modern style of residential architecture. A female narrator speaks in voice-over, describing elements of the mise-en-scène. But the features she describes—marble statues, promenades, grottos, labyrinths, and bridges—do not match those we see on the image track. What we see is in many ways of an opposite style: white walls at right angles, a green lawn, flat but for a patch of wild rushes, and, aside from the tops of a few palm fronds that peek over the horizon, nothing that resembles the intricate ornamentation of which the voice speaks.

The next shot shows a young woman in a sleeveless dress slowly opening a red, pocket-size book and appearing to read silently from it in a fixed medium shot. The narrator proceeds to recite passages and dialogue from a story. Burgin's notes inform us that the text is adapted from Jean-François de Bastide's 1758 *La Petite Maison*, a libertine novella that doubles as an interior decorating manual for liaison houses, offering descriptions of the types of furnishings, wallpaper, lighting, and objects that best facilitate the seduction of prospective lovers. The passage we hear tells of the proprietor Trémicour's arrival at one such house with the young Mélite, whose virtue he hopes to overcome. The relationship between soundtrack and image track in Burgin's video is indeterminate. As the artist notes, the reading woman "may figure the narrator, an eighteenth-century *lectrice*, the heroine Mélite, her actual self, or all at the same time."[8] Visually the image references the lectrice and the type of portrait painting in which a woman is pictured reading a book, often the Bible. This type of picture may invite a feminist inter-

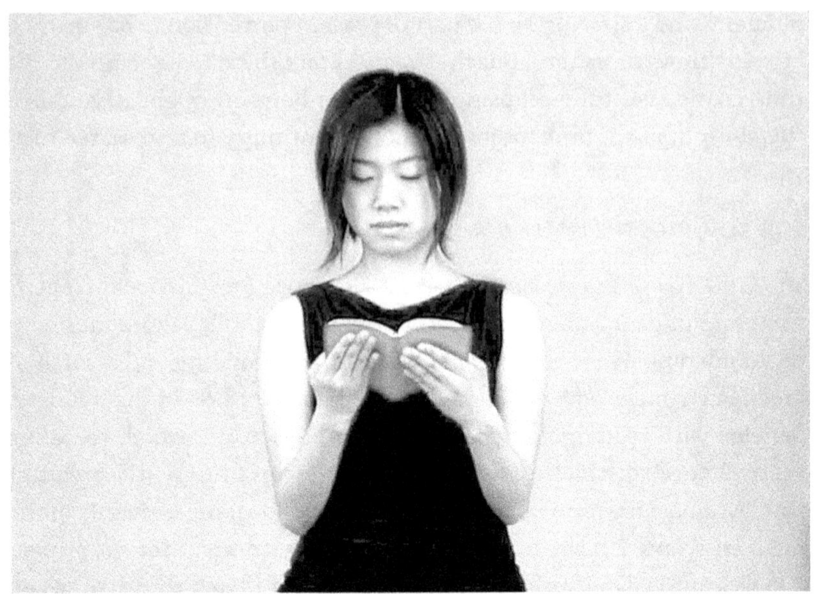

4.3. Still from Victor Burgin's *The Little House* (2005). A women reads from Mao's Little Red Book. Courtesy of the artist.

pretation in that such female figures enjoy access to words and thoughts that are inaccessible to the spectator and that therefore mark a limit to what can be grasped or claimed via the look. The book resembles, and in fact is, a copy of *Quotations from Chairman Mao Zedong*, also known as the Little Red Book.

The next shot brings us to the interior of the building, Rudolph Schindler's Kings Road House in Los Angeles. Schindler, a student of Adolf Loos and, along with Frank Lloyd Wright and Richard Neutra, a pioneer of the California modern architectural style, designed this house in 1921 as a residence for himself. The camera once again pans slowly from left to right. The narrator shifts back into a descriptive mode, and this time what she describes more closely matches what we see: smooth concrete floors, California redwood, and so on. When the voice begins to list the room's furnishings, though—cushions, a Japanese print, a warm fire burning—a gap inserts itself once more between text and image, for the room we see is empty. The next cut reveals a second image of the woman, who clasps her palms together as if reading a book. But her hands are empty; the gesture is only a pantomime. Throughout the remainder of the video, shots of the woman miming the act of reading—or perhaps reading her own palms?—alternate with shots of her reading from an actual book. These in turn are inserted between panoramic shots of empty and nearly empty rooms in the Schindler House. An analogy presents itself between room and book: both, when empty, can be filled with furnishings and words supplied by the imagination.

One image that the mind might supply, triggered by the appearance of Mao's Little Red Book, is that of the founding of the Chinese Communist Party and the secret First Party Congress in Shanghai in July 1921. At this meeting twelve men, including Mao, were planning revolution around a tea table in a brick building in Shanghai, when a French spy interrupted them. The men fled before their identities were revealed, but the still life that they left in their wake—a communal table set with twelve teacups and twelve hastily abandoned chairs—revealed their number. Thus did one of the twentieth century's major historical events spring forth around a dining table, over cups of tea, in a space arranged for communal activity, group reading, and thought. Schindler seems also to have had revolutionary ideas in mind, albeit on a much more modest scale, when he built the Kings Road House, which broke ground just a few months after the founding of the Chinese Communist Party. The idea for the house came to Schindler during a vacation he took with his wife, Pauline, in Yosemite National Park, where the L-shaped arrangement of campsites inspired him to imagine a redesigned type of communal domestic architecture for himself, Pauline, and another couple, Clyde and Marian Chace.

From the image of the woman with the red book and its associations with this historic year of foundations, Burgin's video shifts abruptly back to the eighteenth-century French aristocracy. The narrator recommences the story of Trémicour and Mélite at the petite maison. "The day was ending," she reads, but instead of the candles and extravagant chandeliers she describes, we see beams of bright sunlight glinting through the narrow windows in the concrete walls of the Schindler House. Whereas the previous image resonates with temporal coincidences—1921 and the linking of Shanghai and California through the common element of that year—this shot creates a subtle temporal dis-

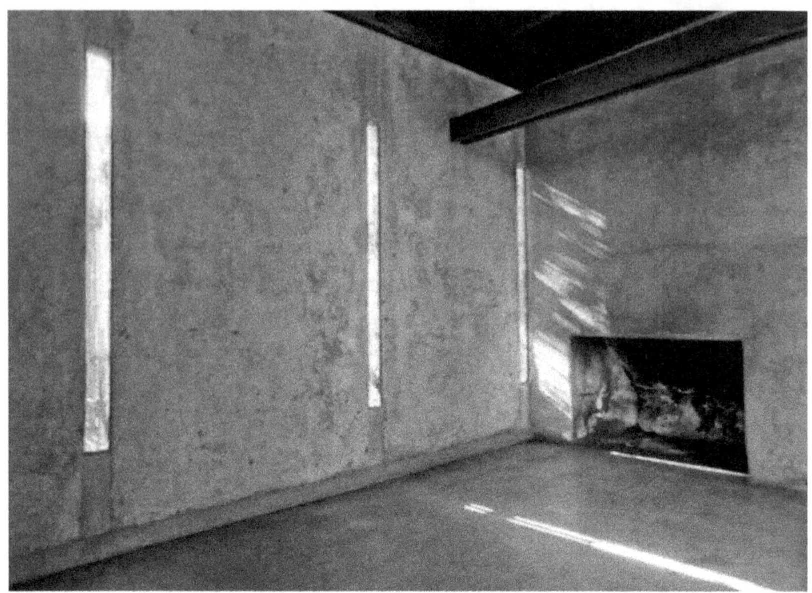

4.4. Still from Burgin's *The Little House*, interior of Rudolph Schindler's Kings Road House in Los Angeles. Courtesy of the artist.

junction as the voice-over speaks of twilight conditions while the image track provides slivers of daylight.

Soon the narrator arrives at a point in Bastide's tale in which Trémicour escorts Mélite into a boudoir. She describes its lavishly mirrored walls, with their "joints concealed," but instead of seamless mirrors we see windows and translucent sliding panels articulated by wooden panes. Exposed wooden beams extend from the ceiling into the courtyard. With its glass walls and lack of proper doors, the room does not really resemble a sleeping chamber. In fact the Schindler House was designed without bedrooms; in their place were rooftop sleeping baskets. Whereas Bastide's narrative describes a movement of retreat into an increasingly recessed, darkened, and private space, Burgin's camera slowly unfurls an architectural plan that opens outward, connecting interior and exterior, earth and sky. Here we may think of the particularly Californian notion of a "design for living": the midcentury gesture of bringing the outside in, domestic space arranged to promote a connection to the natural world along with utopian ideals of physical health, spiritual and mental well-being, and communal values.

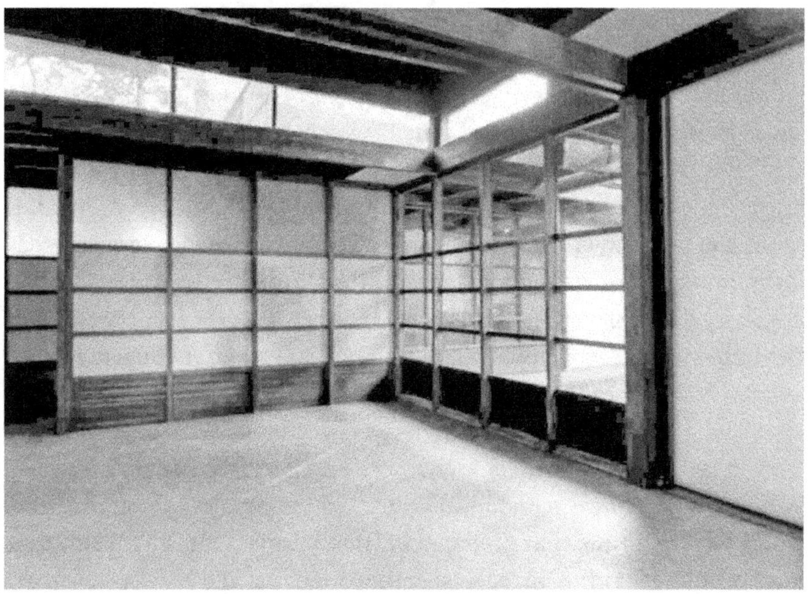

4.5. Still from Burgin's *The Little House*, interior of Rudolph Schindler's Kings Road House in Los Angeles. Courtesy of the artist.

At this point in the video, the viewer may jump to conclude that the relationship between sound and image tracks, and between the eighteenth and twentieth centuries they represent, is purely oppositional: the natural, progressive, communitarian values expressed in the Schindler House as a foil to the artifice, social stratification, and heavily gendered dynamics of the petite maison and Bastide's story. Indeed such a reading seems unavoidable, particularly from a feminist perspective. Building on this reading, the Schindler House and the image track might appear under the sign of the "actual," and the petite maison and voice-over under the sign of the "virtual." But this is where the interpretation goes astray. While the gaps between image and voice, 1921 and 1758, and so on, fall more easily into relief than the points where they overlap, these points do exist.

One of the ways that these points of overlap emerge is through music. In one segment of *The Little House*, Trémicour and Mélite enter a room with botanical decor, and, in purple prose, the narrator describes how it almost produces "the effect of being in a natural wood. . . . The cornices are carved with sweeping festoons of flowers, and painted in colors appropriate to the blooms." The paint, she continues, has been "mixed with fragrances" such that it seems to be "exhaling violet, jasmine, and rose." The synaesthetic experience, the narrator informs us, is augmented by strains of music, which are so sensitive and beautiful that Mélite nearly swoons. Soon we hear a piano on the soundtrack, playing the opening bars of Jean-Philippe Rameau's Allemande from the Suite in A (1728). Burgin notes that since "in Rameau's day the piano had not yet been invented," the choice of instrument "brings together classical and modern, and commemorates the fact that Pauline Schindler was an accomplished musician."[9] The piano would have been a relatively novel, exotic instrument in the 1758 of *La Petite Maison*. (The first pianofortes were made in the early decades of the eighteenth century in Italy, and the earliest known French-made grand piano was built in 1781.) Via Rameau's melody, Pauline Schindler is swept up in a temporal loop to a time that predates Bastide's novella. This loop connects the baroque to minimalism, its seeming opposite, and comments on the association of those styles with their respective time periods and geographical regions.[10] In a kind of synchrony achieved through sound, the piano music could stand simultaneously for what Mélite hears in 1758 or what Pauline Schindler plays in the 1920s.

A form of gentle synchronicity between pasts and presents in *The Little House* emerges through a second conduit: the figure of the reading woman. Following the segment containing the piano music, the narrator begins to describe a "cabinet à la Chinoise." The description of this room, Burgin notes, is not from Bastide's novella, although it is excerpted from a text contemporary with it. Unlike the twentieth-century version evoked by the Little Red Book, the Cathay she describes is decidedly extravagant and sumptuous. Both, though, are virtual in the simple sense, infused with powerful elements of fantasy, to the extent that in a Western imagination, Communist China may function as an abstract political ideal or a site of presumed radical otherness. The narrator continues, "The walls are decorated with painted panels" in which appear "airy landscapes of gnarled trees, precipitous rocks, and fragile pavilions. . . . Beneath a parasol, a young woman is reading." This reading woman provides a link to the one who appears in *The Little House*, suggesting a group of female readers connected to one another across time and space.

A number of temporal and spatial layers accumulate here, as if projected one atop the other: the 1921 of Schindler's Kings Road House and its experiments in communal living, the 1921 of the brick house in which the first Communist Party Congress convened, the 1758 of Bastide's novella and its libertine characters in their petite maison. While the differences suggested by this unlikely grouping are apparent even on a first viewing, the connections among them become visible only with closer attention. It is the video's reading women who open up the indeterminate tenses and spaces that allow these connections to emerge: the narrator who reads aloud from an invisible out-of-field, the woman who opens and closes her red book against an empty backdrop, the woman painted on the orientalist wallpaper who is reading an unknown text beneath her parasol, and, in a sense, Pauline Schindler, whom we may imagine sight-reading a musical score as she plays the grand piano that we hear on the soundtrack. A chorus of virtual images come together here, in the richer, more complex senses of that word: emissaries from the past, fabulations projected onto walls and paper, and stories that may or may not exist on the same diegetic plane.

At the "conclusion" of the video—in scare quotes because the loop form eschews beginnings and endings—the narrator delivers a final line of text: "Mélite rose and hurried into the garden." The loop returns us to the place where it began, ready to begin again the story of Mélite's attempted seduction and flight and ready to reenter the Schindler House from the outside. Burgin informs us that, although the original novella "unambiguously concludes in victory for Trémicour," his own version of *The Little House* "perpetually suspends narrative resolution, fitting the form of the narrative to the structure of the video loop, and leaving Trémicour in unending pursuit of an object of desire that perpetually eludes him."[11] The linear tale of conquest is rewritten as a loop. Like the protagonists of *Vertigo* and *La Jetée*, Trémicour is left forever chasing a woman through the endless labyrinth of his own little theater of desire. While the Sisyphean repetition accurately describes the story of Trémicour and Mélite, the loop takes a different form for the viewers of Burgin's video (as it does, in a best-case scenario, for viewers of any of these texts). In place of an obsessional spiral of chase and evasion, Burgin puts a reprise and a group of female readers who read this spiral differently.

THE LECTOSIGN

In *Cinema 2: The Time-Image*, Deleuze describes a certain type of filmic image that he calls the lectosign: an image that asks to be read rather than simply seen. Deleuze traces this type of cinematic sign to the intertitles of the silent era, but for him the category includes more than filmed images of writing. He describes the lectosign as an "archaeological, or stratigraphic image" that is "*read* at the same time as it is seen."[12] It is a layered image that invites the eye to comb or sift through it in several rounds over time rather than capture it in a flash. This way of "reading" a cinematic image, Deleuze notes, is not the same as the one theorized by Sergei Eisenstein in the silent era, in which shots are edited together grammatically to create syntactical relations that mimic those of verbal language, giving rise to moments of raised consciousness as dialectical opposites collide. In the "new readability" that Deleuze speaks of, it is not a grammatical ordering of montage cells but rather the layers of a single image that are read, the way a geologist might read strata of rock. Deleuze suggests that cinema achieves this new readability in the era of sound, when the image track is liberated from the duty to provide verbal information in intertitles.

What is unearthed through this quarrying of the image as lectosign? It is not simply the past as distinct from the present, as with an archaeological excavation. Nor is it simply occluded or censored data, as in a psychoanalytic depth reading of a text that reveals unconscious meanings encoded as symptoms, meanings that are often in opposition to its manifest or surface ones. Nor, finally, is it a Marxist version of symptomatic reading, wherein the latent content that is exposed through the reader's close critical attention is a hidden ideological construct. For Deleuze stratigraphic reading involves a different sort of uncovering. Paradoxically its movement is not vertical; it occurs across the surface of the image, in a lateral or horizontal gesture. When we read, we are not so much digging or plumbing depths as scanning, scrolling, and connecting. "To read," Deleuze writes, "is to relink instead of link; it is to turn, and turn round." Reading is an act in which our eyes trace a line from left to right and back again over a page-size area, taking in new lines while the previous ones remain close in memory and the coming ones are very near in sight. Reading, Deleuze suggests, "is a function of the eye": not merely a cognitive faculty but an act of perception that requires micro-looping movements.[13] Reading a text in codex form involves a second kind of movement: the turning of pages. It requires relinking and retracing steps since our mind may wander off course until we discover that we have arrived at the end of a paragraph without any conscious memory of how we got there. Conceived of as a type of movement, reading has a kinship with Burgin's scrolling movements and the larger video loops they synecdochize: a slow unspooling and weaving, circling around not as a raptor stalks its prey but as an eye that creates an ever-larger tapestry as it passes back and forth across the weft of the text, seeing a little more of it with each pass of the shuttle. It is not an exhumation but a way to unroll the fabric lined with remembering.

A PRESENT TO THE PAST: *A PLACE TO READ*

A Place to Read (2010) is a digital projection inspired by the Taslik Khave, a coffeehouse and garden in Kanlica, Istanbul, designed by Sedad Hakkı Eldem, built in 1947–48. As in *The Little House*, Burgin looks to architecture as a way to reveal an overlap of pasts and presents: its style is a synthesis of modernism with Ottoman forms of the seventeenth century. Eldem built the structure, which overlooks the Bosphorus Strait, in "an attempt at proof that the old Ottoman motifs still continue to be viable in the Republic of Turkey." As Adolf Max Vogt notes, "The interior space admits, almost in a modern way, a large influx of light, but, in a way much more disciplined than Western modernism, it does not allow any illusion of something like total light; that is, it strictly limits the window openings and leaves the upper half of the space in soothing darkness."[14] The structure was torn down in 1988 to make room for a large Swissôtel. Parts of the structure were moved off site and rebuilt to create a tourist restaurant. At the original site, though, the Swissôtel, a parking structure, outdoor advertisements, and rooftop tennis courts dominate.

Burgin's projection begins with a series of intertitles of white text on black backgrounds that slowly dissolve into one another. The first of these provides an etymology, a character, and a location: "The Turkish word for 'coffee house' is from an Ottoman word that means 'a place to read.' She is reading at a table in a coffee house on a hillside overlooking the Bosphorus." The next title card describes her looking toward the

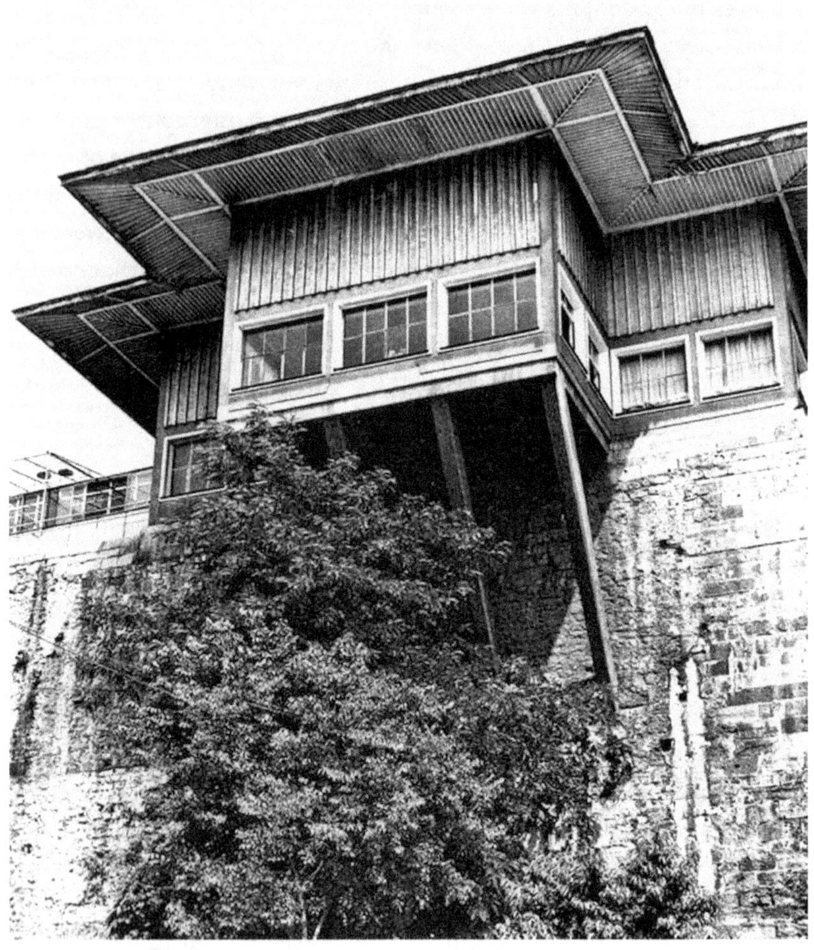

4.6. Taslik Sark Kahvesi (Oriental Coffee House), 1948–50, Macka-Istanbul. Architectural design by Sedad Hakkı Eldem. Photograph © 1986 Suha Özkan.

ferries, tankers, and other vessels on the strait and toward the Dolmabahçe Palace, where Mustafa Kemal Atatürk, founder of the Turkish Republic, died in 1938. In this palace, the title informs us, "the clock always points to 9:05." The clock was stopped in that place to mark the time of Atatürk's death.

Another black frame with white text appears over the course of a slow dissolve, which is Burgin's preferred form of transition to move

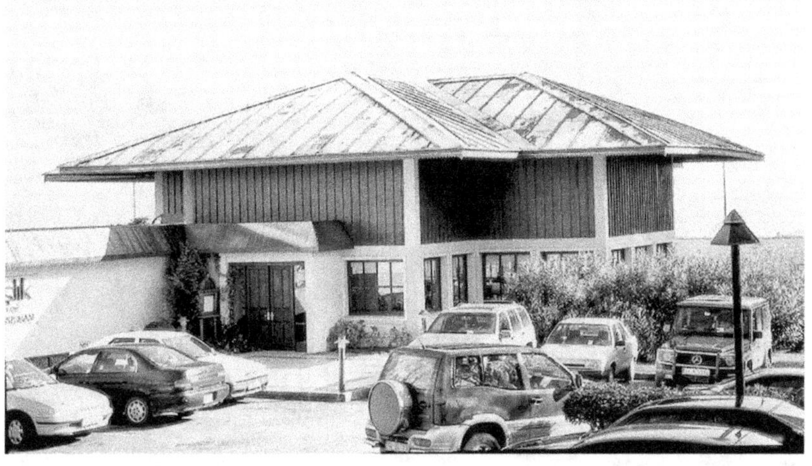

4.7. The site of the original Taslik Khave, overlooking the Bosphorous Strait. Photograph courtesy of Doğan Hasol, Mimarlık Müzesi.

between intertitles in this piece and others (*Solito Posto*, for example). They are lap dissolves, gradual enough so that the texts overlay one another for a short time. The new title informs us that, in the garden of the coffeehouse, "one finds the Ink Tree of which Evliya Çelebi spoke: '. . . a vine they prune back once a year, at which time black and shiny ink flows from where the branch was cut, and they take this to the land of the Franks who use it to print books.'" Çelebi was a seventeenth-century traveler who wandered around the Ottoman Empire for forty years and wrote of his voyages. An interesting circuit of movement between reading and writing begins to emerge: here are ink trees in a garden, at the place where the books the ink is used to print might eventually be read, perhaps even including a copy of the Çelebi book from which this story comes.

This circuit will be further developed over the course of the video. The woman in the café, the next title informs us, is reading a book of fiction that takes place in a parallel universe beset by environmental destruction. Its plot features a murdered journalist and an exploded oil tanker, and in this parallel world "the oceans are rising, and the glaciers are gone from the peaks beyond Lake Geneva." Although we may

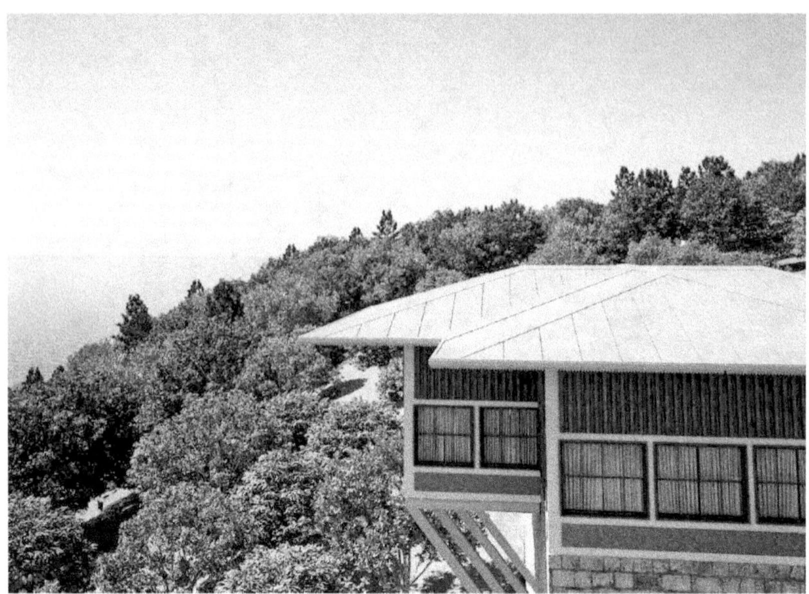

4.8. Still from Victor Burgin's *A Place to Read* (2010), the exterior of the digitally reconstructed Taslik Khave seen from above. Courtesy of the artist.

imagine it to be a work of speculative fiction set in an indeterminate future, this parallel world could still resemble the present one. Already the video invites us to make sense of it by attempting to link the present of our viewing time, the past of Çelebi, and the indeterminate future of the fiction.

Next the video dissolves to a black-and-white, computer-generated image of the café on the hillside overlooking the sea. The building and landscape are rendered in graphic fullness, coming uncannily close to photorealism, yet still bearing tiny artifacts of their status as creations of 3D modeling software. The building is presented in a computer-generated version of a helicopter shot which pans around the structure from above. It reveals sweeping vistas, groves of trees, and a glistening yet eerily calm sea. The feeling evoked by the shot recalls the sense of "imaginary plentitude" and the illusion of omniscient all-seeingness that accompanies the first stage of spectatorial suture in accounts thereof in the apparatus school of film theory.[15]

On the other side of this aerial shot, which is the first of three to show the digitally reconstructed Taslik Khave, the layers of reading and writing become yet more intertwined. The next intertitle reads, "She is writing on the terrace of a coffee house on the Quai des Bergues": a sudden teleportation from Istanbul to Geneva. Burgin relays in an interview that, while doing research for *A Place to Read*, he came across a French translation of Aslı Erdoğan's novella *The Miraculous Mandarin*, which is set in Geneva. This text forms a bridge between the two cities. The "she" of this text fragment, an intertitle informs us, "is writing about a man and a woman whose avatars meet in a virtual world, in a coffee house he has built in a garden overlooking the Bosphorus." The relations among the characters are heavily indeterminate. An initial reading might suggest that perhaps the woman reading in the Istanbul coffeehouse is a fictional character in the book that is being written by another woman in Geneva. The "he" who has built the coffeehouse in a virtual world could be Burgin, in which case he is simultaneously inside and outside the planes of the diegesis—if such a term can even be applied to so layered and porous a text. The next sentences complicate the relations yet further. "Once," the next title reads, "he walked on the floor of the Bosphorus, butterfly fish scattering from sunken caiques. Now the bed is a desert, its riches erased to free disk space for commercial projects. Soon the coffee house also will go." The characters in the book that the Genevan woman is writing, it would seem, inhabit a dystopia of environmental destruction that resembles the one in the book that the woman in the Turkish coffeehouse is reading, perhaps the very same book, or perhaps not. The destroyed world that they inhabit exists on a plane that may be either terrestrial, digital, or both, since the Bosphorus Strait floor has been plundered for "disk space." This destroyed world, we begin to suspect, is a metaphor or allegory, although of what we do not yet understand.

Soon the second of three images of the digital coffeehouse appears. This one is in color. The camera tracks along an inviting concrete path leading to the entrance. Rhododendron flowers, orderly rows of Mediterranean trees, bright grass, and stone half-walls line this path. As in the previous image, the simulation partakes of a photorealism that is nevertheless recognizable as computer-generated, as in a high-budget video game. The trees cast detailed shadows, the natural textures are densely rendered, the contours crisply defined. Only the lack of motion inside the image betrays that this is a place without air or gravity. This

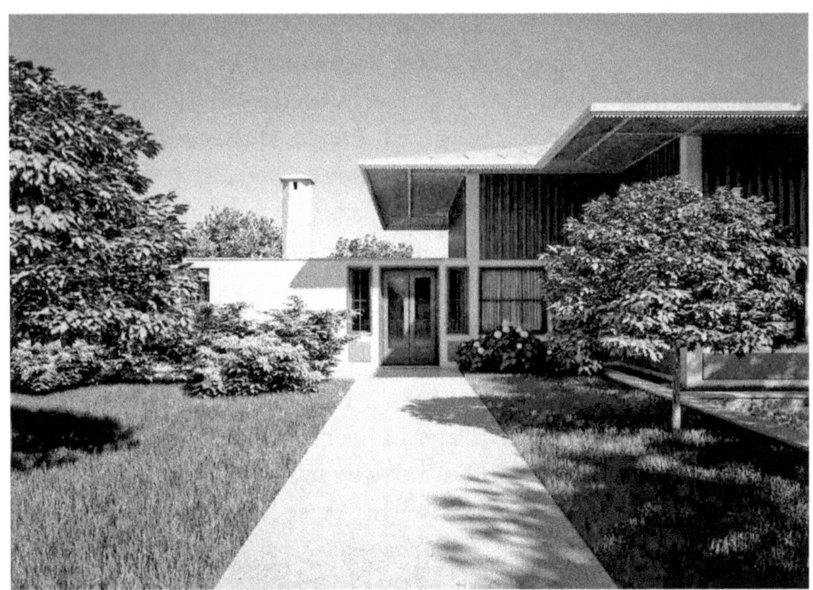

4.9. Still from Burgin's *A Place to Read*, the walkway leading to the digital Taslik Khave coffeehouse. Courtesy of the artist.

shot contrasts with the previous one not only in its use of color but also because it immerses us further into the virtual environment. The camera tracks digitally along the ground at a more or less human height, as if we were strolling along the concrete path rather than circling from a bird's-eye point of view. However, the smooth, steady-cam-like quality of the tracking motion suggests a disembodied perspective rather than the immediacy and palpability of a subjective first-person camera. Writing of Roberto Rossellini's *Germany Year Zero* (1947), Burgin describes the "long traveling shot that moves silently between ruined walls and mounds of rubble down never-ending streets," in which "the camera offers the spectator a feeling of gliding through the debris without touching the ground, the kind of motion conventionally ascribed to ghosts."[16] Burgin compares this motion to that described by Michael Hamburger in W. G. Sebald's *The Rings of Saturn*, as he sedately orbits the ruins of a destroyed Berlin. Although the virtual Taslik Khave is pristine, not decrepit, Burgin in a sense includes a reference to its actual destruction. We cannot visit the ruins of the Taslik Khave because the site has already been built over. But Burgin puts our encounter with its computer-generated double under the sign of ruin by filming it in the ghostly wanderer's point of view and gliding style of movement.

What has been lost with the destruction of the Taslik Khave, this shot begins to make clear, is not only an example of architecture that fuses modern and Islamic styles in interesting ways and ought to have been slated for historic preservation—although this, clearly, is a major loss, whose consequences will never be fully known. Also lost are the virtual contents with which our minds might have filled this building, the books we might have written and read in this space whose name designates it for that activity. While the text titles provide us with an assortment of characters, both loosely contoured characters and historical figures with proper names, the images of the building feel vacant and depopulated, an effect that is enhanced by the lack of audio. The computer-generated tracking and panning shots feel oddly anonymous, haunted. They approach something like a perspectival equivalent of the uncanny valley, that is, a strange sense that this look is on the border between a human and a robotic eye.[17] Like the clock stopped at 9:05, the digital reconstruction—at least at this point in Burgin's video—seems to exist outside of time, subject to what Norman Bryson calls "a certain freezing or glaciation" that is a motif throughout Burgin's oeuvre.[18]

Burgin's practice often operates in such a way as to provide "a story [*histoire*] that no longer has a place . . . for places that no longer have a history [*histoire*]"—to borrow a breathtaking phrase from Deleuze.[19] Often the places in which Burgin works have lost their stories because only their pasts, presents, or futures are clearly visible in their landscapes. The task of the artist in this case is to relink the frozen moment to images from other times and places so that it can be brought back to life. In *Voyage to Italy*, the place is the Basilica in ruins in Pompeii, freeze-framed by the eruption of Mount Vesuvius in its antique past. Burgin supplies it with associations from other centuries: Rossellini's 1954 film of the same title and an 1864 photograph by Carlo Fratacci. Pompeii may be arrested in the past, but these new stories allow us to understand it as part of a still-unfolding history. In *Solito Posto*, it is not the past but the present and future that are overly "present." The video shows images of Mont Stella Park in Milan, where a hill was built on top of the rubble of the city's 1943 bombings, as if in an attempt to bury and forget that history. The video's title (which translates as "usual place") comes from the final words spoken in Michelangelo Antonioni's *The Eclipse* (1962) prior to its long coda of lyrical, semi-autonomous images. This section of Milan is activated by associations with the landscapes that appear in that film, as well as in Antonioni's *The Night* (1961). In an earlier work, *Venise*, Burgin performs a similar operation by connecting three cities together, in part as those cities have appeared in the past and in the imagination. Sponsored by the city of Marseille, the video accesses that place via its associations to a twin, port city of migrants, San Francisco, in part as it appears in *Vertigo*, as well to the Venice that its title echoes.

Even as early as *Photopath* (1967), an installation piece consisting of photographs of a floor pasted onto the floor, Burgin could be said to establish a dialogue between a place's past and the present moment in which the work is experienced. Burgin observes in a recent text that in *Photopath* he was already "looking at the real through the virtual, at the present through the presence of the past."[20] A first reading of the relationship between photo and floor might interpret the former as a deceptive representation papering over the object's concrete reality. This reading is a necessary one, but perhaps only a first step. Viewing the work through another lens allows us to see the relationship as a nonhierarchical layering of perceptions, virtual and actual, that are distinct but that, like decals adhering to a surface, cannot be peeled apart without risk of damage to both. As Bryson lucidly puts it, "Your feelings and recollections do not hover over the surface of the buildings you pass, like a slide on a screen—they infiltrate and fill the built environment, from the inside."[21] The feelings and recollections are not mere smoke and mirrors obscuring the actual buildings, nor are they the whole of our accessible reality. The two cannot be peeled apart. In order to perceive the built environment, we must accept that it is infused from the inside out with virtual associations.

Like Burgin's earlier works, *A Place to Read* supplies stories for orphaned places and places for orphaned stories—"stories" in the double sense of narratives and of history, that is, temporalized existence. The stories come from a mixture of archival sources (Çelebi's wanderings) and fabulous ones (the dystopian novel fragments). The places, in turn, take forms both terrestrial (the site of the Taslik Khave, the Quai des Bergues) and imagistic (the digitally reconstructed coffeehouse, the

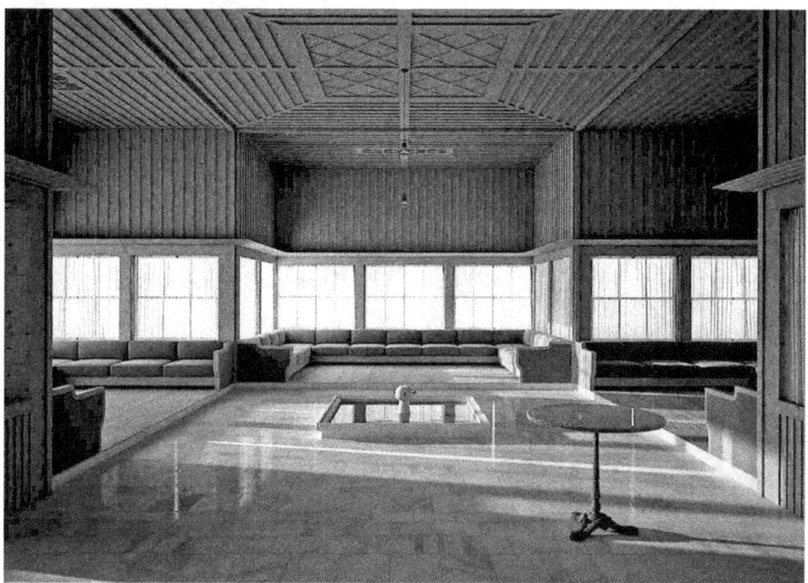

4.10. Interior of the digitally modeled Taslik Khave coffeehouse in Burgin's *A Place to Read*. Courtesy of the artist.

imaginary desert floor of the Bosphorus). In the installation context, Burgin adds additional site-specific elements. In one version of *The Little House*, the audio track was played without images in Schindler's Kings Road House; the building would thereby supply its own images to visitors entering the space.[22] *A Place to Read* was originally installed as a single-channel video in the Archaeology Museum in Istanbul. In an alternate installation in Berlin, the text was stenciled on the wall of a room immediately adjacent to the one in which the images were projected. The graffiti text makes clear the work's connections to the act of reading, to the lectosign, and to the archaeological ruin.

The third image of the Taslik Khave in *A Place to Read* reveals the building's interior from a fixed camera position, in color. We see a square fountain with a calm, glassy surface, a glass-topped round table with an ashtray, banquettes lining windowed walls, and geometric woodwork on the walls, ceiling, and parquet floor, mixing Ottoman styles with the glass boxes of modernism. Then beams of light pass across the frame from right to left, as if the sun were rapidly rising and setting. This arc of moving light and shadow passes twice. The image then darkens to a dusky twilight. The text that precedes this shot reads, "They have counted the sixty-eight steps in the garden, and now look towards the darkening skyline where the four minarets of the Ayasofya and the six of the Sultanahmet mosque stand. The fountain in the coffee house falls silent in its gleaming pool." Here, unlike in *The Little House*, the light and shadows we see on the image track clearly match those described in the text. Even the orientation is correct: the camera is presumably facing the south bank of windows as the sun rises and sets over the digital coffeehouse.

:: :: ::

In an essay entitled "Memory of the Present and False Recognition," Bergson writes about the act of watching a play that one has already seen. He distinguishes this type of "seeing again" from that experienced in the phenomenon of déjà vu. He makes sense of the phenomenon of déjà vu in the following way: what we are experiencing is in fact the present moment, but by a trick of the mind it has fallen under the sign of the past or been inserted into the past's "frame." We feel as though we are divining what is to come, when in fact we are taking it in afresh. Bergson turns to this mental curiosity in order to illustrate that what we call "the past" and "the present" do not unspool in linear succession. Our minds, he claims, generate the two frames simultaneously, and these frames overlap at every point. It is only due to an additional act of cognition, necessary but superadded, that in the experience of reseeing a play we do not experience déjà vu but instead remain conscious of the gap between the first viewing and the encore. As Bergson puts it, "[A] vague feeling of the difference of the frames surrounds, like a fringe, the consciousness I have of the identity of the images, and allows me at every moment to distinguish them."[23]

According to this account, déjà vu is the inverse of the repetition compulsion, and both are explicable by the model that Bergson provides here. In the thrall of the repetition compulsion, the shell-shocked veteran sees Normandy, June 1944, in place of the contemporary moment; the past appears as if it were right here in the present. In the thrall of déjà vu, by contrast, the present appears as though it were the past: we imagine that we have already experienced and can even foretell what is actually still in the process of unfolding. Whereas common sense would attribute both of these to cognitive malfunction, Bergson proposes something like the opposite: that it is our habitual perception of time, Newtonian in origin, with moments succeeding one another as if they were beads on a two-dimensional, perpetually advancing string, that involves a distortion.[24] Burgin expresses a similar idea when he writes that "what we call 'the present' is not a perpetually fleeting point on a line 'through time,' but a collage of *disparate* times, an imbrication of shifting and contested spaces."[25] These disparate times are overlapping sheets rather than discrete fragments: not a mosaic of tiles, but a thickly impastoed collage. In moving-image terms, they are shots connected by lap dissolves rather than straight cuts, overlain from time to time with double exposures.

In the shot of the interior of the reconstructed Taslik Khave, the arc of light that passes across the coffeehouse resembles the beam of a photocopier. It is as if the light were reading the space, and appropriately it reads it twice. This repetition exists in a synecdochal relationship to the video loop; it is a version of the loop within the larger video. Both are scanning movements that relink spaces and times that have been broken apart, whether by commercial development, war, the erasure of disk space and the plundering of ocean floors, or simply by a surplus of images that overcrowd the screen of perception. In order for this relinking to occur, the text that is this virtual coffeehouse must be "reread" by the beam of light. It must be reread in the mode of *reprise*, not vertiginous déjà vu or shell shock—like seeing a play or a film again, but with a separate frame around it. In addition this reseeing must take a particular form. If there is too much forgetting of the prior viewing, it is as if we have never encountered the text before, as though it has no past. On the other hand, if there is too much remembering of it, it is as if the text is frozen, Pompeii-like, at the time of the prior viewing, as though it has no future. Perhaps these are the two states—pastlessness and futurelessness—that the destroyed world referred to in *A Place to Read* allegorizes. Perhaps the virtual is where we end up when we restore temporal continuity to this world. Not too much past, not too much future, but just the right mixture. According to this way of thinking, Burgin's computer simulation of the Taslik Khave is a virtual place not because it was made with 3D modeling software but because it is endowed with this complex temporality.

In Orhan Pamuk's memoir of Istanbul, a text that was a point of reference for Burgin in *A Place to Read*, the author writes of a specific kind of melancholy that comes from living in a place with too much past: "Gustave Flaubert, who visited Istanbul 102 years before my birth, was struck by the variety of life in its teeming streets; in one of his letters he predicted that in a century's time it would be the capital of the world. The reverse came true: After the Ottoman Empire collapsed, the world almost forgot that Istanbul existed. . . . For me it has always been a city of ruins and of end-of-empire melancholy."[26] Pamuk makes clear the particular color of life in a place with too much past and too little present and imaginable future. As those who have lived in the California of midcentury modernism can attest, places with too little past—or rather that endeavor to occlude what pasts they have in favor of an idealized vision of the present or future—also take on a particular hue. Like bell towers from which characters repeatedly fall or spiraling jetties from which they jump—not the kind that wax and wane with the changing tides but the kind that whip in vicious circles—these places need more time, and more stories. Burgin's loops provide them.

CHAPTER 5

The Powers of the Virtual

Discovery, or uncovering, has to do with what already exists. . . . It was therefore certain to happen sooner or later. Invention gives being to what did not exist; it might never have happened.

—Henri Bergson, *The Creative Mind*

The virtual is not the same as the false. They come from two different orders. The true and the false relate what is actual and not actual; the virtual has nothing to do with these. When Deleuze writes of the powers of the false in *Cinema 2: The Time-Image*, he does not simply mean the power of brazen lies, whether the power of those who speak and propagate them or the power of the falsehoods themselves to disseminate and convince the public. Nor does he mean the powers of delusion, seeing or believing in things that are not really there, although this too is a remarkably powerful phenomenon. The power of the false, in the sense I would like to give it here, is more neutral: it is simply the capacity to fabricate or forge something new out of preexisting materials in the world—to "give being to what does not exist," as Bergson puts it in this chapter's epigraph. It is the ability to make or invent something that then really exists as such, regardless of whether it represents something else in the world and regardless of whether it does so accurately or inaccurately. This power thus relates more closely to the virtual than to what we colloquially understand by the word *false*. It is related to what

Bergson calls the creative, and to the faculty of intuition as opposed to that of the intellect.

One might say that this power came into its own with the invention of cinema. As Deleuze puts it, "The cinema does not just present images, it surrounds them with a world."[1] Christian Metz explains that film's mechanisms infuse images with an impression of reality. In typical narrative cinema, all images, even those that are marked off from the rest of the story as flashbacks, eyewitness accounts, and so on, are meant to be accepted as part of the film's diegetic reality. It is extremely rare in conventional cinema to encounter a camera that is an "unreliable narrator" in the literary sense. Metz puzzled over why we suspend our skepticism about these flat, two-dimensional reflections of matter, and he brilliantly uses Freud's account of divided belief to explain how we could know that they are tricks and yet experience them as psychically real at the same time. Deleuze, by contrast, was not bothered by the apparent contradiction. His cinema books operate, from the very start, on the assumption that to make an image is to make something real—not necessarily true, good, accurate, or just, but definitely real. This apparently simple proposition, Deleuze's minor revolution in film theory, opens up all kinds of possibilities for the image. If images are real, they cannot simply be dismissed with a wave of the hand as lies or mirages. We are not fools for having responded in earnest to a two-dimensional light projection; on the contrary, we are exercising a unique power. It is tantamount to saying that cinema is a form of virtual reality.

In his writings on the powers of the false, Deleuze observes that in postwar cinema, the forger emerges as a new kind of emblematic character. Unlike the classical hero, the forger is not motivated by a quest for personal fame or honor. Rather he achieves his greatest purpose when he vanishes anonymously into the image systems created by others. Deleuze cites Orson Welles as an exemplary model of this figure: "Since Welles has a strong personality, we tend to forget that his constant theme, precisely as a result of this personality, is to be a person no longer."[2] Deleuze suggests that *F for Fake*, Welles's essay film about famous forgers, is the culmination of this theme. Here, Deleuze notes, Welles becomes fully Nietzschean: he approaches the category of the false in an extramoral sense.[3] It is no longer a question of lying or telling the truth but of making images and stories that ask to be understood and taken seriously on their own terms, within the worlds with which they surround themselves.

F for Fake is a film about characters who work with preexisting images in the world, playing with them, riffing on them, and inserting new entries into the groups of which they are a part. Elmyr—the prolific, highly skilled forger of Matisses, Modiglianis, and Picassos—is one of the characters portrayed in this film. Importantly Elmyr does not copy existing paintings by these famous artists; he makes new ones in the style of their work. His forgeries are thus originals in one sense. But he does not get credit for them; the artists he forges do. He thereby "becomes a person no longer," and this is precisely what Deleuze means by this declaration: he vanishes anonymously into other artists' worlds and expands their oeuvres in the process. These paintings' existence in the art market might detract from the economic value of the authentic ones, but they add exponentially to their value as wellsprings of ideas. It is as if "Picasso" were a mode that included a surplus of shapes, figures, and forms that the artist never in fact painted but easily might have, which Elmyr then taps into and brings to light in his compositions.

A whole set of contemporary art practices has grown out of this proposition of Deleuze's, some taking direct inspiration from it, others participating more intuitively. Some of these practices directly involve forgery in an extramoral sense: the creation of images attributed to people who never in fact made them or of documents that relate to events and histories that in fact never occurred. In an essay on the artists Michael Blum, Walid Raad, and others, Carrie Lambert-Beatty terms these "parafictional" works.[4] Similar practices include speculative fiction, presenting images in the guise of history that would not normally appear there, and other modes of image making and storytelling that draw on real events and people in the world. Forgery, in the sense I am exploring, might simply be a method of creativity that acknowledges its debt to materials from the past rather than pretending to arise out of a void. I would suggest that this method of image making is better understood by the name *virtual* than *false*.

WHAT MIGHT BE: *THE MAKES*

Eric Baudelaire's *The Makes* (2009) casts a glance backward to the cinema of midcentury Europe. Its route to the past, though, is an unexpected one. *The Makes* is a forged documentary, and its ostensible topic is a series of films that Michelangelo Antonioni produced during his nonexistent Japanese period. The video is staged as an interview with the real-life film critic Philippe Azoury, who provides a kind of oral history about this supposed phase in Antonioni's career. Azoury appears at a table on which lie vintage actor headshots, film stills, and Japanese film publicity materials—ephemera that are allegedly artifacts of these films. In fact they are found photographs that Baudelaire collected and worked with while in Japan. The camera occasionally departs from Azoury to show these fragments in a closer view, providing enough time for the viewer to invest them with a sense of reality. Aside from the occasional black screen and a brief interlude in which a simple musical motif is heard, the video does not really depart from the filmic conventions that would be expected of this style of documentary. Close viewing, though, reveals moments in which the fiction is broken—clues that the history being told is a fake, and openly so. At one point, an off-screen voice is heard asking "Can you start over?" as Azoury appears to fumble

5.1. Philippe Azoury in a still from Eric Baudelaire's *The Makes* (2009). Courtesy of the artist.

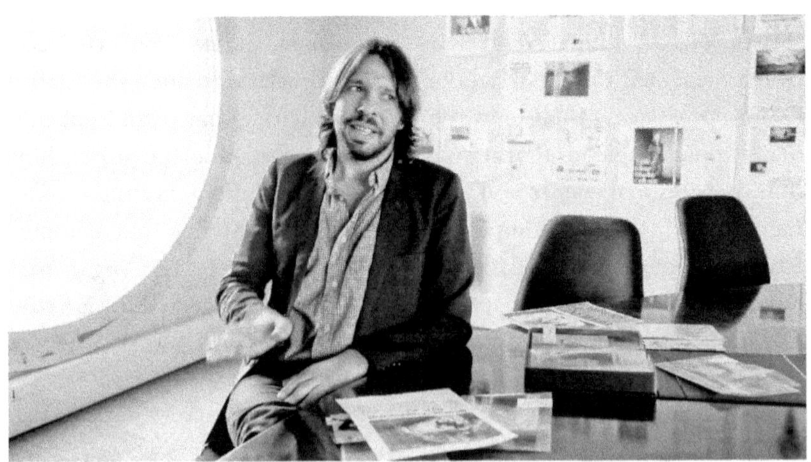

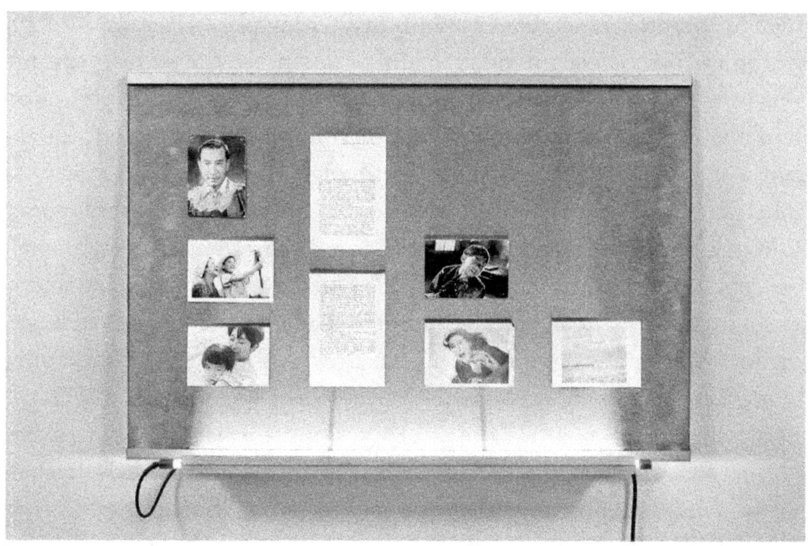

5.2. Eric Baudelaire, *The Makes (That Bowling Alley on the Tiber)*, installation view (2009). Courtesy of the artist.

a line. The critic speaks earnestly about Antonioni, but his demeanor is at times comical. On occasion he coyly avoids the camera's gaze, like a child acknowledging that he knows that we know he is fibbing.

While the history told in this work is a fictive one, the films in question are not fabricated out of thin air. They come from a book by Antonioni called *That Bowling Alley on the Tiber* in which the director wrote notes, descriptions, and ideas for films that were never made, in some cases because he didn't have time, in some cases because they would be unfilmmable or go beyond the limits of cinema. *The Makes* is thus an exercise in imagining films that might or might not be. Baudelaire's video is accompanied by a group of mixed-media works of the same title: illuminated glass vitrines containing pages from *That Bowling Alley on the Tiber* alongside the found photographs of Japanese actors that constitute these virtual films' archive. The vitrines, which resemble those that used to house publicity posters in the lobbies of movie theaters, lend materiality to the fiction.

In one sense *The Makes* involves a quest to find Antonioni. But in another, the film aims to miss the director. Baudelaire does not look for Antonioni in all the right places—Italy, for example, or the locations of his film shoots. He searches for him in a wrong place: Japan. Although Antonioni had indeed intended to film in Japan, the closest he ever came was in 1972, when he traveled to China as the first foreigner permitted to make a film there since the country's communist walling-off. The result was his sprawling documentary *Chung Kuo: Cina*, a film that is as much about the process of encountering an unknown place as it is about China as such. Interactions with foreign people and places play a small yet crucial role in Antonioni's narrative films as well, and his characters' encounters with alterity often prompt an about-face, a metamorphosis, or the undoing of stagnation.[5] In keeping with the spirit of Antonioni's work, *The Makes* stages an encounter between Italian texts and Japanese still photographs, and the meeting is transformative on both sides.

The Makes is a parafictional text and a forgery in the Deleuzian sense. While not precisely forging new Antonioni films in the way that Elmyr forges Picassos or that Welles forges stories about Picasso, the video works with the director's preexisting, unmade scenarios and supplies found images to them. Close viewing of *The Makes* reveals that the images do not merely illustrate the script fragments and fill in the blanks; the relationship is more complex. The video begins with a close-up of hands placing black-and-white images of Japanese actors in a pile, one by one. The shot resembles the one that begins Antonioni's *Story of a Love Affair* (1950), in which a wealthy husband hires a private investigator to probe his wife's past and shows the detective a series of photos of her. As in *Blow Up* (1966), though, the detective fiction frame is only an excuse for Antonioni to tell a different kind of story. *The Makes* seems to promise a similarly investigative frame, that of archival film research. But this is a ruse as well: no new facts about Antonioni's career will be unearthed, only unrealized possibilities and speculative scenes.

In some cases the found images closely match the scenarios and can plausibly be imagined as frame enlargements from the films. Azoury begins by describing a lost film called *Four Sailors*; accordingly he shows us photos of four sailorish actors and a ship. As the video continues, though, the fragments begin to grate against the films from which they are supposedly torn. This gap is widest in the segment on *The Silence*, a story of a husband and wife who have nothing more to say to each other, whose silence Antonioni proposes to film. In the prelude to the segment, Azoury places some still photographs in a pile, one at a time:

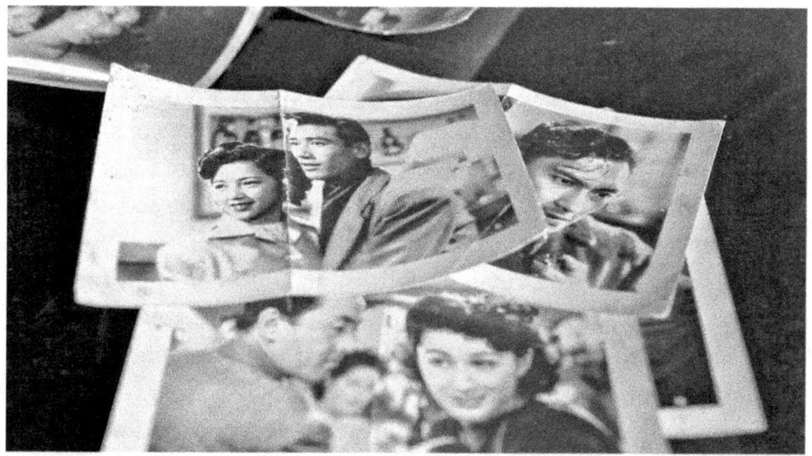

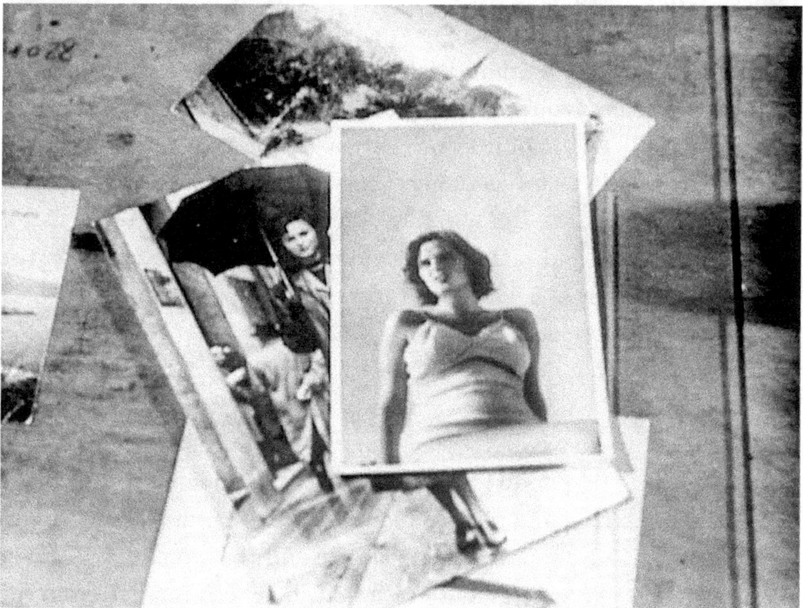

5.3. A pile of photographs in Baudelaire's *The Makes*. Courtesy of the artist.

5.4. A pile of photographs in *Story of a Love Affair*, directed by Michelangelo Antonioni (1950).

a modern, disaffected-looking couple, a couple in traditional Japanese dress, more alienated couples with creases in the photographs that emphasize their separation. One photo shows a couple who look as though they might have come over from a samurai film. Still, it's possible that this could be their story; by this point in the video, the fictions begin to smooth each other's edges, and we have been primed to accept a great deal of dissonance into the frame.

One segment of the video deals with an Antonioni film fragment called *Don't Try to Find Me*. Antonioni writes in *That Bowling Alley on the Tiber* that this title is meant as a caveat to his reader: Don't play hide and seek with Michelangelo Antonioni, don't try to find him. In his fictive oral history, Azoury recounts that during this film's production, Antonioni struggled with direction, reverting to a more theatrical Italian style of acting even though he had recently found a restrained Japanese style that was more appropriate to the types of films that he had always made. Azoury notes, though, that one scene stands out as quintessentially Antonioni: a husband has spoiled his happy family by distancing himself, when suddenly a fog intercedes, like the fog in Antonioni's native Ferrara.[6] Here, finally, Azoury remarks, we sense Antonioni's presence as a director. That finding, though, is propped on the image of a lost man—a man who is disappearing into a fog. It is only when Antonioni gets lost that he is found, that is, that his cinema can be rediscovered in a new way. This seems to be, in part, the project of *The Makes*: to make way for the emergence of nascent, potential images by looking for them where they are not.

In a sequence that occurs toward the end of the video, Azoury selects one photograph from the pile: a Japanese couple standing under a tree, with the man in a modern, Western suit and the woman in a traditional, Japanese kimono. Azoury says that the photo is taken from the scene in *The Silence* in which Alain Delon and Monica Vitti, having met at the Tokyo stock exchange, wander flirtatiously through the streets of Tokyo, with Vitti pausing to float an origami boat in a rain barrel at the side of the road. Minus Tokyo and the origami, Azoury seems to be describing the memorable scene between Delon and Vitti near the conclusion of Antonioni's *The Eclipse* (1962), but this is not what we see in the photo. The thick layers of superimposition require unfolding: *The Eclipse* appears as *The Silence*; Japanese actors appear as Vitti (as her

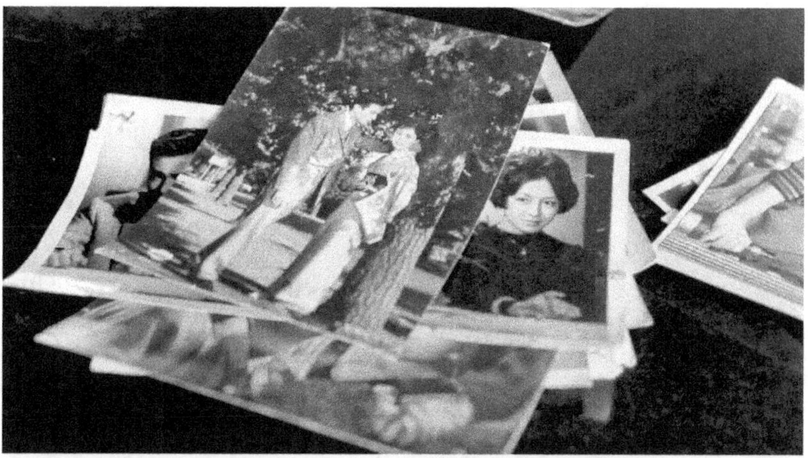

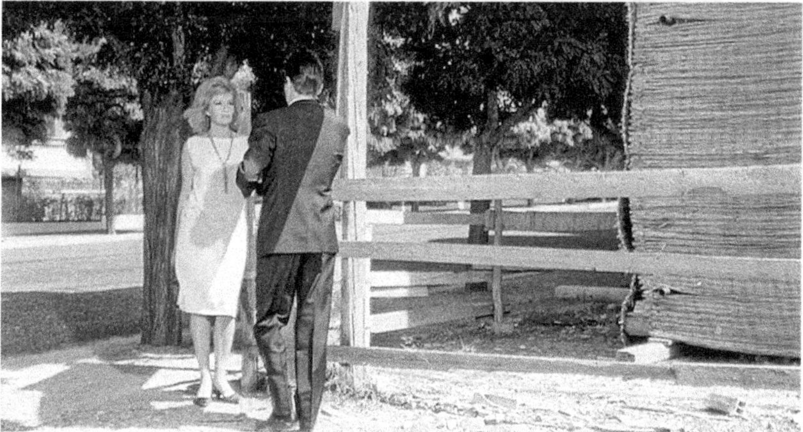

5.5. A still photo of a couple standing by a tree in Baudelaire's *The Makes*. Courtesy of the artist.

5.6. Monica Vitti and Alain Delon in *The Eclipse*, directed by Michelangelo Antonioni (1962).

character Vittoria) and Delon (as his character Piero). In addition the scene in question from *The Eclipse* already involves several superimpositions. Piero's image is eclipsing that of Vittoria's former lover, whom she has just left, and their initial playful meeting will soon be eclipsed by a repetition of the scene—another date that Vittoria and Piero plan, at the same street corner, at eight o'clock the next evening, to which neither of them shows up.

Antonioni's camera shows up, though, and films the empty street corner. In Antonioni's films, this gesture is a kind of ethical principle: to go to the places where "the people are missing."[7] We see him do this immediately after *The Eclipse*, in *Red Desert* (1964), where he uses wandering panning shots to reveal empty and anonymous spaces, places the characters can't or won't go. In *The Makes*, Baudelaire's gesture is similar to Antonioni's: the artist goes to Japan, a place where Antonioni is not, and forges a collaboration among the director's writing fragments, found Japanese images, Antonioni's actual films, and other texts that they reference. The result is, in a way, the opposite of an eclipse: it draws open a curtain, revealing a portal into a virtual film history that is simultaneously a fictive invention and the illumination of a potential that, in retrospect, was already there within cinema.

One might counter this reading of *The Makes*—and indeed similar readings of contemporary film and video works that combine fiction and documentary practices—with the accusation that they betray history and disregard fact or that they unjustly attempt to pull the wool over their viewers' eyes. But as should be clear by now, apprehending the virtual requires that we think in a different way. The story of Antonioni's sojourn in Japan is, let me be clear, fiction; it is simply not true. *The Makes* is a virtual film history, similar to the way that Elmyr's Picassos are virtual Picassos: it depends on an existing group of films for its existence, it draws on their frames of reference, and it is in dialogue with this archive of actualities to which it does not belong. But in the same way that Elmyr's Picassos are not merely simulations or mirages of paintings, but real paintings, so the stories and images in *The Makes* are real, even if they are untrue. They are forged, real, and virtual all at the same time.

TENUOUS FRAMES: *PERSONA PERFORMA*

The Singaporean-born, Berlin-based artist Ming Wong's primary gesture is to remake scenes from classical Hollywood and European New Wave cinemas with the aim of teasing out their potentially queer, racial, and politically subversive elements. His video installations and live performances continue along a path taken by R. W. Fassbinder, Tom Kalin, and Todd Haynes, where unexpected performing bodies appear in familiar narrative scenarios. Similarly to these directors, they are often direct remakes of scenes or narratives from films by Douglas Sirk and other directors. They do not engage in a documentary mode, nor do they present themselves as forged films by these directors. Nevertheless they too are a form of virtual cinema: they are virtual Sirks, Polanskis, Bergmans, and so on.

In *Life of Imitation* (2009), Wong casts Singaporean actors in key scenes from Sirk's *Imitation of Life* (1959). They reenact scenes in drag, occupying the roles of Sarah Jane and Annie Johnson in varying permutations. Similarly in *Making Chinatown* (2012), Wong himself plays the roles of Jake Gittes, Evelyn Mulwray, Noah Cross, and Katherine Cross from Polanski's film, making the Chinese body visible in a film where, although referenced in the title, it is largely an absent presence. These casting choices expand the repertoire of identities that film screens normally accommodate. But they do much more than this. The performing body becomes a vehicle through which identity is rendered collective, transitional, and mutable, while still retaining its visual, gestural, and linguistic particularities. These works do not simply advocate on behalf of diversity, inclusiveness, or even hybridity. Rather they present identity as a time-based work in progress.

Wong's *Persona Performa* is a work of film, video installation, and live performance, which was included in the 2011 Performa festival and mounted at the Museum of the Moving Image in Queens, New York. Its source material is provided by Ingmar Bergman's 1966 film, which tells the story of Elisabet Vogler (Liv Ullmann), an actress who has fallen abruptly into a state of elective muteness during a performance of *Electra*, and Alma (Bibi Andersson), her nurse. On the advice of Elisabet's physician, the pair retreat to the remote island of Fårö. There they become locked in a dynamic of identification, desire, and passive and active aggression, fueled by Elisabet's refusal to speak. Bergman's use of nondiegetic imagery, a split screen, exposed celluloid, and similar techniques famously made this film a landmark of experimental narrative.

Persona Performa departs from its source material, leading it off the confined island of Fårö into a space of extreme openness. It undoes the rivalrous dyad formed by the two women by multiplying the number of players. Wong's restaging, notably, continues a theme that is already present in *Persona*, that of the tenuousness of singular personhood. His most apparent intervention is to multiply Elisabet and Alma into twelve pairs, casting twenty-four amateur actors from the borough of Queens in their places. The actors were selected in part to maximize the range of ethnicities, countries of origin, genders, body types, and languages spoken. They dance and act out vignettes from Bergman's film, undergoing a series of permutations of gender and race. The staging is both queer and brown, the latter in the sense defined by José Muñoz: a feeling that resists crystallizing into a category or fixed position. As Muñoz puts it, "Feeling brown is a mode of racial performativity, a doing within the social that surpasses limitations of epistemological renderings of race."[8]

Wong's combinatory use of media forms is also queer and brown in this sense. It reanimates cinema by juxtaposing it with video, dance, and live performance, such that the medium resists crystallizing into a fixed ontology or form. Upon entering the museum's lobby, visitors are greeted by a large video installation taking up the left-hand wall, the *Persona Performa Panorama*. The video shows the faces and hands of the actors, but they have been splintered by vertical frame lines in mirror-fracture effect. We may be reminded of the convention of displaying actor's headshots in the lobby of a theater, introducing playgoers to the real people behind the characters we are about to see before we become

5.7. Ming Wong's *Persona Performa* (2011), lobby installation shot at the American Museum of the Moving Image, the *Persona Performa Panorama*. Courtesy of the artist.

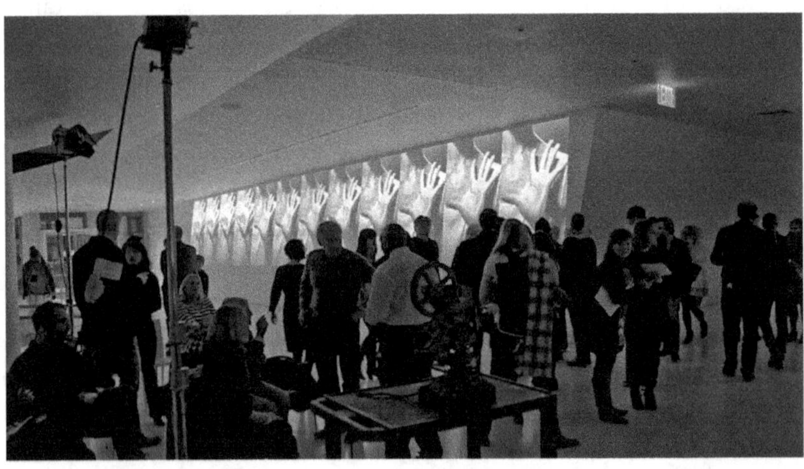

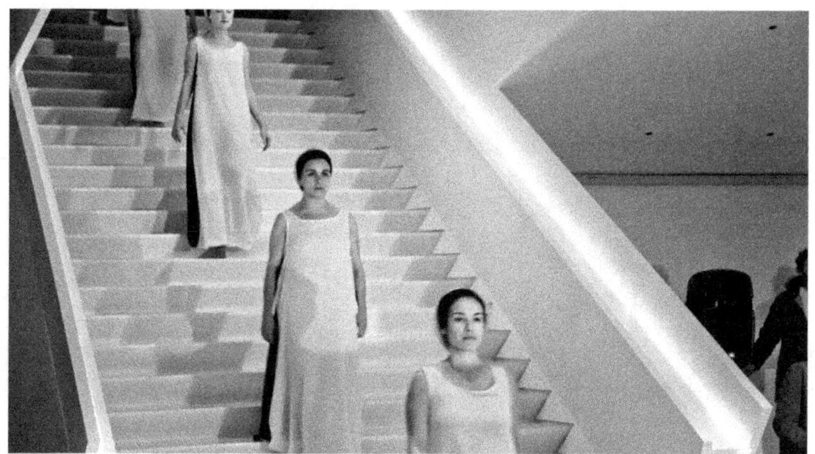

5.8. Dancers descend the staircase at the American Museum of the Moving Image in Wong's *Persona Performa*. Courtesy of the artist.

immersed in the fictional world. In Wong's lobby installation, though, the actors are already in the fragmentary state that they will occupy for the duration of the performance.

Soon we enter the museum's central gallery space with its white walls, modernist angles, and glass panels with views onto a courtyard. This space was redesigned in 2011, and Wong's piece is tailored to its new architecture. We advance toward a wide staircase, and on the mezzanine we encounter a 16-millimeter film shown from a projector positioned in the middle of the room, the whirr of its gears audible. The film is a remake of a single shot from Bergman's film, in which the faces of Alma and Elisabet appear spliced together in a single frame. At least one of Wong's actors appears to be Asian and male, but their genders and races are indeterminate, made more so by the black-and-white film stock, splicing, and identical costuming. The transitional space of the mezzanine leads to another upstairs gallery where Bergman's original film is projected—a smaller, more black box–style room tucked away in a corner. In a third upstairs gallery, with sunken seating and windows, a dance film plays, a color, digital video made during rehearsals for the piece.

Through the windows we catch a glimpse of the courtyard, and if our timing is right, we will see an extremely tall, commanding figure in dark

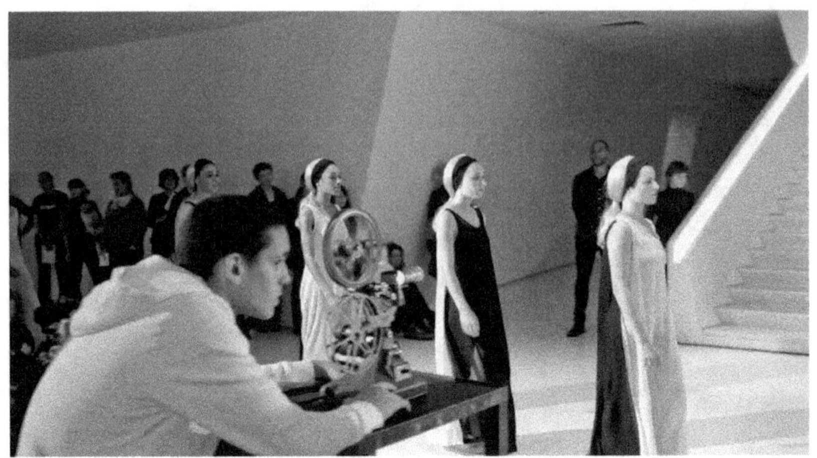

5.9. A scene from the opening half of Wong's *Persona Performa* with dancers and a film projector. Courtesy of the artist.

robes slowly moving around the outdoor space. This figure is Death, a reference to Bergman's *The Seventh Seal* (1957) and *Prison* (1949), a brief clip from which appears in the prelude to *Persona*. The reference may strike us as comical: we glimpse Death only darkly, through glass. Such humor is common in Wong's work, which has a playful, camp touch. Putting this dancer in the museum courtyard animates a space normally allocated to static sculpture, in effect cinematizing it with the inclusion of a statuesque but moving entity. Bits of rocky seaside landscape are projected onto the glass panels; these confirm that the space is being turned into a museum-size cinematic apparatus.

At the start of the live performance component of the work, dancers begin to descend the museum staircase one at a time, perhaps in a nod to Duchamp. As they descend, an allegory is set in motion: the twenty-four dancers are like frames of film, and their movement through the space resembles that of a spool of celluloid winding through a projector. The sound consists of a track of mechanical ticks, like a camera shutter clicking, along with occasional clinks of glass. A 16-millimeter projector runs nearby, providing another source of audio. The projector runs clear film, casting light on the actors. Upon descending the staircase, each dancer looks briefly toward the projector as if searching for someone in its empty light. When all twenty-four performers have assembled, they

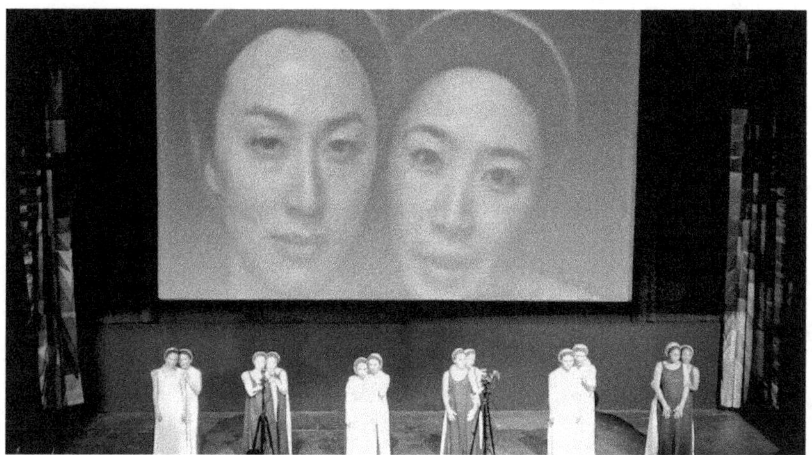

5.10. Inside the auditorium at the American Museum of the Moving Image during the second half of Wong's *Persona Performa*. Courtesy of the artist.

begin a dance in a row of pairs, clasping, embracing, locking arms, then switching places before moving on to the next partner in the line and repeating the same movements. Upon reaching the end of the line, each dancer snaps off the chain and runs away, as if the film reel had broken off abruptly, as in Bergman's film.

The second act of the performance takes place in the museum's large auditorium with more traditional seating and sightlines. Again the dancers form pairs, and they begin to recite bits of dialogue from *Persona*. Each one speaks the text in a different language or dialect to a mute partner. Occasionally the partners trade off. As they speak, a camera mounted in front of the stage films them, and these images are projected in a live stream above their heads. The digital simulcast allows for different pairs to be selected from the series of twelve with their audio amplified above the murmur of voices. The lines of dialogue that the actors speak add a twist to Bergman's original, which is about the misunderstandings and psychical projections that can accrue in the space of silence. They speak Alma's lines to the mute Elisabet, which vacillate between idealization—"Many people have told me that I'm a good listener. Funny, huh? No one's ever bothered to listen to me. Like you are now. You're listening. I think you're the first person who's listened to me"—and denunciation: "My words mean nothing to you. People like you can't be reached. I wonder whether your madness isn't the worst kind. . . . I know how rotten you are." These lines take on an entirely new significance when spoken in the native languages of the diverse group of actors. Bergman's classic of European modernist film, Wong seems to say, can be recast to reflect the experience of the contemporary migrant to Queens, New York, attempting to navigate a soundscape of enigmatic foreign languages and in turn being perceived as foreign with each attempt at speech. On the one hand, these new migrant Elisabets are romanticized as the perfect passive servants, silently absorbing whatever is thrown their way; on the other, they are denounced as mad or rotten if they show signs of resistance. The racially, linguistically marked immigrant figure is a screen for a range of projections involving black-and-white thinking.

Bergman's script does not say whether the *Electra* during which Elisabet has gone mute is the Sophoclean tragedy or the comedic version by Euripides. However, a line of dialogue states that she fell silent while attempting to stifle the urge to laugh, suggesting that it was the Sophoclean version, in which laughter would be inappropriate. Sophocles's Electra is marked by an excessive and long-lived mourning: her father, Agamemnon, has been brutally murdered by her mother, Clytemnestra, and Clytemnestra's suitor Aegisthus, the usurping king of Mycenae, and she has continued to mourn his death long past the customary grieving period. As a result of her mourning, Electra is punished and confined to quarters, where she nonetheless persists in loud, wailing lamentations that carry beyond the palace walls. In answer to the first question that the Chorus poses to her—"Electra, child of the wretchedest of mothers, why with ceaseless lament do you waste away, sorrowing for one long dead?"—she provides a voluminous response. In a series of wild free anapests punctuated by the iambic pleadings of the Chorus, she replies first that her lament is madness, then that it is her heart's desire, that it is honorable, and finally that it is the only proper recourse for a well-bred girl.[9] Unlike her sister Chrysothemis, Electra refuses to comply with those in power, to be silent and obey. As Ann Batchelder notes, the word used here for "obeying" is *akoustea*, to listen.[10] In Sophocles's play, it is not so much the content of Electra's speech that offends, although this is also a problem; it is the very shrillness and long duration of her lament, which signal her refusal to submit to quiet passivity. Electra's cries are a form of verbal protest, the only kind available given that in her world, heroic deeds and acts of vengeance can be undertaken only by men.

Understood in this context, Electra's wailing is an act of fearless speech, or *parrhesia*. As Foucault describes it, parrhesia is a form of free speech, a speech-act of a sort, that is marked by frankness and truth and accompanied by a sense of both duty and risk.[11] Elisabet's muteness, in turn, can be thought of as a form of fearless *silence*: silence as protest, willfully pursued against doctor's orders and against the demands that the public places on the great actress. In *Persona Performa*, the actors' costuming in long, classical robes and their slightly Grecian hairstyles suggest a reference to the themes of the Sophoclean tragedy. In this version, both fearless speech and fearless silence come into play: the vulnerable speech of the play's Almas, who risk incomprehension in their native languages, and the bold silence of the Elisabets, who refuse to respond to such caricatured descriptions of themselves. A series of additional twists on the dialogue emerge as the scene shifts from pair to pair. When the scene is played by two smiling women of color, Alma's praise might read as part of a moment of genuine intimacy; when the same lines are spoken by a white performer to an actor who mimes not being able to understand English, the scene becomes a satire about monocultural assumptions. Alma's denunciations, in turn, can be read in nearly opposite ways depending on what language and accent they are delivered in and to whom.

Wong's piece for the Performa festival was not as critically acclaimed as his prior and subsequent work, including his installation for the Singapore pavilion at the Fifty-third Venice Biennale, which included *Life of Imitation*, and the *Making Chinatown* show at REDCAT gallery in Los Angeles. The reactions to *Persona Performa* can be read symptomatically. One critic wrote that the large number of actors and their racial and sexual diversity disrupted the "existential dread" and the "good, dark stuff" of Bergman's original film, substituting for it "a feel-good . . . Gap ad . . . kind of sentiment."[12] Nothing could be further from Wong's aesthetic than a United Colors of Benetton style of multiculturalism; the work is full of acerbic commentary. Indeed *Persona Performa* has more satirical bite than many of Wong's previous works, most patently during the act in which the characters speak Alma's lines and infuse them with the second, politicized layer of meaning that seems to have been lost on the reviewer. This second meaning corresponds to the fearless, risky speech and silence that is already a topic in Bergman's film but that is made more bitterly evident in the contemporary American context in which Wong restages it.

Nevertheless it is true that *Persona Performa* has a certain "feel-good" quality to it, or more precisely a playfulness and light touch. Wong seems to say that just because the inhabitants of Queens are working class, diverse, and largely of foreign origin does not mean that they are immune to the alienations and existential crises that afflict Bergman's pale, twin protagonists; on the contrary, such crises may be the norm rather than the exception. At the same time, the work's choreography suggests an alternative way of making sense of these affects. What if identity were always already a crisis, a work in progress, or a time-based performance? The dancing frames that lock together and unlock from one another, that clasp and separate, allegorize this notion of identity as a time-based, interactive work, with each frame and figure emerging as a character through movement and dialogue.

The glass windows that become film frames, the film that emerges simultaneously with its pro-filmic event, and the empty spinning projector that make up the mise-en-scène of Wong's *Persona Performa* are as important to the work as are the human figures. In a sense they are ready-made versions of the apparatus-exposing images that Bergman includes in *Persona*: the visible projector, found footage, glimpses of naked celluloid, and so on. Only in this case the apparatus that is being exposed is not specific to the medium of film; perhaps it is the conceptual channels and glasses through which we view the world even in the absence of an intervening camera. As Susan Sontag argues, Bergman was perhaps less interested in baring the device for didactic purposes than the reception of *Persona* would suggest: "Bergman seems only marginally concerned with the thought that it might be salutary for audiences to be reminded that they are watching a film (an artifact, something made), not reality."[13]

This point is important, since it illuminates certain political and feminist ramifications of both works. As critical viewers, we may have grown accustomed to thinking of film as "only a representation," false, partial, and potentially infused with ideological content that must be exposed by the intelligent filmmaker or spectator. Sontag, though, helps us to understand that Bergman's departures from illusionistic convention don't really operate in the service of exposing artifice, nor of helping us to distinguish fabulation from truth. As Sontag notes, *Persona*'s viewers may find themselves "unable to decipher whether certain scenes take place in the past, present, or future; whether certain images and episodes belong to reality or fantasy. . . . Sorting them out is a minor achievement, and it quickly becomes a misleading one." Certain images might represent daydreams or hallucinations, but, as Sontag suggests, they are still "possible, and may even have taken place" in the film's diegetic reality.[14] These images are virtual: they cannot be vouchsafed as true or false; they simple might or might not be.

We can contrast this indeterminate enunciation with that of Polanski's *Repulsion* (1965), a film that makes fairly clear that we have been witnessing the delusions of a madwoman, or Cukor's *Gaslight* (1944), which reveals in the end that we have not been, or Fincher's *Fight Club* (1999), whose ending resolves any indeterminacy by revealing that the two major characters are aspects of a single personality. *Persona* allows similar construals to glimmer to the surface at times—Is Alma going mad as she endures Elisabet's silence? Has this scene taken place, or was it a hallucination? Are Elisabet and Alma two aspects of the same person?—only to submerge them again. It presents them as real questions that nevertheless cannot be answered definitively for the film as a whole, only, perhaps, tentatively for a given scene. This principle also applies to Wong's *Persona Performa*: questions of identity and its attributes, and of which images belong to the register of diegetic truth and which are infused with subjective fantasy, are not exactly unanswerable, but they can only be answered moment by moment, provisionally, in time-bound ways.

In *Time and Free Will*, Bergson adds the self or ego to his list of forms that can be approached as if they were static over time, as the intellect would prefer, or as if they were caught up in the vicissitudes of temporal change that are revealed through intuition. As one might expect, he takes the position that we are not the same people throughout our lives, that our identities are not singular and unchanging over time. We live in stages. But these stages cannot be set up end to end on a timeline as though they succeeded one another in a linear, developmental way, each coming to a clean close prior to the next one commencing. Bergson suggests that we are made up of a succession of states that are distinct but that mutually interpenetrate, reaching forward and backward, forming a continually evolving whole in which past and present loop through and overlap one another. "Pure duration" he writes, "is the form which the succession of our conscious states assumes when our ego lets itself *live* . . . when it forms both the past and the present states into an organic whole [*quand il s'absitent d'établir une séparation entre l'état présent et les états antérieurs*], as happens when we recall the notes of a tune, melting, so to speak, into one another."[15] As in the case of Bergson's melody, our egos are not isomorphic with themselves: we cannot break off a chunk of our biography or reorder its chapters without fundamentally altering the composition of the whole. Bergson continues, "Pure duration might well be nothing but a succession of qualitative changes, which melt into and permeate one another, without precise outlines."[16] We are not identical with ourselves over time, nor are we a jumble of shattered fragments. The through-line that makes us ourselves is not a timeline laid out in an orderly column but rather a messy, looping circuit that wanders in unpredictable ways through our pasts, presents, and futures.

As we have seen, Bergson turned to the metaphor of the cinematograph to critique ways of thinking that isolate select points on a line and then attempt to string them into a unified, moving whole.[17] With its twenty-four still frames per second, Bergson argued, the cinema offers only an illusion of continuous movement; in fact it is composed of discrete instants, locked into frames, all of which are already given from the start and fated to unspool on the reel the same way each time. He suggests that, like the cinema, a model of thought based in such an illusion fails to take account of the true nature of time, which is smooth, frameless, not perfectly linear, and, most important, admits of chance and change. At first glance *Persona Performa* might seem to partake of the cinematographic model that Bergson critiques: each figure is a discrete frame, carefully numbered and queued up, as if they were boxes on a census form or figures in a multicultural amusement park ride. But through Wong's use of blurred enunciation, multiple media, overlapping dialogue, and graceful dance movements, the figures in *Persona Performa* come across less as a tally of separate personae, each one dis-

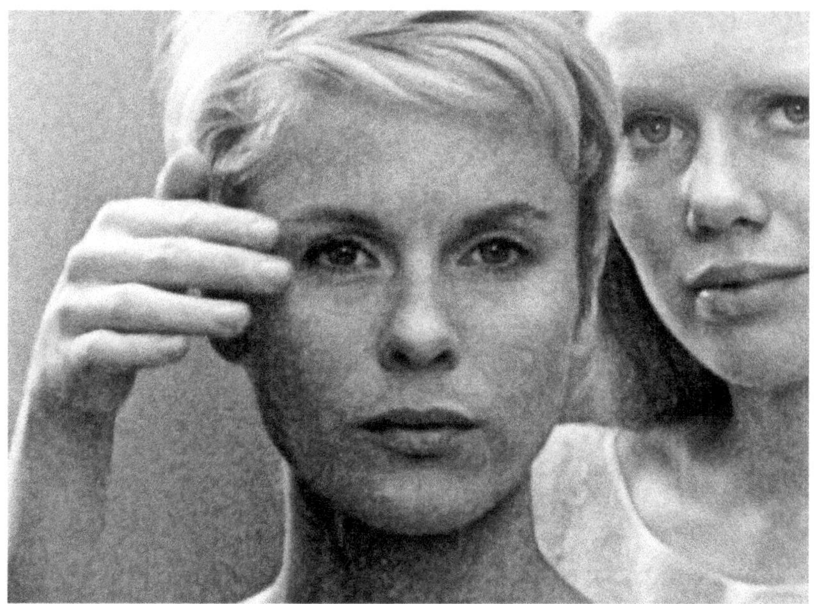

5.11. Alma and Elisabet in *Persona*, directed by Ingmar Bergman (1966).

connected from the next, than as states that melt into one another. In Wong's reinterpretation of Bergman's film, outlines are rendered yet more imprecise, the frame yet more tenuous than it already is in the original. On the one hand, it is a *virtualization* of Bergman's film, in the sense described here by Pierre Lévy: "Virtualization . . . calls into question the classical notion of identity, conceived in terms of definition, determination, exclusion, inclusion, and excluded middles. For this reason virtualization is always heterogenesis, a becoming other, and embrace of alterity."[18] On the other, it also *unvirtualizes* the film, or more specifically elements of it that are revealed to have been latent there but that might never have become visible were it not for Wong's restaging with this new setting and cast of players.

Sontag closes her essay on Bergman's *Persona* with the image of Elisabet and Alma locked in an embrace in close-up. For Sontag it is an image of vampirism: the parasitical activity of the actress who pilfers material from others for her craft, and the clinging activity of the fan who admires and copies the star's gestures and attributes. Gwendolyn Audrey Foster reads this image as a portrait of lesbian desire, drawing on the

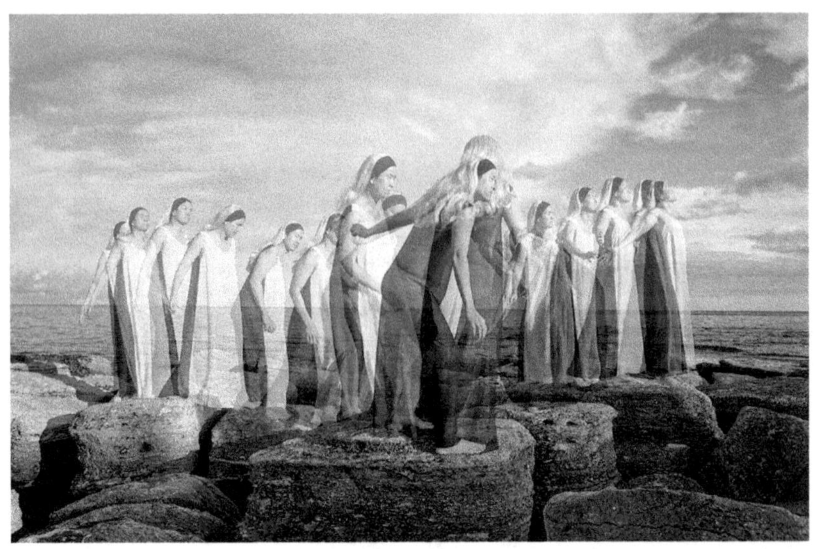

5.12. A publicity still for Wong's *Persona Performa*. Courtesy of the artist.

psychoanalytic model of the negative Oedipus complex for her interpretation.[19] There is a third possibility that I would like to add to these, one suggested by Leonardo's well-known painting *Virgin and Child with Saint Anne*.[20] Wong's own practice, which relies on techniques of appropriation, restaging, and reenactment, could be described as vampirical according to one reading. Like Alma, the devoted fan, he mimics the postures of cinema's great fading stars, and like Elisabet, the great actor, his performance relies on preexisting materials. *Persona Performa* also teases out the queer elements in Bergman's film by permuting the genders of the actor pairs. But it is finally the third of these readings that gets us onto new terrain: like Leonardo's Virgin and Saint Anne, Wong's figures melt into one another in such a way that the self is neither parasitic on the other nor bound up in the thrall of identification and desire. Rather the figures are coextensive with one another: echoing each other formally and occasionally becoming one, while still retaining distinct outlines.

Wong sometimes installs his work in multiple versions that respond to the specific sites in which they take place. The version of *Persona Performa* that he created for the Museum of the Moving Image draws expressly from the local population there. A future version, the artist suggested in an interview, might return the work to the island of Fårö, thereby implicitly connecting this isolated place to the other spaces in which the work has been performed.[21] This gesture would surely be in keeping with the principle of connectivity and continuity and of differences that saturate each one into the next like the movements of a dance.

:: :: ::

As discussed at the beginning of this chapter, the artist Elmyr forges Picassos; we see him making them in Welles's *F for Fake*. I suggested, though, that Elmyr's paintings can be understood not just as counterfeit Picassos but as virtual ones. They are *almost* Picassos, so close as to be indistinguishable. They are not poor copies or substitutes for any given authentic Picasso; they are images that, through their form alone, suggest an interpretation of the artist or a reenactment of his painting: they implicitly think about what "Picasso" means and what this group of images can convincingly include. Elmyr's forgeries, I would claim, are not cheap imitations of creative work, but creative acts in the strongest sense of the term, because he not only makes new pictures; he changes the existing ones too, compelling us to rethink their place in relationship to the interloper who is now a part of the group.

In a similar way Baudelaire's *The Makes* is perhaps better understood not as a fake documentary but as an exercise in making virtual cinema. Unlike Elmyr, Baudelaire does not fully create the virtual Antonioni films that *The Makes* is about; he merely describes and illustrates them, just enough so that they become credibly imaginable. But the effect is similar: whether or not we are tricked by the documentary frame, we are invited to reimagine film history with a new tetralogy or more of Antonioni films. *Persona Performa* continues this logic with yet another strategy: the frame of actuality is dropped altogether. Instead Wong imagines another Bergman, a virtual Bergman, revealing hidden potentials, detours, and political resonances in his oeuvre that are, in a sense, created by Wong at the same time as he unearths them, since they retroactively appear there as the new work unspools.

These two contemporary artworks teach us something important about the powers of the virtual. The virtual, it seems, does not require fully realized, indistinguishable forgeries to do its work. It can plant ideas with just a few fragments of script and some mildly credible film stills. It can even operate on suggestion alone. Significantly it also does not require that we accept the virtual work as authentic, even on first glance. We do not unthink the thoughts we have had about Picasso once we discover that a given painting was actually executed by Elmyr. We may reinterpret the image in light of the new information, perhaps seeing things in it that ought to have tipped us off, but this is a continuation of thought, not an erasure thereof. It relates to what Bergson meant when he called negation "an affirmation of the second degree."[22] The same is true for *The Makes*: it retains its power of suggestion about the European New Wave's journeys abroad even once we realize that it is not based in historical fact, indeed even if we know before we view it. Most surprising of all, the virtual operates even in a restaged work like *Persona Performa*, where there is never any suggestion that we will be looking at a real Bergman film or learning about ones that were lost. The new way of looking at *Persona* that we might glean from this experience is in no way lessened or negated. After seeing *The Makes*, even while fully knowing it to be fictional, we might see *Blow Up* in a new light; after seeing Wong's installation and performance, perhaps we cannot view *Persona* in quite the same way again. It is more than that our interpretations of these films have changed; the films themselves have somehow changed, as if they were new. This is the power of the virtual: to trace a looping circuit through the 1966 of *Persona* and back again, so that its past and future course is altered by images crafted in the current moment.

SUBSTANTIVE DURATION: *RODEN CRATER*

Erin Shirreff's *Roden Crater* (2009) is a 14.5-minute video loop and an example of a nondigitalic work of new media art. It is nondigitalic in the same way that certain works of cinema can be non-"cinematographic," as Bergson put it. The video's subject is the geological formation of the same name, a dome-shaped, extinct volcanic cinder cone with an interior crater. The cone is approximately three miles in diameter and 400,000 years old. It lies near the Painted Desert outside Flagstaff, Arizona, and the land it occupies is owned by the artist James Turrell, who purchased it in 1977 with the help of the Dia Foundation. Since the late 1970s Tur-

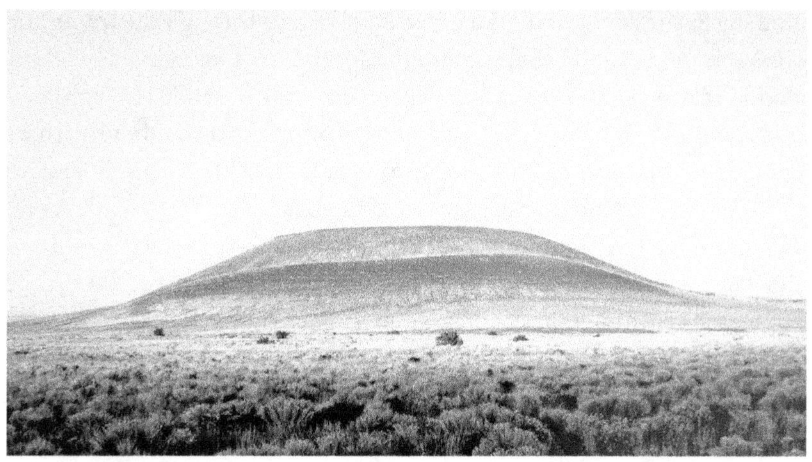

5.13. Erin Shirreff, *Roden Crater* (2009), video still. 14:34 minute loop, silent. Courtesy of the artist.

rell has been developing a now legendary earthwork at this site, a cosmic-scale observatory that takes inspiration from prehistoric archaeo-astronomical sites like Newgrange, Angkor Wat, Machu Picchu, and the Mayan and Egyptian pyramids. In the Roden Crater project, Turrell continues to work with ideas, architectural elements, and optical effects similar to those he has used in smaller-scale sculptural installations: "skyspaces" in which carved apertures frame sections of naked sky and "Ganzfeld pieces" that induce perceptual deprivation, a state of temporary blindness or optical hallucination caused by exposure to a uniform visual field.[23] The project has been cloaked in mystery, in part due to the extreme inaccessibility of the site. As one visitor put it, "Be aware that the desert is not a forgiving place, and that the crater is remote, many miles from the nearest paved road. You can die trying to get there."[24]

Throughout Shirreff's video, the cinder cone appears in approximately the same framing and point of view, a landscape in a fixed medium-long shot. As the video rolls, breathtaking alterations of illumination and color slowly infuse the image, as if the crater were placidly enduring a slow succession of changes in the weather, lighting, and seasons. The work is unabashedly delicious to the eye, sublime and stunning. Each color and lighting scheme morphs into the next as a slow, continuous dissolve; there are no apparent cuts or edits. Occasionally flashes of light or patches of shade move through the frame and create more dramatic changes in illumination, suggestive of lens flare, clouds casting shadows, or an approaching storm. While the light and hue change visibly, the crater remains equanimous throughout with its gently rounded top always tracing the same arc. The image seems to pulse with life. As one critic writes, Shirreff's *Roden Crater* solicits an awareness of the "temporal register" of the viewing time, "the duration and rhythm of recognition."[25] Calmly persisting, the landscape appears to be undergoing those miniscule changes that take place in what Robert Smithson calls "geologic time": changes that are undetectable to the human eye, mathematically insignificant across the span of a human life, and perhaps not even radical over the course of an entire species' tenure on Earth, but whose existence suggests the Bergsonian idea that even the largest, most solid earthly objects, like the planet as a whole, are in a state of constant motion and entropy through which they nevertheless endure. Smithson, in a dazzling essay, describes geologic time thus: "The strata of the Earth is a jumbled museum. Embedded in the sediment is a text that contains limits and boundaries which evade the rational order. . . . In order to read the rocks we must become conscious of geologic time, and of the layers of prehistoric material entombed in the Earth's crust."[26] With its massive yet not particularly unique or breathtaking silhouette, the Roden crater seems not simply to endure, but to *abide*.

Roden Crater has the appearance of a time-lapsed moving picture, and its richly vibrant colors and grain suggest fine celluloid film stock. Its referent, though, is not a direct image of the crater but rather a digital image that Shirreff culled from the Internet. She printed this image, then reshot it hundreds of times in her studio under different lighting conditions and edited the stills together to produce a continuous take of digital video. The time-lapse effect is real, in a way, but it comes not from changes in the light and weather patterns around the actual crater but from lighting changes artificially produced in the studio. It is the photograph, not the crater, that is being "weathered," exposed to harsh light at one turn and dappled in shadow at the next. *Roden Crater* is a work of digital sampling that has been filtered back through an analog, photographic process. By these combined means and materials, it taps into the virtual.

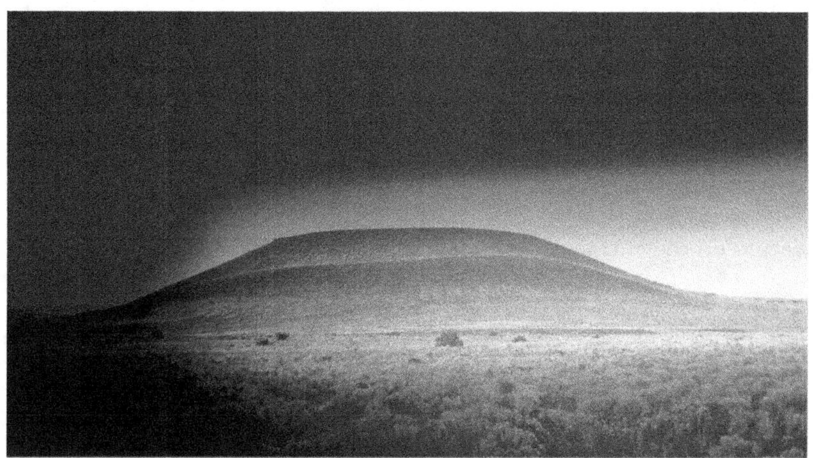

5.14. Shirreff's *Roden Crater*, video still. Courtesy of the artist.

Turrell saw that there was something special about the Roden cinder cone that made it an ideal place for an astronomical observatory. "I had this thought to bring the cosmos closer, down to the space that we occupy," he stated in an interview. "A lot of people come to art and they look *at* it. This is one of the problems with contemporary art. You don't actually enter the realm that the artist is involved in, you have a little more of a distance."[27] One could not wish for a more precise description of immanence. The view from inside the crater reveals something that is usually hidden: that we are in the atmosphere, that sky and earth are not fully separate from one another, that there is continuity between them. This perspective is a powerful one, unusual in the conventional landscape genre. It reveals that the gaseous, apparently substanceless sky is on a continuum with the solidly material, and that our viewing position—unlike the satellite's-eye view of Earth from outer space—is also inside of this earthly matter and atmosphere. It is not surprising that Shirreff also works in sculpture; her affinity for tangible matter is palpable. Rather than set up her digital video works as a foil to her sculptural works, she bestows on them an equal affinity for that matter. To the airy nothing of the electronic image, readily available to anyone with a computer and an Internet connection, she imparts a sense of presence, singularity, gravity, felt duration, and reality.

Curiously, many reviews of Shirreff's *Roden Crater* have emphasized an opposite quality, describing the work as one that plays up its own digitally reproduced aspects and irreality: its airy nothingness, as opposed to its earthy materiality. One critic describes Shirreff as working within the "realm of reproduction and mediated experience."[28] Another writes that in this work, as in others in Shirreff's 2010 solo show at the Lisa Cooley Gallery, "we are dealing with replicas. . . . All the action occurs on the surface . . . where the artificial nature of the works is revealed. Once the sleight of hand is exposed, and the viewer realizes what he is actually looking at, the stand-in nature of the works becomes apparent."[29] Writing of the glare of the camera's flash on the reshot source image, a third writer suggests that "the repeated flare of the apparatus . . . undoes any illusion of viewing actual on-site footage and returns to the viewer an acute awareness of the 'vehicle of communication' itself—the mediated image."[30] It is as if these authors were describing a work of situationist détournement, one that bares its devices and winks at its viewers.

The fact that contemporary art critics would experience *Roden Crater* in this way seems indicative of a profound disenchantment with images that besets the digital age. The safe, go-to viewing position is one that wraps itself in an assiduously Cartesian distrust of visual media and its potential to propagate illusions and replicas. That a work so compellingly visual, so unencumbered by language and theory, and so infused with a sense of duration that, for some, it borders on the spiritual, could be received as if it were a work of conceptual media critique calls for an explanation. Benjamin's "The Work of Art in the Age of Mechanical Reproduction," or rather its popularity and reception in subsequent decades, may be partly to blame for how baked-in the Cartesian distrust of the image has become. The text can leave readers stalled between original and copy, critical of the former's elitism but wary of the latter's easy availability and capacity to dissemble. The logical response to this quandary is to approach images in general with extreme skepticism. This response, though, results from a specific reading of Benjamin, one that assumes that the primary danger of the replica is its potential to trick viewers into accepting it as an original, and that the primary danger of the aura is its potential to induce a cult-like, subservient fascination.

Ever since Benjamin's popularization in studies of film and the contemporary visual arts, we have come to think of images made using mechanical and electronic devices, especially those capable of serialization or mass production, as if they were "mechanical reproductions" in the sense he describes. But this way of thinking confuses matters on several points. First, it sets so-called hand-made, unique objects in opposition to those made with the aid of tools or machines. Second, it creates an artificial divide between primitive tools or machines and modern technologies. Third, it fails to understand the difference between a copy that attempts to replace or serve as an adequate substitute for its source and one that functions as something else. Finally, it disregards the possibility that even a bad reproduction can rise to the status of an original; that is, it can accumulate aura.[31] The postmodern position according to which there are no originals and all is copy or simulacrum aspires to think its way past this impasse, but without an accompanying account of the virtual, it succeeds only in universalizing the demand for skepticism.

Benjamin famously defined the aura in section 3 of "The Work of Art in the Age of Mechanical Reproduction" as a quality that inheres in a "natural object" viewed at "the unique phenomenon of a distance, however close it may be."[32] In section 2 of that text, he introduces his discussion of the aura by way of a related concept: authenticity. He defines "the authenticity of a thing" as "the essence of all that is transmissible from its beginning, ranging from its substantive duration to its testimony to the history which it has experienced." Authenticating a work of art of course means analyzing the object's history and provenance. More broadly, though, Benjamin seems to be saying that authenticity and aura are related to "substantive duration," that is, to time-based existence. The replica—say, a digital photograph of the Roden Crater—sacrifices its authenticity, the accumulated history and patina of the original rock, in order to "meet the beholder halfway." With recording technology, Benjamin writes, images and sounds left the cathedral and the auditorium to enter the studios and drawing rooms of his era; in our era they leave the studio and drawing room to meet us even closer, on gadgets that fit in our pockets. Benjamin writes of the desire of the contemporary masses to bring things closer, satisfying a desire for instant gratification; portable digital technologies, as the story goes, fulfill this promise.[33]

In Shirreff's *Roden Crater*, though, the cinder cone's longevity and remoteness are brought along with it when it meets the beholder in the museum gallery or on a computer screen. This meeting is not, as in Benjamin's critique of the reproduction, a "halfway" meeting; it is a whole one. This is because Shirreff's *Roden Crater* is not a reproduction. It is simply an image. It does not pretend to substitute for the actual crater nor claim to put it within reach. Shirreff's *Roden Crater* is not a stand-in for the earthwork by Turrell or the rock formation in the Painted Desert, nor is it simply a poor copy of these, not even one that dutifully exposes itself as such. The crater appears in this work not as a pin dropped on a satellite map nor as a jpeg file found on a Google image search, both of which tend to give the illusion of having no author, no provenance, and no history; rather it carries the substantive duration of the worldly crater along with it: the felt sense, if not the actual clock time, of 400,000 years of rugged abidance through as many seasons of fire, rain, drought, light, and darkness. This is not an imposter Roden Crater; it is another Roden Crater, a new one, and a virtual one.

Here again the virtual shines a light through the impasse thrown up by the shadow of the false and the true. The virtual work's existence does not take away from the actual Roden Crater; it adds to it, and not just by providing a kind of advertisement for it but by making a real contribution to the repertoire of its iconography. The fact that it was created out of a single digital file does not diminish or invalidate the work; it enriches it because it thereby reminds us that something solid and powerful can be created out of so few pixels. One doesn't get closer to the real by increasing the number and density of pixels. One gets there by way of the virtual: by coming close while preserving the unique phenomenon of a distance.

AVID FELLOW FEELING: *FOR ALAN TURING*

I conclude this chapter with a return to the figure with whom I started, Alan Turing, and from whom we will hear once more via a work of recombinant electronic music. In 2006 the electronic band Matmos released an EP called *For Alan Turing*. The album was commissioned by Robert Oysterman and David Eisenbud of the Mathematical Sciences Research Institute in Berkeley, California, and was first performed at the dedication ceremony of Shiing-Shen Chem Hall there in March 2006 for an audience of mathematicians. The EP was sold in a limited edition of one thousand, each copy hand-signed by the musicians, Drew Daniel and M. C. Schmidt. It followed closely from the band's previous record, *The Rose Has Teeth in the Mouth of the Beast* (2006). Each of the tracks on that album is dedicated to a queer icon; the song titles include "Roses and Teeth for Ludwig Wittgenstein," "Snails and Lasers for Patricia Highsmith," and "Rag for William S. Burroughs." Like the tracks on *The Rose Has Teeth*, the three pieces on *For Alan Turing*—"Enigma Machine for Alan Turing," "Messages from the Unseen World," and "Cockles and Mussels"—are dedicated to their eponym and draw from his biography for their content, form, and source materials.

Turing's final project in the field of cryptology was a prototype for a secure-speech machine. The machine, developed at Hanslope Park with Robin Gandy, with collaboration from Bell Labs, was designed to encode speech for transmission over radio waves.[34] It provided the prototype for the Vocoder used in electronic music of the 1970s and popularized forty years later by T-Pane in the form of Autotune. Turing ran a contest to name this machine and chose the winning entry, Delilah, for its reference to the biblical deceiver-seductress. In a classified report, Turing refers to the machine as "she."[35] Delilah encrypted the voice using sampling: rather than transmit the whole sound wave, she would transmit select points along the curve, which the receiving machine would then reconstruct, as in a game of connect-the-dots.

While digital in design, Delilah had an important analog aspect, for she depended on the transmission of amplitudes, their shapes and curvatures. Her name also suggests some of the same conflations that we find in the Apple Computer icon between the rational and the sensuous, the scientific and the mythological. Similar technology is used to anonymize the human voice to protect privacy during testimony, removing vocal identifiers such as gendered vocal ranges, regional accents, and so on. In her own way, Delilah was thus a project with queer overtones, a project about covert communication that involved mixed signals of gender. She was in some ways the opposite of the Turing Test: her purpose was not to determine a gender or mark of human identity but rather to erase these things and thereby render indeterminate the distinction between communication and electrostatic gibberish.

"Enigma Machine for Alan Turing" begins with the pounding of a dissonant, slightly metallic-sounding chord. A faint clicking sound becomes audible. This high-pitched noise would be at home representing the chatter of 1950s-era B-movie science-fiction insects. Another mechanical sound is heard: the clicks of an old-fashioned dial rotating into place. Perhaps this dial opens a combination lock, powers a mechanical spring motor, or tunes into a radio frequency. A third percussion element soon enters, sounding vaguely like a switch flipping or thudding into on and off positions in a hollow shell. This track provides a rhythmic bass line for a layer of rapid, arithmetical, baroque invention-style piano arpeggios. The arpeggios, which briefly play solo, are soon joined by a selection of electronic tracks that resemble the beeps and whirrs of a video game—or perhaps, once again, audio effects supplied for a midcentury B-movie, in this case one in which the script called for computer sounds or distorted radio transmission waves. The piano merges with these sounds and at times becomes indistinguishable from them, suggesting a relationship between two kinds of keyboards: piano and computer.

Matmos's audio work proceeds according to the method of *musique concrète*, a practice developed by the theorist and composer Pierre Henri-Marie Schaeffer in the 1940s. Musique concrète mixes conventional instruments with sounds and noises sampled from acoustical objects in nature and the world. Drawing on radio and magnetic tape recording technology developed during World War II, it was one of the first sound genres to fuse digital and analog aesthetics. As Schaeffer put it, musique concrète operates in the interest of "plastifying music, of rendering it plastic like sculpture."[36] In Matmos's work, digital and analog sound aesthetics—electronic bleeps and piano notes, distortion crackle and mechanical thumps—are at times audible as distinct tracks, but at times they blend together. The clicking sounds on "Enigma Machine for Alan Turing" were sourced from recordings of an Enigma machine in operation.[37] A digital tool, the Enigma, is here used as an analog instrument, a "plastic" or substantive object that makes sounds. Its sounds are then redigitized in the final recording mix. The piano parts, which might seem at first to represent the analog or "concrete" aspect of the music, have in turn been digitized in two ways. First, the piano is an electronic one, played by M. C. Schmidt. Second, after the melody was composed, its notes were enciphered by Matthew Curry using an emulator running Enigma's polyalphabetic encryption methods, using only the letters A through G so as to be playable on a musical scale. These notes were then replayed in their encoded form.[38]

The second song on the EP, "Messages from the Unseen World," has a distinctive vocal track. A male, British voice (David Tibet of Current 93) repeatedly speaks the words "The universe is the interior of the light cone of creation." This is a quotation from one of four postcards of cryptic poetry that Turing wrote and sent to his friend and colleague Robin Gandy in the early 1950s and which represent some of the final documents Turing produced prior to his death. Watery low tones and harmonics of unclear origin similar to those heard in the previous song sustain the musical track, interrupted by staticky crackling sounds and a high-pitched electronic ringing. As this approximately seven-and-a-half-minute song progresses, the vocal track becomes increasingly distorted and choppy, as if the speaker were attempting to make radio contact from a distant galaxy. By midsong the repeated lyric is no longer intelligible. The vocal has morphed into a series of clipped, nonsensical but rhythmically adept percussive vocalizations. At the end of the song, though, the voice becomes distinct one final time to speak the concluding lines of Turing's poem, a line with unmistakably subversive, queer implications: "The exclusion principle is laid down purely for the benefit of the electrons themselves, who might be corrupted and become charges or demons if allowed to associate too freely."

The title "Messages from the Unseen World," also quoted from Turing's postcards to Gandy, invokes a second principle of musique concrète, that of the acousmatic. The term *acousmatic*, revived in the 1950s by Schaeffer, refers to "sound that is heard without its cause or source being seen"; this category of sound is familiar to students of film theory by way of Michel Chion, who uses it to describe sounds that emanate from spaces off-screen or *hors-champ* without necessarily being extradiegetic.[39] In musique concrète, the unseen, unidentified elements of the acousmatic are the material or plastic objects whose sounds are sampled and then transformed through mixing and collage. In some of Matmos's recordings, these objects remain unidentified or distorted—abstracted, in a way—such that the sounds can no longer be attributed to a specific material. The term originates from the Greek *akousmatikoi*, a pedagogical technique used by Pythagoras in which students were required to listen to his lectures in silence while he spoke from behind a screen or veil. Epistolary forms like postcards, indeed written forms in general, likewise involve a situation in which the author is absent in image and body and present only as language. This situation becomes yet more pronounced in a keyboard exchange where not only the body, face, and voice disappear but also the traces that would be left by handwriting.

In acousmatics the composer aims to keep the sources of sound hidden, like Pythagoras behind his screen, in order to decouple the listening experience from knowledge about its origins that might interfere with or precondition the listener's reception and experience of the music. It involves a depersonalization, a removal of the markers of identity and attribution that would allow the listener to identify the audio source. As a musical duo and couple who produce work under a single epithet, often with their individual contributions not absolutely specified, Matmos embody this principle in their practice. They also embody it in their name, which was inspired by the seething lake of evil slime beneath the city of Sogo in the 1968 film *Barbarella*, but which also translates from the Swedish for "mashed food"—or, as Rick Moody and Michael Snediker put it, "*purée*, which more exactly describes *matmos*."[40] These vivid metaphors connect to another aspect of acousmatics: the abstraction of sound, a mincing up and blending of distinct objects and a movement away from figural reference that loosely approximates the movement of abstraction in the visual arts. Finally, the acousmatic register aligns in some ways with the operations of closeting and passing. An Enigma machine passes as a snare drum, in a gesture that parallels a gay man passing as straight, a woman passing as a man, or a computer passing as human, tropologically if not in social significance and consequence.

The final song on *For Alan Turing* seems in many ways like a departure from the electronic aesthetics of the previous two tracks. "Cockles and Mussels" follows a simple, standard time signature and features a melodic refrain in a major key and identifiable guitar and violin tracks.[41] It also contains a rendition of the seventeenth-century Irish song "Molly Malone," the unofficial anthem of the city of Dublin, sung by Clodagh Simonds. According to his biographers, Turing played this tune on the fiddle and drank wine on the day in 1952 that detectives from Scotland Yard came to arrest him at his home. The song tells the story of a fishmonger who wandered the streets of Dublin hawking her cart of shellfish. She died of a fever, but her ghost continued to roam the city, pushing her barrow. A character by the same name appears in the eighteenth-century song "Apollo's Medley." This second Molly Malone, like the first, is a lost love object, and forgetting the loved one is potentially fatal: "But poison be my drink/If I sleep, snore or drink/Once forgetting to think/Of your lying alone."

Matmos's version of "Cockles and Mussels" invokes all three of these melancholy tales—those of Turing, the seventeenth-century Molly Malone, and her eighteenth-century counterpart—while situating them in a narrative about the voice and its impersonal sources. From the first track of *For Alan Turing* to its third and final one, there is a progression backward in time, from the 1940s of the Enigma machine to the folk tale refrain of Malone. The songs' aesthetics mirror this movement with a shift from the more electronic, computerish sounds of the first track to the acoustic, lyrical, and melodic elements of the final track. The album also moves from a register in which meaningful human vocalizations are absent to one in which they take center stage. The middle song, "Messages from the Unseen World," dramatizes these transitions internally, with its combination of digital and acoustic elements, and through the masking and unmasking of Tibet's vocals with a layer of distortion that settles and later dissipates.

There is a sense in which all of the voices on *For Alan Turing*, whether bell-clear or muffled, are voices that speak from beyond the grave, or at least from a radically alternative space and time. Molly Malone's cry of "Cockles and mussels, alive, alive, oh" forms the song's chorus, and at the song's end, it is repeated by her wandering ghost. There is yet a further layer of remove, since the repeated chorus takes the form of indirect discourse. The song is written in the past tense, and the singer is both quoting his memory of Molly's singing and "channeling" the refrain now sung by her ghost.

A key dimension of Matmos's album is its dedication to Turing, which in effect makes it a kind of gift and correspondence. As with the songs on *The Rose Has Teeth in the Mouth of the Beast*, these tracks are two-way; they have a sender and a recipient. Or rather they have multiple senders and recipients: Matmos, who are already two, along with their collaborators (Curry, Tibet, Simonds, et al.) and all the objects and instruments found in the world that contribute their sounds; the album's dedicatee, the audiences addressed within the songs, and the listeners of Matmos's music. A host of senders and receivers are referenced, explicitly or implicitly, within each song: the cryptographers on both sides of the war, Gandy and his postcards, the detectives who arrested Turing, Molly Malone and her auditors on the streets of Dublin, and so on.

How do these senders and recipients differ from one another? The messages sent by military officers are in a sense one-way: their purpose is to impart orders and strategic information. Turing's relationship with Morcom too became one-way at the moment that his friend ceased to live. Turing's encoded references to his sexuality in his private writings and the cryptic poems he sent to Gandy were also in a sense one-way communications, the former until scholars began to interpret and respond to them, the latter due to their extremely elliptical contents. What Matmos accomplish in *For Alan Turing* is to restore multidirectional movement to these unidirectional communications, to make them more "sociable" in Simmel's sense. What is significant in all these correspondences is not who sends what to whom but the very fact and form of the address: the communication of a communicability, which represents, as Simmel suggests, "the play-form for the ethical forces of concrete society." *For Alan Turing* is, as Simmel puts it, "a gift to the group—but a gift behind which its giver becomes invisible."[42] As with Deleuze's forger, who "becomes a person no longer" as he vanishes anonymously into a world of images, sociable speech involves a creative act, the creation not of a proposition or argument but of an implied group or virtual community.

In *For Alan Turing*, Matmos take preexisting analog material—the physical, plastic sounds of the enciphering machine; the poetic postcards that Turing wrote to Gandy—and convert it into a digital format. There it is remixed and transformed, and the original sounds and voices are multiplied. But these techniques do not make a statement about digital media as an endless series of copies of copies, its extensibility to infinity, nor do they testify to remix culture as a prison in which contemporary aesthetic creation is inevitably confined. Rather they reinsert the found material into relationships with the present world and into moving, durational time.

CHAPTER 6

Another World Is Virtual

Virtual is not opposed to real; what is opposed to the real is the possible.

—Gilles Deleuze, "The Method of Dramatisation"

A familiar slogan for movements of social change is the phrase "Another world is possible." This slogan is filled with thrilling promise. What is this other world that is possible? Is it better than this one? How do we get there? There are other worlds we can picture as a kind of logical exercise in speculative fiction, when we imagine what would result if certain historical events had gone another way—say, if Alan Turing had lived to see the 1980s, or if he had never been born. A computer could run these historical simulations given the right inputs. Great works of science fiction too have begun from such premises. But there is also another world we can picture, just barely on the cusp of the imagination, whose causes and effects are not predictable even by the most powerful computational tools. It can be glimpsed in art and fiction. This world is still blurry in form; it is not yet what it might become; its laws and boundaries are still unclear. It is not impossible, but it is also not possible, technically speaking. It is virtual.

The virtual is perpetually open. What it includes cannot be counted or listed, and it can never be grasped synchronically. Here, finally, we arrive at one of Bergson's most important and most radical observations: If there is to be room for free will, change, progress, or genuinely new and unexpected developments in the world, it must be true that not everything in the universe can be quantified and rendered in a calculable form. As Bergson puts it in *The Creative Mind*, "Even those few who have believed in free will, have reduced it to a simple 'choice' between two or more alternatives, as if these alternatives were 'possibles' outlined beforehand. . . . They therefore still admit even if they do not realize it, that everything is given."[1] If everything is given from the start, nothing radically new can spontaneously appear.

Bergson is an ardent believer in free will. It is one of his most passionate tenets, and it is intimately related to his most pressing concern: time. To get at the relationship between these two concepts, take the experience of physical pain. The circuit between stimulus and reaction is so short that there is no time for free will. We are affected by a perception of pain, and we cannot choose not to feel it. We can reduce our level of reactivity to it, we can train ourselves to ignore it, we can take medication for it, but the initial awareness of the sensation is not under our conscious control. Like a plant compelled by its heliotropism to turn toward the sun, an injured being whose nervous system transmits a signal of pain is in reflex mode and experiences no significant delay between cause and effect.

Now imagine a game of chess between players who are skilled enough to consider their options and think several moves in advance before touching a piece. The chess player has an interval of time between the perception of the board and the decision about how to respond to it. True, this player may also experience immediate, uncontrollable affects, but the rules of the game insert a cushion of time between these autonomic reactions and any action the player might take that would produce a binding outcome. Elizabeth Grosz, paraphrasing Bergson, describes this cushion of time as "a disconnection, a hesitation, the possibility of a different reaction to the same stimulus, a minimal freedom . . . the means for the interposition of a delay."[2]

This delay is where the virtual arises. It exists for all sentient beings that have the capacity to pause or hesitate before acting and, in that interval, to connect the present moment to memories of the past and sketches of the future. In Bergson's view, this interval is the source of free will. This is why computers, however intelligent, do not have free will and are not privy to the virtual. At least at this point in their development, they cannot pause and ponder before executing a script and entertain the possibility of running it another way—or not running it at all. Objects in rearview mirrors appear farther away than they actually are for good reason, since the perception of a distance allows the driver to respond calmly, using deliberate thought. This distance, which is ultimately more temporal than spatial, is a virtual air bag, a gap in which alternate trajectories, possibilities, and forking paths can be inserted. The virtual lives in this interstice, the time in which awareness arises: in the pause that relaxes the tight apertures of our viewfinders. In this interval, and only in this interval, we can access the ability to slow down, speed up, redirect, or swerve away. This interval is thus our sole passport to free will.

THE POSSIBLE AND THE POTENTIAL

The deterministic view of time against which Bergson's philosophy is directed implies that we are powerless to avert catastrophes once their preconditions have been set in motion. Quentin Meillassoux offers an elegant paraphrase of this deterministic view: "Time, then, is the throw with which the die offers us one of its faces: but in order for the faces to be presented to us, it must be the case that they pre-existed the throw. The throw manifests the faces, but does not engrave them."[3] A "possible" is like the face of a die: the options 1 through 6 preexist the throw. These options can be tallied and assigned a probability. For this reason possibility is not one of the modes of the virtual; it is part of a closed system in which outcomes can be calculated and thus in a sense foretold.

Tom Stoppard's *Rosencrantz and Guildenstern Are Dead* begins with a game of coin toss in which Rosencrantz calls heads ninety-two times in a row and wins every time.[4] However improbable this result, it is neither impossible nor unpredictable, since there were always only two options. If the future consisted of a set of possibilities and outcomes that could be determined in advance, even if that number were unimaginably large and even if the odds were wild, the universe would essentially operate like a coin toss or roll of dice. As Meillassoux writes, "Time is not the putting-in-movement of possibles, as the throw is the putting-in-movement of the faces of the die: time creates the possible at the very moment it makes it come to pass. . . . [It] throws the die, but only to shatter it, to multiply its faces, beyond any calculus of possibilities."[5]

With Meillassoux's help, we now see that the example of a game of chess is not, as it turns out, a space in which radical free will can be exercised. There is a little freedom in chess, to be sure, much more than that enjoyed by the heliotropic plant, but because chess is a closed system, it is still a calculus of possibilities. The number of possible board positions is staggeringly large: in 1950 the mathematician Claude Shannon estimated it at 10^{43}, a figure that came to be known as the Shannon number. Subsequent research calculates the game-tree complexity of chess at an unimaginable 10^{123} possibilities, which exceeds the computed number of atoms in the observable universe by forty-two powers of ten. One could go on from there and attempt to compute yet another colossally unimaginable number configuring the states of possibility for all these atoms. But like the cinematograph, none of these would be an apt analog for a universe in which not everything is given synchronically at once. Time potentializes matter, morphing the dice and pawns and restructuring the grid, so that at the very moment we think we have identified and counted the variables, they will have already changed and our computations will have to begin afresh. In Bergson's perhaps too antiscientific view, this axiom is as true for the universe in its totality as for any one microscopic bit of matter.

Meillassoux goes yet further than Bergson in his embrace of temporal contingency. For Meillassoux there is indetermination not only in matter and life—the possibility for change, for the radically new and unexpected—but also within the very laws of nature. Virtuality, for him, is related to the "pure power of the chaos of becoming," and there is no metalaw mandating that nothing will violate the laws of physics, mathematics, science, and so on.[6] We might wake up tomorrow to find not only that our dice now have twelve faces instead of six but that 6 plus 6 no longer equals 12. Whether or not one embraces Meillassoux's radical contingency, it is a logical extension of the Bergsonian principle that the only law that remains the same for all time is that nothing remains the same for all time. Presumably even this law might be broken; like characters in *Groundhog Day* or *The Edge of Tomorrow*, we might wake up tomorrow to find that it is exactly like today, that change has been eliminated from the universe. For Bergson, though, time is change, and change can take place only in substantive, durational time.

An interviewer once asked Bergson, as an erudite man of letters, to predict the future of literature after the Great War. Bergson could not answer the question as it was posed. "I saw distinctly that he conceived the future work as being already stored up in some cupboard reserved for possibles," he wrote in a reflection on the interview.[7] Instead of hazarding a guess, Bergson responded in the following way: "The work of which you speak is not yet possible. . . . I grant you at most that it *will have been possible*. . . . It will have been possible today, but it is not yet so."[8] Pierre Lévy makes a point germane to this anecdote: "The possible is already fully constituted. . . . The realization of the possible is not an act of creation in the fullest sense of the word, for creation implies the innovative production of an idea or form."[9] Along similar lines, Brian Massumi offers this formulation: "Possibility is a variation *implicit in* what a thing can be said to be when it is on target. Potential is the *immanence* of a thing to its still indeterminate variation, under way."[10]

Massumi introduces an important idea here: the potential, essentially an analog, time-based cousin of the possible, which is, however, of a different order. Giorgio Agamben defines the potential as a power or capacity that sets things in motion that are not preconstituted. In "On Potentiality," he suggests that this power comes in two varieties: generic (a child could grow up to be "anything") and existing (a specific faculty, knowledge, or ability).[11] He adds that an existing potential also implies the potential to *not* do: a person who has the ability to play the violin also has the ability to not-play the violin; a factory worker who can operate a machine also has the potential to not-operate the machine. In "Bartleby, or On Contingency," Agamben lists two additional types of potentiality. He illustrates the first of these with Herman Melville's Bartleby the scrivener, who neither does nor not-does, but instead, in his well-known catchphrase, "would prefer not to." He slacks, he demurs; basically he fails to live up to his potential. Agamben argues that Bartleby "dwells obstinately in the abyss of potentiality and does not seem to have the slightest intention of leaving it."[12] By this ruse Bartleby, at least in Agamben's reading, is able to remain a vast source of unrealized potential.

Agamben's fourth type of potentiality is, ostensibly, fully open-ended. He calls it "pure potentiality." Less defined than existing potentiality, which is restricted to a particular faculty or ability, and less determinate than generic potentiality, which still implies a set of options (however privileged its upbringing, a child cannot really grow up to be "anything"), pure potentially is completely undifferentiated. It is also less airtight than Bartleby's stratagem, which works only by a kind of flaw of logic and only for as long as Bartleby can successfully defer. Agamben borrows a metaphor from Aristotle's *De Anima*, that of the *grammateion* or blank tablet on which nothing is written, for his description of this final type of potential: "How is it possible, in actuality, to think a pure potentiality? . . . The potential intellect . . . is not a known object but simply a pure knowability and receptivity (*pura receptibilitas*). . . . It is as if the letters, on their own, wrote themselves on the writing tablet."[13]

The sentient, aware mind, at its most receptive to the virtual, resembles this writing tablet. Like the virtual, potentiality is intimately related to durational time. It requires a long circuit between perception and reaction—a large cushion of indetermination—for the genuinely new to develop and appear on the tablet. In *Creative Evolution*, Bergson writes, "Time is invention or it is nothing at all."[14] In *The Creative Mind*, he suggests that "time is this hesitation"—a hesitation that makes room for "searching" and "groping." The reverse is also true for Bergson: time gives, but it also, fortunately for us, withholds. Time is "what hinders everything from being given at once"; it is the factor that ensures that for a given hour, decade, or lifespan we will not be provided with a preset menu of options for what will happen. The menu will be written over the course of the meal, or perhaps even after the meal is over. There will be no plot synopsis. Time is indetermination, and it is the proof "that there is indetermination in things."[15] It is what ensures that we cannot always calculate the odds for what will appear next on the tablet.

Deleuze offers a reading of Melville's Bartleby that provides a necessary counterpart to Agamben's theory of the potential. Technically speaking Agamben's account of potentiality still keeps one toehold in the possible. Deleuze's reading draws not on Aristotle but on Spinoza, in whom he sees a kinship with the school of thought associated with American pragmatism. For Spinoza there is no such thing as a purely empty tablet: “One never commences; one never has a *tabula rasa*; one slips in, enters in the middle; one takes up or lays down rhythms.”[16] In our world as it currently stands, there is no way to return to zero, no magic eraser. But we can blur and soften some of its most worn-in grooves. According to Deleuze, Bartleby’s formula offers one way to do so: “I PREFER NOT TO . . . will proliferate around him and contaminate the others, sending the attorney fleeing. But it will also send language itself into flight, it will open up a zone of indetermination or indiscernibility in which neither words nor characters can be distinguished.”[17] Robert Musil wrote of the man without qualities; Bartleby, for Deleuze, is a man without references. The references he lacks are both employment-related (like Hitchcock’s thieving Marnie, he is hired without any) and linguistic. His declaration ostensibly refers to the task of copying, but this preference gradually expands until the list of things that he would prefer not to do is quite long and what it refers to rather unclear. In Deleuze’s reading, this formula opens up a space of potentiality in which the structures that subtend the relationship between supervisor and employee are reorganized and in which the two characters finally become indistinguishable.

All of this occurs by the simplest of means: because Bartleby’s formula frustrates possible replies. It is a baffling response to a direct order. “I would prefer not to” subtly undermines the very set of options implied by a command or request and thus steers the conversation in another direction. In Agamben’s reading of Bartleby, the abyss of potentiality preexists Bartleby’s statement; Bartleby merely dives into it and refuses to leave. In Deleuze’s reading, by contrast, Bartleby’s formula actually *creates* the space of potentiality. It does so, strangely, not by adding more choices to the list of possibilities but by destroying this list. “I will perform this task” and “I won’t perform this task” are two items on a menu-tree, two buttons to click, two responses to an imperative that we can use a limited form of free will to choose between. But they don’t exercise free will’s most radical power, which is to dissolve the imperative, deflect it off course, casually drop a wrench into the system, and thereby make room for something completely different. Bartleby’s formula exercises precisely this form of free will: it is a passive, nonviolent resistance, a kind of sit-in or occupation of language that makes room for another world, even if not yet actualizing it.

ANTIPHON: THE PEOPLE'S MICROPHONE

When Occupy Wall Street first appeared in the news in September 2011, the movement took many by surprise. To many it felt radically new, a manifestation of genuine change. The political tactics, the use of open-air spaces for the day-to-day business of living together, and the communal spirit that informed the enterprise were not invented out of thin air; in fact many of these were quite ancient. The methods of direct democracy that the Occupy movement advocated and modeled were not a brand-new invention either. The simple message that wealth inequality had reached unsustainable levels was, one hopes, already fairly evident to anyone who had read the financial pages in the past few years, or wandered through a residential neighborhood plagued by foreclosures, or responded to an offer of credit and been dinged by its Byzantine terms of service. In spite of the fact that none of this news was exactly shocking, the Occupy movement's appearance on the world stage struck many with the force of an absolutely novel revelation. It seemed so different and new that many were baffled and alienated by some of its basic strategies.

I conclude this book with a discussion of a "new medium" that became something of a signature instrument for the Occupy movement: the people's microphone. This medium was initially perceived by many as strange and silly, a novelty gimmick. The people's microphone is a means for amplifying speech in large crowds, and its mechanics are straightforward: all those within earshot repeat loudly and in unison what the speaker who has the floor has just said. In smaller groups, a single repetition can suffice for all to hear. In assemblies of hundreds or thousands, several rounds may be necessary for the message to reach those on the outskirts. It's a surprisingly effective medium, one that works best when the speaker delivers her message in short segments, without fillers or contorted grammar. The human mic is an ingenious solution to the problem of mass communication at sites where amplified sound is banned, including the original Occupy Wall Street encampment at Liberty Plaza in New York. It was used in the occupation of the Madison, Wisconsin, capitol building in February 2011 and was documented on video in use over a decade earlier in the World Trade Organization protests of 1999 in Seattle.[18] Regardless of who used it first in current times, versions of it have likely been in use for centuries. It is a simple extension of a familiar medium: the human voice.

In a time marked by the ubiquity of cell phones, texting, tweeting, and similarly instantaneous forms of communication, the people's microphone struck many as a rather primitive, cumbersome, even laughable system. As Richard Kim notes, meetings and group decision-making processes conducted by these means can be "incredibly, agonizingly, astonishingly slow."[19] In spite of the obvious drawbacks, people were compelled and mesmerized by the new form of conversation. Some speakers opted to use the people's mic even when a megaphone was ready to hand and sanctioned by permit. Frances Fox Piven, speaking at Occupy Philadelphia on November 8, 2011, began her remarks through the human mic before switching to an electrically powered microphone. She made several adjustments before discovering the right angle at which to hold the microphone, and some of her words were lost to the ether in the process. Her example suggests that, at times, the human mic functions more intuitively than technologically reproduced sound, with no crackle, no feedback, and no electric shock. While state-of-the-art technology, notably live-streamed video feeds, was certainly instrumental to the success and a signature element of the Occupy movement, which began with a call from *Adbusters* magazine and its readership of hackers, the movement relied on digital technology largely to amplify and form a continuous stream with extremely primitive, analog tactics on the ground.

More important, the performative, ritual, and relational capacities of the people's microphone vastly exceed its utility as a way to spread information. It is less a tool than a mode of speech. It involves a special kind of speech-act, an actualization of principles *in viva voce*. There is amplification, but also reverb, chorus, equalization, and distortion. It is a kind of speech at once radically new and ancient, evocative of the choruses of Greek drama, the antiphonal cadences of Gregorian chant, and the liturgical call-and-response of certain religious ceremonies. These calls-and-responses are liturgical in the etymological sense of the word: *leitourgos* = "work of the people," from *leito-*, "public," and *ergon*, "work" or "deed."

The human microphone goes up to eleven. Or rather, it doesn't go up—it goes across, horizontally, radiating in concentric circles, or fan-

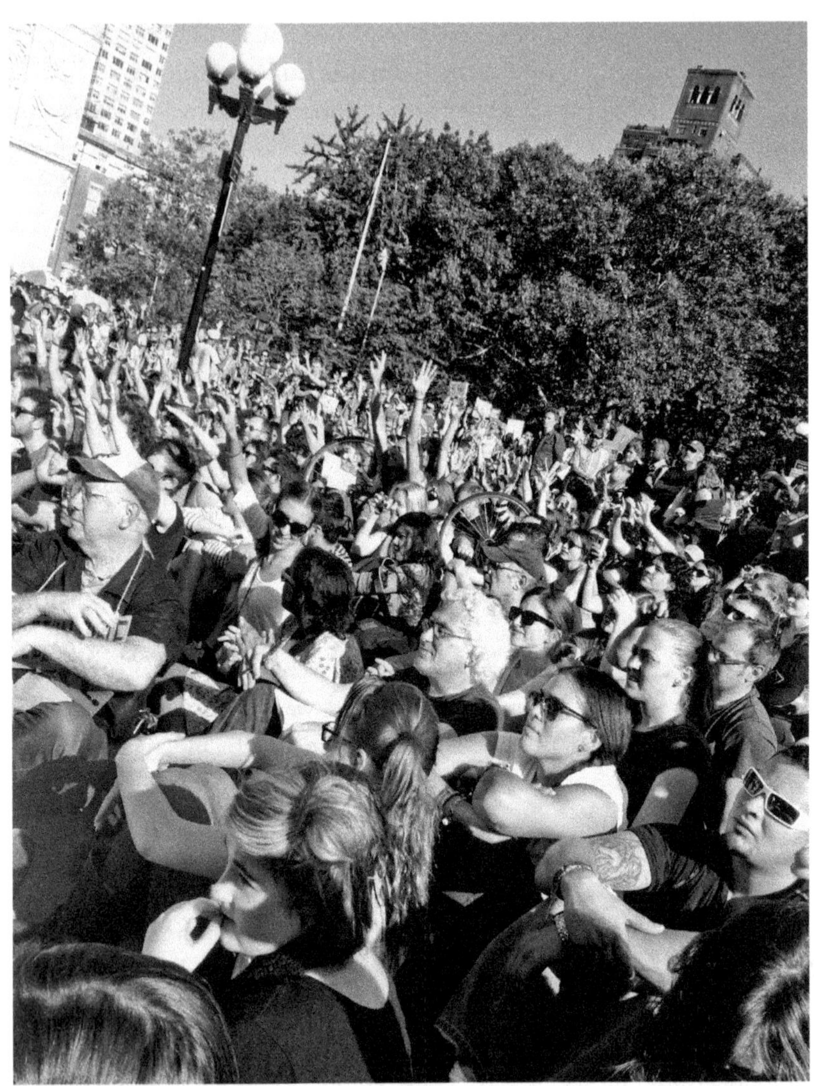

6.1. An Occupy general assembly at Washington Square Park, New York City, October 8, 2011. Photograph by the author.

ning out in a wedge-shaped pattern. In this medium, speech skips away and comes back mirrored, but also transformed, by the crowd. Through collective speech the people's mic shifts away from sovereign, solitary personhood. There is "something inherently pluralistic about the human mic," writes the *Nation*'s Richard Kim, something that "exudes solidarity over ego."[20] It also marks a shift away from the idea that our speech belongs to us, as if it were a commodity, as if, when others reiterate it, it is somehow used up or stolen rather than bolstered and enhanced. The mode is not appropriation but forwarding, reposting, retweeting, making bigger and better.

The human mic not only amplifies; it also enacts. It is related to what J. L. Austin calls a performative utterance: a statement that actualizes what it invokes.[21] Each use of the people's microphone carries with it an implicit enactment of the very thing being demanded: *This* is what democracy looks like. Kim calls this a "prefigurative politics . . . living in the conditional tense."[22] Each fragment of speech amplified by the people's mic expresses a desire for, and also models, anticipates, and genuinely creates, a pluralistic democratic process. In this way it resonates with the Militant Sound Investigations of the group Ultra-red, whose mission statement asks, "If we understand organizing as the formal practices that build relationships out of which people compose an analysis and strategic actions, how might art contribute to and challenge those very processes? How might those processes already constitute aesthetic forms?"[23] The people's mic is, in a word, an instrument of potentiality.

Speakers using the people's microphone often spontaneously adopt a slightly mannered way of speaking: a strict and even tempo, exaggerated and somewhat simplified tonal cadences, clearly articulated consonants, firm breaks between syllables. It's the way one might speak to a class of elementary foreign-language students or a computer with voice-recognition software. The style of delivery is a bit sing-songy and might be mistaken for sarcasm were it not for the resoundingly earnest and affirmative echo from the crowd. This mannered, even affected style of enunciation at times recalls the alienation effects of Bertolt Brecht's epic theater: nonnaturalistic, overtly stylized ways of speaking, moving, and gesturing intended to promote critical consciousness in lieu of mute absorption.[24] Every utterance is already on the path to becoming a quotation; every phrase is becoming a text to be pondered. Each remark has the potential to rise to the dignity of a slogan or chant, and yet it is also provisional, in quotation marks, and offered up for clarifying questions and friendly amendment. There's something contradictory about this way of speaking, something tentative and on the brink of existence, as if each utterance were prefaced by the question "If someone were to say this, would you be willing to hear it, repeat it, and let it reverberate across a crowd?"

Some media outlets poked fun at the human microphone by comparing it to a scene in Monty Python's *Life of Brian* (1979) in which the unthinking repetition of words reveals a mentality of absurd, mindless group-think. ("You're all individuals," pleads the speaker, to which the crowd replies in unison, "Yes, we're all individuals." "You've all got to work it out for yourselves," "Yes, we've got to work it out for ourselves.") What the people's mic makes evident, though, is precisely that we are *not* all individuals—at least not in the sense of autonomous, independent, self-sufficient beings who can remain unaffected by the fates and actions of others. Common sense reveals this to be true, even from a purely selfish perspective: when my neighbor is ill and has no medical care, I am at risk of becoming ill via contagion; when my neighbor's home is foreclosed upon, my own property and municipality will suffer loss of value as well; when my neighbor's children have no access to quality education, my children too will suffer because everyone grows up to shape the future through their thoughts and actions, however well- or ill-informed.

Like Brecht's alienation effects, the human microphone distances us not from each other, but from ourselves—more specifically from the fiction of the self as entirely autonomous and independent. There are indeed problems that we have got to work out for ourselves, but economic inequality is not one of them. We can solve a problem like Wall Street only in concert with one another. The working-out happens not when speakers sing to the choir—to an already convinced, already constituted public—but when differences are aired that are not strictly assignable to any one individual. Moreover the choir does not preexist this process: as with Bartleby's potentiality, it is created at the moment in which it collectively speaks, and it comes into being through this practice. It is not a repetition, but more properly a refrain, an encore, or a chorus.

The very phrase *preaching to the choir* implies a prefabricated position that is merely mirrored back to the speaker by an unthinking chorus. In classical Greek theater, though, which also required the transmission of dialogue to large audiences without the use of modern technology, the function of the chorus was not merely to repeat and amplify but to explicate, comment on, or express what the main actors could not say. Greek choruses employed "synchronization, echo, ripple, physical theatre and the use of masks" to assist in transmitting but also transforming the message.[25] Occupy actions incorporate elements of physical theater in various forms—giant puppets, choreographed flash mobs, and carefully scripted sit-ins—for example, the one that took place at Philadelphia's Wells Fargo bank on November 18, 2011.[26] Whether by design or accident, such actions come off simultaneously as a perfectly staged live performance for a lucky audience of unsuspecting bankers and as ready-made films aimed at a fleet of cell phone cameras.

As in the Greek chorus, there are masks aplenty in Occupy movement actions. The most visible and distinctive of these is perhaps the Guy Fawkes style donned by members of the Anonymous hacker collective. Its creepily effacing qualities resemble those of the Venetian *bauta* mask (seen on film with similar effect in Stanley Kubrick's *Eyes Wide Shut*). The eighteenth-century function of the bauta was to facilitate a "general, direct, free, equal and secret" ballot-casting process.[27] In spaces where police rules forbid anonymity, Anonymous members wear the mask on the back of the head, signaling a desire for equalization in spite of police orders to identify themselves. Bandanas and scarves worn across the nose and mouth sadly provide little protection against the military-grade pepper spray and tear gas that have been used on nonviolent protestors, but they do provide a degree of anonymity, and their colors and patterns sometimes indicate allegiance with other political and revolutionary movements. Gas masks and goggles are more effective against airborne agents; they also produce a chilling, vaguely paranormal theatrical effect. As the French sociologist Roger Caillois notes, "Wearing a mask is intoxicating and liberating. . . . The mask occupies a central place in the social paroxysms called festivals, in magico-religious practices, or in the as yet crude form of a political system."[28] Although this grouping of the magical with the political might seem off-putting to those who favor rational-secular approaches to a politics that seem already too deeply plagued by religious dogmatism, there is something about the festival form, including its sacred and magical aspects, that could have the potential to reanimate politics. Caillois describes the function of the festival thus: "All living things must be rejuvenated. The world must be created anew. . . . Social institutions are not exempt from this alternation. They must also be periodically regenerated."[29]

Like the Greek chorus, the Occupy movement's general assemblies involve synchronization, echo, and refrain or repetition with a difference. The community organizer Matthew Remski explains, "The repeaters, unburdened by the anxiety of creation, actually improve the clarity of the orator's rhythm and intonation as they fall into a shared pulse."[30] Sometimes the repetitions take a typewritten form. Several of the Occupy chapters broadcast their general assembly meetings over livestreamed video on sites like globalrevolution.tv, livestream.com, and ustream.tv. Chat boxes to the side of the video frame provide a space for comments from viewers that scroll by quickly. Often a commentator spontaneously assumes the role of captioner, transcribing the remarks spoken through the human microphone for the hearing impaired, for those who have tuned in late, or for posterity. It's a fourfold translation, from original speaker to human microphone repeaters to video stream to text. The succinctness and protracted pace of speech make possible a highly accurate, word-for-word transcription: an accessible set of meeting minutes that emerge in real time.

At times some among the virtual peanut gallery of chat-box commentators become participants, even creators and framers, of the events on the ground. Viewers type their support in capital letters from cities around the world: "We've got NEW ZEALAND here!" Or, in an oft-repeated reference to *Medium Cool* and the Democratic National Convention protests of 1968, "The whole world is watching!"[31] Many commentators know the camera operator by name and, like a gaggle of backseat directors, beg her to move into the light or please steady the camera because we're getting seasick over here. They ask her to go to interview a familiar protestor, as if calling in a song request to a radio DJ. And when violence ensues, they form a cadre of thousands of virtual witnesses. The wall between spectators and actors, actors and directors, virtual and actual bodies, chorus and stars is dismantled.

The people's microphone creates something similar to what narratologists call free indirect discourse. In literary studies the free indirect mode refers to a form of writing in which the narrator's voice becomes, to a degree, fused with those of the characters. The resulting prose seems to be articulated from an array of points of view that remain distinct from one another and yet are shared. The narrator and the characters within the diegetic world all seem to share a certain mental wavelength in which the reader too is included. Free indirect discourse opens up the enunciative aperture so that otherwise discrete positions become implicated and intertwined in a kind of coresponsibility.[32]

In his writings on cinema, Deleuze defines the free indirect as a mode of discourse that "does not allow itself to be fixed with the first person." He suggests that this style has a political dimension, for in spreading its enunciation across a group, it operates to constitute a wider people. The free indirect utterance has "several heads"; it works "to plant the elements of a people to come . . . to constitute an assemblage which brings real parties together in order to make them produce collective utterances as the prefiguration of the people who are missing." These collective utterances resonate across previously disconnected spaces, creating new alliances and equalizing relations across the group. Such discourse, Deleuze writes, "will create the interaction between individuals or groups who are far away, dispersed, indifferent to each other, as in a song which crosses spaces, places, and people."[33] All of this could be a description of the people's microphone.

The slogan "We Are the 99%," the Tumblr photolog that goes by that name, and the cache of handmade signs that have frequently tiled the space of Occupy sites, both on the pavement and on the web, also participate in a form of free indirect discourse. The protest signs produced for this movement tend to have an immediately recognizable, distinctly DIY aesthetic: simple, even child-like in design, painted or inked on canvases of flimsy paper, thinning bed linens, or rain-soaked cardboard boxes with their creases and flaps still visible. The messages range from crisp demands ("Jobs Not Cuts!") to appeals to logic ("You can't give people freedom, that's a contradiction, people gotta get freedom for themselves") to personal testimony ("Graduated in 2002 from a state university, still owe $23,000. I could really use that $200/month to pay my mom's hospital bills"). We are all implicated and addressed by these messages: the workers and the job creators, the you who can-

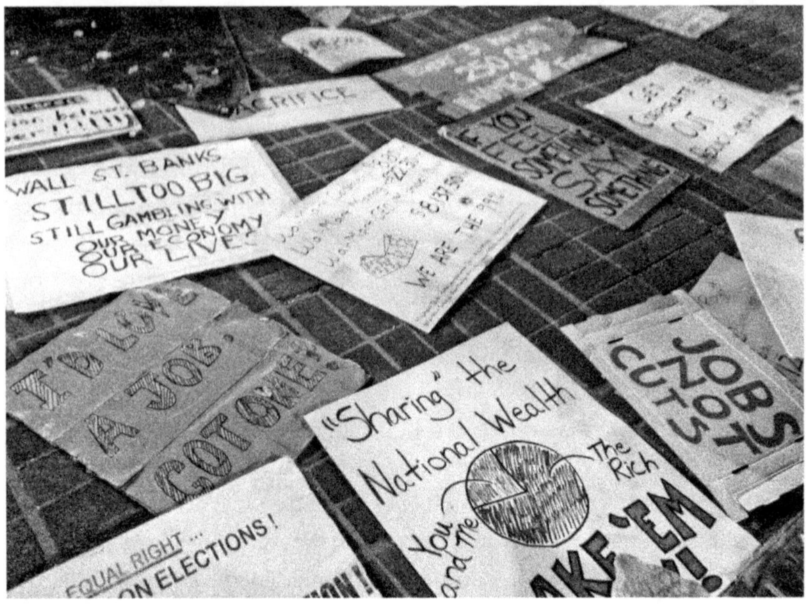

6.2. Signs on the pavement at Occupy Baltimore, October 22, 2011. Photograph by the author.

not give freedom and the people who must get it for themselves, the college graduate, the hospitalized mother, and the bankers extracting their monthly fees.

These signs tend to collect in piles around Art Committee tents, strewn with fresh Sharpies, pots of paint and crayons, where anyone can make a sign, take one, exchange one for another; photograph it, post it online, or print it out in many copies. This fact adds an additional dimension of freedom and indirectness to the discourse. Each message has an individual, handcrafted, occasionally even autobiographical aspect to it, but also an aspect that shows the author's situation to be far from unique, attesting to a pervasive pattern of economic inequity affecting millions. The signs are interchangeable, in a sense equivalent to one another, yet each one feels necessary and irreplaceable. They suggest a form of anonymity that is paradoxically intensely personal, constituting a people through a mass of constantly fluctuating voices and pronouns: first, second, third, singular, plural.

Occasionally the human microphone distorts the speaker's original words as it travels through the crowd, as in a game of telephone. An element of foreignness is introduced into the text, which nevertheless never fully corrupts it. But, as it turns out, a strong, clear utterance—or even a rambling, half-baked one—can withstand a certain amount of distortion when the crowd is with the speaker and when the attitude is one of trust and receptivity. Drum circles also create noise and interference, at times deafening. But even this noise can be meaningful, as a historic callback to earlier movements and marches, as an incentive to increase the volume and energy level, or as a metaphor for leaderlessness.[34] A friend's elderly father remarked on seeing the drummers at Zuccotti Park in Manhattan, "There's no conductor, no score: they autosynchronize!" Or, to quote Ira Livingston quoting the Invisible Committee's *The Coming Insurrection*, "Revolutionary movements do not spread by contamination but by resonance . . . the shape of a music, whose focal points . . . succeed in imposing the rhythm of their own vibrations.[35] They do so in spite of military LRADs or long-range audio devices, sound

6.3. "You can't give people freedom, that's a contradiction, people gotta get freedom for themselves." Occupy Pittsburgh, October 28, 2011. Photograph by the author.

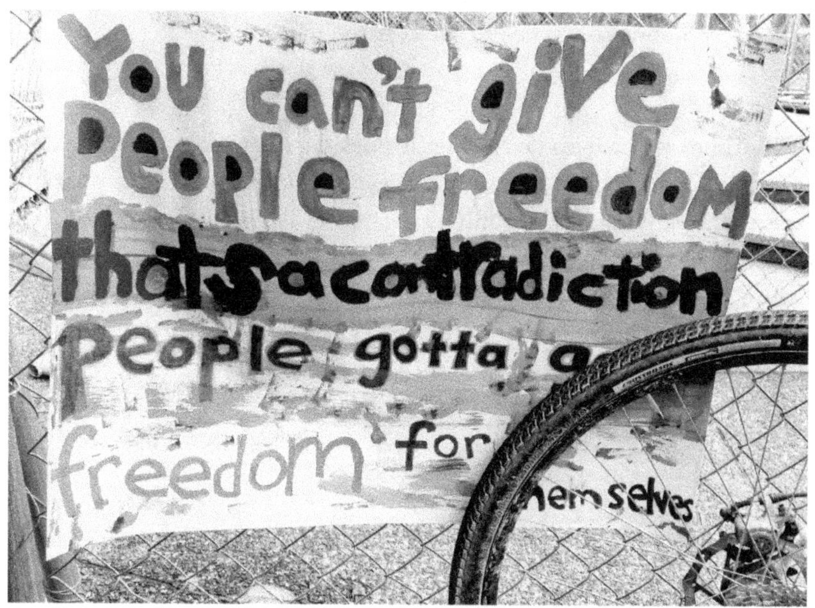

cannons, deafening helicopters, and all the other acoustic and stealth weapons that stand in the way of the people's microphone, the speech-act, and free indirect discourse. This movement enacts what in another context Grosz describes as "the becoming-art of politics . . . a politics of surprise, a politics that cannot be mapped out in advance, a politics linked to invention, directed more at experimentation in ways of living than in policy and step-by-step directed change, a politics invested in its processes."[36]

At Occupy Berkeley—home of the Free Speech movement, as a few commemorative structures on campus proudly proclaim—poets, writers, orators, and teachers were beaten by police. Not far away, at Occupy Davis, students seated peacefully on the ground were repeatedly pepper-sprayed. Their protest of the assault took the form of an eerily silent vigil as the university chancellor left a press conference. At Occupy Philadelphia, a stone's throw away from Love Park, police on horseback trampled a woman while she attempted to videotape them. These incidents say something about the world we live in, its fear of open, ricocheting speech bringing change. The human microphone is truly potential, both agent and exemplar of that change. It is also truly virtual, a metaphor that is more than a metaphor, a medium that is no mere simulation, since it actualizes the potential that it imagines for as long as someone continues to speak through it.

:: :: ::

Sometimes we have to undo what is possible in order to open the door to what is potential. When we destroy our notions of what is possible, the accompanying impossibilities disappear along with them. Another world might not be possible; as Stewart Brand put it, this "little blue, white, green, and brown jewel-like" planet is, for now, all we've got. Another world may not be possible. But another world is virtual.

NOTES

INTRODUCTION

1 Arendt, *The Human Condition*, 1.

2 Volker M. Welter has written an illuminating essay, "From Disc to Sphere," about the iconography of Earth seen from outer space; some of the information here draws on his research. He notes that the August 1959 photograph is but one of many to have been declared the "first" of its kind, each of which claimed the title based on differences "with regard to distance from Earth, technical equipment used, and size of surface captured" (24).

3 Arendt, *The Human Condition*, 11.

4 Leonard, "Stewart Brand on the Long View," 104.

5 Lacan, "The Mirror Stage," 78.

6 Diedrichsen and Franke, *The Whole Earth*, accessed February 7, 2015, http://www.hkw.de/en/programm/projekte/veranstaltung/p_87732.php.

7 Leonard, "Stewart Brand on the Long View," 104.

8 Arendt, *The Human Condition*, 251.

9 This is the first appearance of the term, according to the *Oxford English Dictionary*.

10 Garb, "Virtual Reality," 119, 118.

11 Garb, "Virtual Reality," 119, 120.

12 Turing, "On Computable Numbers."

13 *How We Became Posthuman*, 13. Along with Hayles there are numerous scholars and practitioners working in media studies and related areas who examine the fate of embodied, gendered, raced, and variously abilitied and economically resourced encounters with digital media and the

Internet. Books that have especially informed my thinking on this topic include Nakamura, *Cybertypes*; Flanagan, *Reload*; Trinh, *The Digital Film Event*; Galloway, *Gaming*, in particular the chapter on the embodied first-person point of view; Everett, *Digital Diaspora*; Juhasz, *Learning from YouTube*; Chun, *Programmed Visions*.

14 Rodowick, *Reading the Figural*, 39. In *The Ticklish Subject*, Slavoj Žižek has suggested that the self-same, masterful Cartesian subject is a straw man and that Descartes's theory of the subject is in fact far less monolithic, a point well taken. However, I adopt this shorthand for consistency, even if I have oversimplified the matter by calling this subject "Cartesian."

15 Sobchack, *Carnal Thoughts*, 153–54, 159.

16 Lim, *Translating Time*, 48.

17 Grosz, *Time Travels*, 105.

18 Baudrillard, *Passwords*, 41–42.

19 *Roget's International Thesaurus* (New York: Thomas Y. Crowell, 1960), 2.8, p. 2, 5.6, p. 3.

20 *Oxford English Dictionary*.

21 Shields, *The Virtual*, 25; Deleuze, "The Method of Dramatisation," 99. Also cited in Grosz, *Time Travels*, 108.

22 Lévy, *Becoming Virtual*, 16.

23 Massumi, *Parables for the Virtual*, 58.

24 Hayles, *How We Became Posthuman*, 20.

25 Deleuze, *Cinema 2*, 258.

1. KEYS TO TURING

For the solution to the encrypted epigraph at the start of this chapter, run the text through a three-rotor Enigma machine emulator with the rings set to AMT, ground setting AAA, without steckering.

1 For a discussion of the gendering of computers and systems of control during World War II, see Chun, *Programmed Visions*, 29–34.

2 See Wardrip-Fruin, "Digital Media Archaeology."

3 "The Thinking Machine," 26.

4 Hodges, *Alan Turing*, 168–70. Hodges is Turing's preeminent biographer, and throughout this chapter I rely heavily on his meticulous research and narrativization of Turing's life, for which he draws on primary documents in the Turing archive at King's College Cambridge, interviews with Turing's associates, letters, radio transcripts, official government records, and other published and unpublished material, including Turing's own research papers, which Hodges, a mathematician by training, explicates with admirable clarity.

5 Turing, "Computing Machinery and Intelligence."
6 For a nontechnical account of the Loebner Prize competition, see Christian, *The Most Human Human*.
7 For example, Christian recounts the tale of Dr. Robert Epstein, who fell in love with a chatbot that had been passing for a Russian woman named Ivana (*The Most Human Human*, 8–9).
8 Hodges, *Alan Turing*, 473.
9 Zach, "Alan Turing and the Decision Problem."
10 Letter to James Atkins, quoted in Hodges, *Alan Turing*, 129.
11 See Sara Turing, *Alan M. Turing*.
12 Raszl, "Interview with Rob Janoff." Jobs did state in an interview that "he wished he had thought of that" (e.g., the reference to Turing). See Isaacson, *Steve Jobs*, xviii.
13 Isaacson, *Steve Jobs*, 63.
14 Halberstam, "Automating Gender," 440, 445.
15 Hodges writes that "with his new friend Venable Martin, [Turing] went to H. P. Robertson's lectures on relativity in the new year of 1937. . . . At one point he 'indirectly indicated' an 'interest in having a homosexual relation,' but his friend made it clear that he was not interested. Alan never broached the subject again and it did not affect their relationship in other ways" (*Alan Turing*, 127).
16 Hodges, *Alan Turing*, 206.
17 Turing quoted from Wilde's *The Ballad of Reading Gaol*: "Yet each man kills the thing he loves,/By each let this be heard,/Some do it with a bitter look,/Some with a flattering word,/The coward does it with a kiss,/The brave man with a sword!" Hodges, *Alan Turing*, 216.
18 Hodges, *Alan Turing*, 232.
19 Quoted in Hodges, *Alan Turing*, 457.
20 This dialect is used in Morrissey's 1990 pop song "Piccadilly Palare": "so bona to vada . . . your lovely eek and your lovely riah" (so good to see you . . . your lovely face and your lovely hair).
21 Hodges, *Alan Turing*, 370–71, 479.
22 Turing solved Hilbert's *Entscheidungsproblem* simultaneously with Alonzo Church and was thus not technically the first to solve it.
23 This example comes from a graphic novel by Doxiadis and Papadimitriou, *Logicomix*.
24 I have vastly oversimplified Turing's solution; for a more detailed analysis and explication, see Petzold, *The Annotated Turing*.
25 Zach, "Alan Turing and the Decision Problem."
26 Hodges, *Alan Turing*, 127.
27 Phillips, *On Flirtation*, 41.

28 Quoted in Hodges, *Alan Turing*, 48.

29 Turing Digital Archive, document AMT/K/1/20, on the death of his best friend, Christopher Collan Morcom, http://www.turingarchive.org.

30 Laplanche, *New Foundations for Psychoanalysis*, 126–28.

31 Eperson, a master at Sherborne, quoted in Hodges, *Alan Turing*, 38.

32 Simmel, "Sociability," 136–37.

33 Hodges, *Alan Turing*, 168.

34 Hodges, *Alan Turing*, 170. The precise number of possibilities added by steckering is 1,305,093,289,500.

35 Copeland, *Colossus*, 378.

36 Hodges, *Alan Turing*, 427.

37 As Hodges notes, he was more likely to be found "pottering in the wilderness of nature than arranging the trim lawns of suburbia" (*Alan Turing*, 427).

38 The existence of Bletchley Park became public knowledge in 1974 with the publication of F. W. Winterbotham's *The Ultra Secret*.

39 Turing did in fact see a Jungian psychoanalyst, Franz Greenbaum, but after his time at Bletchley Park. See Hodges, *Alan Turing*, 480.

40 The *Oxford English Dictionary* identifies an etymology from the "Arabic *çifr*, the arithmetical symbol 'zero' or 'nought' . . . a subst. use of the adj. *çifr* 'empty, void,' < *çafara* to be empty. The Arabic was simply a translation of the Sanskrit name *śūnya*, literally 'empty.'"

41 Bergson, *The Creative Mind*, 36, 340.

42 Turing's PhD dissertation, quoted in Hodges, *Alan Turing*, 144.

43 Turing Digital Archive, document AMT/C/29, "Nature of Spirit," essay written during a visit to Clock House, April 1932, http://www.turingarchive.org.

44 Bergson, *Creative Evolution*, 93, 46, 154–55.

45 Bergson, *The Creative Mind*, 37.

46 Grosz, *Time Travels*, 98–99.

47 Bergson, *Creative Evolution*, 155–56, 165.

48 Elizabeth Grosz reminds us that Darwin's primary intervention was to situate humans alongside other life forms as part of a multiplicity, marked by "difference of degree and not kind" (*Becoming Undone*, 16).

49 Bergson, *Creative Evolution*, 288. In Bergson's words, "Negation . . . is an affirmation of the second degree."

50 Bergson, *Creative Evolution*, 165, 176.

51 Bergson, *The Two Sources*, 43, 44, 46.

52 Benjamin, "Theses on the Philosophy of History," 253.

53 Hodges, *Alan Turing*, 415.

54 Turing, "Computing Machinery and Intelligence," 433.

55 See Halberstam, "Automating Gender"; Hayles, *How We Became Posthuman*, xiv.
56 Ian Bogost, "The Great Pretender: Turing as a Philosopher of Imitation," *Atlantic*, July 16, 2012.
57 Simmel, "Sociability as the Autonomous Form of Sociation," 52.
58 Agamben, *Means without End*, 58.
59 Bersani, "Sociability and Cruising," 10.
60 Simmel, "Sociability as the Autonomous Form of Sociation," 50, 53.
61 Simmel, "Sociability," 137.
62 Simmel, "Sociability as the Autonomous Form of Sociation," 53.
63 Simmel, "Sociability," 131.
64 Simmel, "Coquetry," 176, my translation.

2. CHRISTIAN MARCLAY'S TWO CLOCKS

1 Deleuze, *Cinema 1*, 1–2.
2 Bergson, *Creative Evolution*, 305.
3 Bergson, *Matter and Memory*, 9.
4 On the jigsaw puzzle, see Bergson, *Creative Evolution*, 340, and *The Creative Mind*, 36. On the mosaic, see *Creative Evolution*, 89, and "Intellectual Effort," 228.
5 Bergson, *Creative Evolution*, 340.
6 Bergson, *Creative Evolution*, 89–90.
7 Bergson, *Creative Evolution*, xiii, 155, 306, 31.
8 Bergson, *Matter and Memory*, 94. Bliss Lim also makes note of Bergson's "aural," musical metaphors (*Translating Time*, 46).
9 Bergson, *The Creative Mind*, 55.
10 Balász, *Theory of Film*, 62. The following citation in this paragraph are also from this page.
11 Tyler, "Dragtime and Drugtime."
12 A. O. Scott, "In *The Clock*, You Always Know the Time," *New York Times*, July 16, 2012.
13 Roberta Smith, "As in Life, Time Is Everything in the Movies," *New York Times*, February 3, 2011.
14 Heath, "Narrative Space," 29–30.
15 Daniel Zalewski, "The Hours: How Christian Marclay Created the Ultimate Digital Mosaic," *New Yorker*, March 12, 2012, 53.
16 See Gunning, "An Aesthetic of Astonishment."
17 Zaleswski, "The Hours," 55.
18 Bergson, *The Creative Mind*, 9.
19 Deleuze, *Francis Bacon*, 93, 94, 95.

20 Massumi, *Parables for the Virtual*, 137.
21 Bergson, "Memory of the Present and False Recognition," 165.
22 Bergson, *Matter and Memory*, 9. Grosz glosses this axiom thus: "While matter may well exceed the images we have of it . . . the images that our perception gives us of it are nonetheless of the same kind as our images" (*Time Travels*, 105).
23 Bergson, "The Soul and the Body," 58.
24 Bergson, *Matter and Memory*, 13.
25 Bergson, *Matter and Memory*, 79–82.
26 Bergson, "'Phantasms of the Living,'" 95–96.
27 Bergson, *The Two Sources*, 315.
28 Deleuze, *Cinema 2*, 68–69.
29 Bergson, "Dreams," 106.
30 Deleuze, "The Method of Dramatisation," 99.

3. MATTER, TIME, AND THE DIGITAL

1 Benjamin, "On Some Motifs in Baudelaire," 185. In the original German, "passing moment" is *Erlebnis* and "experience" is *Erfahrung*.
2 Bergson, *Mind-Energy*, 95, 129.
3 Bergson, *Creative Evolution*, 245.
4 Bergson, *Creative Evolution*, 246.
5 Bergson, *Creative Evolution*, 251.
6 Rodowick, *Reading the Figural*, 212.
7 Manovich, *The Language of New Media*, 28.
8 Bazin, "The Ontology of the Photographic Image," 14; Barthes, *Camera Lucida*, 80.
9 Kracauer, *Theory of Film*.
10 Arendt, *The Human Condition*, 183.
11 Anne Rutherford, "The Poetics of a Potato Documentary That Gets under the Skin," *Metro Media and Education Magazine* 137 (Summer 2003): 127.
12 Deleuze, *Francis Bacon*, 124–25.
13 Deleuze and Guattari, *A Thousand Plateaus*, 27.
14 As Massumi notes, the emblem is capacious but not perfect: "Even the supposedly liberating paradigm of the 'rhizome,' as commonly construed, repeats the founding gesture of empirical reduction. It takes a multidimensional experiential process and reduces it to a spatial configuration" (*Parables for the Virtual*, 175).
15 Manovich, *The Language of New Media*, 295.
16 Elsaesser and Hoffman, preface, 16.
17 Callenbach, "*The Gleaners and I*," 48.

18 Kinder, "Designing a Database Cinema," 348–49, 350.
19 Deleuze and Guattari, *A Thousand Plateaus*, 7.
20 Baudrillard, *The System of Objects*, 24.
21 Hollis Frampton, quoted in Manovich, *The Language of New Media*, 133.
22 Laplanche, "The Kent Seminar."
23 Laplanche, "Seduction, Persecution, Revelation," 169.
24 Kinder, "Designing a Database Cinema," 351.
25 In French the line is more poetic: "Si on ouvrait les gens, on trouvrait des paysages. Moi, si on m'ouvrait, on trouvrait des plages."
26 Merleau-Ponty, quoted in Silverman, *World Spectators*, 143.
27 Silverman, *World Spectators*, 143.
28 Silverman, "The Author as Receiver."
29 Béar, "French Resistance," 48.
30 Torlasco, *The Heretical Archive*, 35.
31 "Exhibition: Agnès Varda: *Les Veuves de Noirmoutier*," press release, Carpenter Center Gallery, Harvard University, March 12, 2009.
32 Barthes, "The Third Meaning," 59.

4. BEYOND REPETITION

1 Burgin, *Components of a Practice*, 93. Burgin also discussed this form in the course of a series of talks given at the Jeu de Paume, Paris, in February 2010. A condensation of the talks was subsequently published as "Interactivité et non-cinématique," *Trafic* 79 (Autumn 2011) and in English as "Interactive Cinema and the Uncinematic."
2 Burgin, "Diderot, Barthes, *Vertigo*," 176.
3 Wollen, "Godard and Counter-Cinema."
4 Burgin, *Components of a Practice*, 91.
5 Burgin has described *La Jetée* as a film that "rejects the 'radical opposition' between film and photography" and that demonstrates how "the experience of looking at [a photographic] image belongs to the subjective register of *durée*" ("The Noise of the Marketplace," 282).
6 Freud, "Repeating, Remembering, Working-Through," 154.
7 Bergson, *Mind-Energy*, 113.
8 Burgin, *Components of a Practice*, 158.
9 Burgin, *Components of a Practice*, 158.
10 For an important study of the baroque's relationship to digital aesthetics (as opposed to minimalism), see Murray, *Digital Baroque*.
11 Burgin, *Components of a Practice*, 158.
12 Deleuze, *Cinema 2*, 245.
13 Deleuze, *Cinema 2*, 245.

14 Vogt, *Le Corbusier*, 55.
15 See Dayan, "The Tutor-Code of Classical Narrative Cinema"; Heath, "On Suture"; Oudart, "Cinema and Suture"; Silverman, "Suture."
16 Burgin, "Monument and Melancholia," 316.
17 See Mori, "The Uncanny Valley."
18 Bryson, "Victor Burgin and the Optical Unconscious," 44.
19 Deleuze, *Cinema 2*, 258.
20 Burgin, "Questions," 268.
21 Bryson, "Victor Burgin and the Optical Unconscious," 42.
22 Installed at the Schindler Kings Road House, West Hollywood, November 2007 to March 2008. See Burgin, *Components of a Practice*, 158.
23 Bergson, "Memory of the Present and False Recognition," 174.
24 The reference to Newtonian time is Burgin's, not Bergson's. See Burgin, "Brecciated Time," 212.
25 Burgin, "Brecciated Time," 182. This term comes from Freud's description of dreams as like pieces of breccia or composite rock, a metaphor that resonates nicely with the notion of a "stratified" image.
26 Pamuk, *Istanbul*, 6.

5. THE POWERS OF THE VIRTUAL

1 Deleuze, *Cinema 2*, 68.
2 Deleuze, *Cinema 2*, 145.
3 Nietzsche, "On Truth and Lie in a Nonmoral Sense."
4 Lambert-Beatty, "Make-Believe."
5 For example, the central character in *The Night* (1961) reaches a turning point after visiting a burlesque show featuring an African contortionist. Daria, the heroine of *Zabriskie Point* (1970), decides to leave her corporate job and in her imagination blows up her boss's house after an encounter with a Mexican servant. In *The Passenger* (1975), David Locke's time in the Saharan desert landscape seems to prompt a desire to exchange his identity for that of another man.
6 On fog in Antonioni's cinema, see Bellour, "D'un autre cinéma," 5.
7 Deleuze, *Cinema 2*, 216.
8 Muñoz, "Feeling Brown, Feeling Down," 687.
9 Sophocles, *Sophocles II*, 131.
10 Batchelder, *The Seal of Orestes*, 64–65.
11 Foucault, *Fearless Speech*, 11–19, adapted from a series of lectures at the University of California, Berkeley, in 1983.
12 Dan Duray, "You Say Persona, I Say Performa: Ming Wong Does Bergman at the Museum of the Moving Image," *New York Times*, November 14, 2011.

13 Sontag, "Bergman's *Persona*," 78.
14 Sontag, "Bergman's *Persona*," 64, 68, 71.
15 Bergson, *Time and Free Will*, 100. French source: *Essai sur les données immédiates de la conscience* (Paris: Librariries Félix Alcan et Guillaumin Réunies, 1911).
16 Bergson, *Time and Free Will*, 104.
17 See for example Bergson, *The Creative Mind*, 7, and *Creative Evolution*, 306.
18 Lévy, *Becoming Virtual*, 34.
19 Foster, "Feminist Theory and Lesbian Desire in *Persona*."
20 Kaja Silverman provides an extended reading of this image that puts it in dialogue with a digital work, James Coleman's installation at the Louvre's 2003 exhibition of Leonardo's work. I have that reading of the painting in mind here. See "The Twilight of Posterity," in *Flesh of My Flesh*, 133–67.
21 Studio visit with the artist, Berlin, July 24, 2012.
22 Bergson, *Creative Evolution*, 288.
23 "James Turrell: Roden Crater and Autonomous Structures," press release, Pace Gallery, New York, March 14, 2013.
24 Jori Finkel, "Shh! It's a Secret Kind of Outside Art," *New York Times*, November 27, 2007.
25 Meade, "Erin Shirreff," 3.
26 Smithson, "A Sedimentation of the Mind," 110.
27 James Turrell, quoted in *Art in the Twenty-First Century*, season 1, episode 2 (PBS, 2001).
28 Gartenfeld, "Erin Shirreff," 115.
29 Gritz, "Erin Shirreff," 131.
30 Meade, "Erin Shirreff," 6.
31 On the aura that sometimes accrues to degraded, multigeneration dubbed video tapes, see Lucas Hilderbrand, *Inherent Vice: Bootleg Histories of Video and Copyright* (Durham, NC: Duke University Press, 2009), 161–90.
32 Benjamin, "The Work of Art in the Age of Mechanical Reproduction," 222. I am grateful to Kaja Silverman for drawing the connection between this work and Benjamin's essay during a conversation at the Institute of Contemporary Art in Philadelphia in conjunction with the exhibition *Still, Flat, and Far*, December 5, 2010.
33 Benjamin, "The Work of Art in the Age of Mechanical Reproduction," 221, 220, 223.
34 Hodges, *Alan Turing*, 274.
35 For a copy of the original document, see "Alan Turing's Delilah Report," Turing Archives, accessed September 6, 2012, http://www.turing.org.uk/sources/delilah.html.
36 Quoted in James, "Expansion of Sound Resources in France,"79n91. See

also "Music concrète," Wikipedia, accessed September 9, 2012, http://en.wikipedia.org/wiki/Musique_concr%C3%A8te.

37 The Enigma machine was recorded at Cryptography Research in San Francisco.

38 In the inaugural performance, the Enigma machine was played live with the enciphering of the musical notes conducted simultaneously (author conversation with Drew Daniel, Berlin, July 2012).

39 Chion, *The Voice in Cinema*, 18.

40 Moody and Snediker, "On the Doctoral Dissertation of One Electroacoustic Musician (Fragments)," 88.

41 Stanley Kubrick used this song in the opening scene of *A Clockwork Orange*, where it is sung by a drunkard before he is beaten to death by droogs.

42 Simmel, "Sociability as the Autonomous Form of Sociation," 53.

6. ANOTHER WORLD IS VIRTUAL

1 Bergson, *The Creative Mind*, 8.

2 Grosz, *Time Travels*, 98–99.

3 Meillassoux, "Potentiality and Virtuality," 73.

4 Stoppard, *Rosencrantz and Guildenstern Are Dead*, 11–18.

5 Meillassoux, "Potentiality and Virtuality," 73–74.

6 Meillassoux, "Potentiality and Virtuality," 75.

7 Bergson, *The Creative Mind*, 81, excerpted from Bergson's lecture "The Possible and the Real," delivered in 1920.

8 Bergson, *The Creative Mind*, 82.

9 Lévy, *Becoming Virtual*, 24.

10 Massumi, *Parables for the Virtual*, 9.

11 Agamben, "On Potentiality," in *Potentialities*, 179.

12 Agamben, "Bartleby, or On Contingency," in *Potentialities*, 254.

13 Agamben, "Bartleby, or On Contingency," 251.

14 Bergson, *Creative Evolution*, 341.

15 Bergson, *The Creative Mind*, 75.

16 Deleuze, *Spinoza*, 123.

17 Deleuze, "Bartleby; or, the Formula," 76.

18 See Sammons, "I Didn't Say Look"; Rustin Thompson, *30 Frames a Second: The WTO in Seattle*, documentary, 2000.

19 Richard Kim, "We Are All Human Microphones Now," *Nation Blogs*, October 3, 2011, accessed March 22, 2012, http://www.thenation.com/blog/163767/we-are-all-human-microphones-now.

20 Kim, "We Are All Human Microphones Now," 1.

21 Austin, *How to Do Things with Words*.

22 Richard Kim, "The Audacity of Occupy Wall Street," *Nation*, November 21, 2011.
23 Ultra-red, "Mission Statement." I thank David Buuck for the reference.
24 Brecht, "Alienation Effects in Chinese Acting."
25 "Greek Chorus," Wikipedia, accessed March 22, 2012, http://en.wikipedia.org/wiki/Greek_chorus.
26 See Quan Nguyen, "Occupy Philadelphia Confronts Wells Fargo," *Philadelphia Inquirer*, November 18, 2011; "Occupy Philly: Foreclosure on Wells Fargo Bank (Uncensored Version)," YouTube, November 18, 2011, accessed March 22, 2012, http://www.youtube.com/watch?v=PUxKxPMz6HY.
27 "Carnival of Venice," Wikipedia, accessed March 22, 2012, http://en.wikipedia.org/wiki/Venetian_mask.
28 Caillois, *Man, Play, and Games*, 75, 97.
29 Caillois, *Man and the Sacred*, 101–2.
30 Matthew Remski, "Mic Check: How the Occupy Movement Creates Empathy through Communication," *Tikkun Daily Blog*, October 18, 2011, accessed March 22, 2012, http://www.tikkun.org/tikkundaily/2011/10/18/mic-check-how-the-occupy-movement-creates-empathy-through-communication/.
31 For a good set of resources on *Medium Cool*, see the website for the film *"Look out Haskell, it's real": The Making of Medium Cool* (Paul Cronin, UK, 2001), accessed March 22, 2012, http://www.thestickingplace.com/projects/projects/mediumcool/.
32 For more on free indirect discourse, see King, "Free Indirect Affect in Cassavetes' *Opening Night* and *Faces*."
33 Deleuze, *Cinema 2*, 242, 223–24, 227.
34 For more on the history and theory of drum circles, see Arnold, "The Sound of Hippiesomething."
35 Livingston, "Darth Vader and Occupy Wall Street."
36 Grosz, *Time Travels*, 2.

BIBLIOGRAPHY

Agamben, Giorgio. *Means without End: Notes on Politics*. Trans. Vincenzo Binetti and Cesare Casarino. Minneapolis: University of Minnesota Press, 2000.

———. *Potentialities*. Trans. Daniel Heller-Roazen. Stanford: Stanford University Press, 1999.

Arendt, Hannah. *The Human Condition*. Chicago: University of Chicago Press, 1998.

Arnold, Gina. "The Sound of Hippiesomething, or Drum Circles at 'Occupy-WallStreet.'" *Sounding Out!*, November 7, 2011. Accessed March 22, 2012. http://soundstudiesblog.com.

Austin, J. L. *How to Do Things with Words*. Cambridge: Harvard University Press, 1975.

Balász, Béla. *Theory of Film: Character and Growth of a New Art*. Trans. Edith Bone. New York: Dover, 1970.

Barthes, Roland. *Camera Lucida*. Trans. Richard Howard. New York: Hill and Wang, 1981.

———. "The Third Meaning." In *Image—Music—Text*. Trans. Stephen Heath. New York: Hill and Wang, 1977.

Batchelder, Ann G. *The Seal of Orestes: Self-Reference and Authority in Sophocles'* Electra. Lanham, MD: Rowman and Littlefield, 1995.

Baudrillard, Jean. *Passwords*. London: Verso, 2003.

———. *The System of Objects*. Trans. James Benedict. London: Verso, 1996.

Bazin, André. "The Ontology of the Photographic Image." In *What Is Cinema?* Vol. 1. Trans. Hugh Gray. Berkeley: University of California Press, 1967.

Béar, Liza. "French Resistance: Agnès Varda." *Interview* 39.5 (2009).

Bellour, Raymond. "D'un autre cinéma." *Trafic* 34 (June 2000).
Benjamin, Walter. "On Some Motifs in Baudelaire." In *Illuminations: Essays and Reflections*. Trans. Harry Zohn. New York: Schocken, 1968.
———. "Theses on the Philosophy of History." In *Illuminations: Essays and Reflections*. Trans. Harry Zohn. New York: Schocken, 1968.
———. "The Work of Art in the Age of Mechanical Reproduction." In *Illuminations: Essays and Reflections*. Trans. Harry Zohn. New York: Schocken, 1968.
Bergson, Henri. *Creative Evolution*. Trans. Arthur Mitchell. New York: Dover, 1998.
———. *The Creative Mind: An Introduction to Metaphysics*. Trans. Mabelle L. Andison. Mineola, NY: Dover, 2007.
———. "Dreams." In *Mind-Energy*. Trans. H. Wildon Carr. New York: Henry Holt, 1920.
———. "Intellectual Effort." In *Mind-Energy*. Trans. H. Wildon Carr. New York: Henry Holt, 1920.
———. *Matter and Memory*. Trans. Nancy Margaret Paul and W. Scott Palmer. New York: Zone Books, 1991.
———. "Memory of the Present and False Recognition." In *Mind-Energy*. Trans. H. Wildon Carr. New York: Henry Holt, 1920.
———. "'Phantasms of the Living' and Psychical Research." In *Mind-Energy*. Trans. H. Wildon Carr. New York: Henry Holt, 1920.
———. "The Soul and the Body." In *Mind-Energy*. Trans. H. Wildon Carr. New York: Henry Holt, 1920.
———. *Time and Free Will: An Essay on the Immediate Data of Consciousness*. Trans. F. L. Pogson. London: George Allen and Unwin, 1921.
———. *The Two Sources of Morality and Religion*. Trans. R. Ashleu Audra and Cloudesley Brereton. Garden City, NY: Doubleday, 1954.
Bersani, Leo. "Sociability and Cruising." *Umbr(a): Sameness*, no. 1 (2002).
Bersani, Leo, and Adam Phillips. *Intimacies*. Chicago: University of Chicago Press, 2008.
Brecht, Bertolt. "Alienation Effects in Chinese Acting." In *Brecht on Theatre*, ed. and trans. John Willett. New York: Hill and Wang, 1977.
Bryson, Norman. "Victor Burgin and the Optical Unconscious." In *Victor Burgin*. Barcelona: Fundació Antoni Tàpies, 2001.
Burgin, Victor. "Brecciated Time." In *In/Different Spaces: Place and Memory in Visual Culture*. Berkeley: University of California Press, 1996.
———. *Components of a Practice*. Milan: Skira Editore, 2008.
———. "Diderot, Barthes, *Vertigo*." In *Situational Aesthetics: Selected Writings by Victor Burgin*, ed. Alexander Streitberger. Leuven: Leuven University Press, 2009.
———. "Interactive Cinema and the Uncinematic." In *Screen Dynamics: Map-

ping the Borders of Cinema, ed. Gertrud Koch, Volker Pantenburg, and Simon Rothöler. Vienna: SYNEMA—Gesellschaft für Film und Medien, 2012.

———. "Monument and Melancholia." In *Situational Aesthetics: Selected Writings by Victor Burgin*, ed. Alexander Streitberger. Leuven: Leuven University Press, 2009.

———. "The Noise of the Marketplace." In *Situational Aesthetics: Selected Writings by Victor Burgin*, ed. Alexander Streitberger. Leuven: Leuven University Press, 2009.

Caillois, Roger. *Man, Play, and Games*. Trans. Meyer Barash. Urbana: University of Illinois Press, 2001.

———. *Man and the Sacred*. Trans. Meyer Barash. Urbana: University of Illinois Press, 2001.

Callenbach, Ernest. "*The Gleaners and I*." *Film Quarterly* 56.2 (2003).

Chion, Michel. *The Voice in Cinema*. Trans. Claudia Gorbman. New York: Columbia University Press, 1999.

Christian, Brian. *The Most Human Human: What Talking with Computers Teaches Us about What It Means to Be Alive*. New York: Doubleday, 2011.

Chun, Wendy. *Programmed Visions: Software and Memory*. Cambridge, MA: MIT Press, 2011.

Copeland, B. Jack. *Colossus: The Secrets of Bletchley Park's Codebreaking Computers*. Oxford: Oxford University Press, 2006.

Dayan, Daniel. "The Tutor-Code of Classical Narrative Cinema." *Film Quarterly* 28.1 (1974): 22–31.

Deleuze, Gilles. "The Actual and the Virtual." Trans. Eliot Ross Albert. In *Dialogues II*, ed. Gilles Deleuze and Claire Parnet. London: Continuum, 2002.

———. "Bartleby; or, The Formula." In *Essays Critical and Clinical*. Trans. Daniel W. Smith and Michael A. Greco. Minneapolis: University of Minnesota Press, 1997.

———. *Bergsonism*. Trans. Hugh Tomlinson and Barbara Habberjam. New York: Zone Books, 1988.

———. *Cinema 1: The Movement-Image*. Trans. Hugh Tomlinson and Barbara Habberjam. Minneapolis: University of Minnesota Press, 1986.

———. *Cinema 2: The Time-Image*. Trans. Hugh Tomlinson and Robert Galeta. Minneapolis: University of Minnesota Press, 1989.

———. *Francis Bacon: The Logic of Sensation*. Trans. Daniel W. Smith. Minneapolis: University of Minnesota Press, 2002.

———. "The Method of Dramatisation." *Bulletin de la Société française de Philosophie* 62 (1967).

———. *Spinoza: Practical Philosophy*. Trans. Robert Hurley. San Francisco: City Lights Books, 1988.

Deleuze, Gilles, and Felix Guattari. *A Thousand Plateaus: Capitalism and Schizophrenia*. Trans. Brian Massumi. Minneapolis: University of Minnesota Press, 1987.

Diedrichsen, Diedrich, and Anselm Franke. *The Whole Earth: California and the Disappearance of the Outside*. Exhibition brochure. Haus der Kulturen der Welt, Berlin, April 26–July 1, 2013.

Doxiadis, Apostolos, and Christos H. Papadimitriou. *Logicomix: An Epic Search for Truth*. New York: Bloomsbury, 2009.

Elsaesser, Thomas, and Kay Hoffman. Preface to *Cinema Futures: Cain, Abel, or Cable? The Screen Arts in the Digital Age*, ed. Thomas Elsaesser and Kay Hoffman. Amsterdam: Amsterdam University Press, 1998.

Enwezor, Okwui. "Documenta 11, Documentary, and 'The Reality Effect.'" In *Experiments with Truth*. Curated by Mark Nash. Fabric Workshop and Museum, Philadelphia, 2004–2005.

Everett, Anna. *Digital Diaspora: A Race for Cyberspace*. Albany: State University of New York Press, 2009.

Flanagan, Mary. *Reload: Rethinking Women and Cyberculture*. Cambridge, MA: MIT Press, 2002.

Foster, Gwendolyn Audrey. "Feminist Theory and Lesbian Desire in *Persona*." In *Ingmar Bergman's* Persona, ed. Lloyd Michaels, 130–46. Cambridge: Cambridge University Press, 2000.

Foucault, Michel. *Fearless Speech*. Los Angeles: Semiotext(e), 2001.

Freud, Sigmund. "Repeating, Remembering, Working-Through." Trans. Joan Riviere. In *The Standard Edition of the Complete Psychological Works of Sigmund Freud*. Vol. 12: *1911–1913*. London: Hogarth Press and the Institute of Psychoanalysis, 1958.

Galloway, Alexander. *Gaming: Essays on Algorithmic Culture*. Minneapolis: University of Minnesota Press, 2006.

Garb, Yaakov. "Virtual Reality." *Whole Earth Review* 57 (Winter 1987): 118–20.

Gartenfeld, Alex. "Erin Shirreff." *Art in America*, February 5, 2010.

Gritz, Anna. "Erin Shirreff." *Frieze*, January 1, 2010.

Grosz, Elizabeth. *Becoming Undone: Darwinian Reflections on Life, Politics, and Art*. Durham, NC: Duke University Press, 2011.

———. *Time Travels: Feminism, Nature, Power*. Durham, NC: Duke University Press, 2005.

Gunning, Tom. "An Aesthetic of Astonishment: Early Film and the (In)credulous Spectator." *Art and Text* 34 (Spring 1989).

Halberstam, J. "Automating Gender: Postmodern Feminism in the Age of the Intelligent Machine." *Feminist Studies* 17.3 (1991).

Hayles, N. Katherine. *How We Became Posthuman: Virtual Bodies in Cybernetics, Literature, and Informatics*. Chicago: University of Chicago Press, 1999.

Heath, Stephen. "Narrative Space." In *Questions of Cinema*. Bloomington: Indiana University Press, 1981.

———. "On Suture." In *Questions of Cinema*. Bloomington: Indiana University Press, 1981.

Heidegger, Martin. *Being and Time*. Trans. John Macquarrie and Edward Robinson. San Francisco: Harper and Row, 1962.

Hodges, Andrew. *Alan Turing: The Enigma*. New York: Walker, 2000.

Isaacson, Walter. *Steve Jobs*. New York: Simon and Schuster, 2011.

James, Richard S. "Expansion of Sound Resources in France, 1913–1940, and Its Relationship to Electronic Music." PhD dissertation, University of Michigan, 1981.

Juhasz, Alexandra. *Learning from YouTube*. Cambridge, MA: MIT Press, 2010.

Kinder, Marsha. "Designing a Database Cinema." In *Future Cinema: The Cinematic Imaginary after Film*, ed. Jeffrey Shaw and Peter Weibel. Cambridge, MA: MIT Press, 2003.

King, Homay. "Free Indirect Affect in Cassavetes' *Opening Night* and *Faces*." *Camera Obscura* 19.2/56 (2004): 104–35.

———. *Lost in Translation: Orientalism, Cinema, and the Enigmatic Signifier*. Durham, NC: Duke University Press, 2010.

Kracauer, Siegfried. *Theory of Film: The Redemption of Physical Reality*. Princeton: Princeton University Press, 1960.

Lacan, Jacques. "The Mirror Stage as Formative of the *I* Function as Revealed in Psychoanalytic Experience." In *Écrits*. Trans. Bruce Fink. New York: Norton, 2006.

Lambert-Beatty, Carrie. "Make-Believe: Parafiction and Plausibility." *October* 129 (Summer 2009): 51–84.

Laplanche, Jean. "The Kent Seminar." In *Seduction, Translation, and the Drives*. London: ICA, 1993.

———. *New Foundations for Psychoanalysis*. Trans. David Macey. Cambridge, MA: Basil Blackwell, 1990.

———. "Seduction, Persecution, Revelation." In *Essays on Otherness*. New York: Routledge, 1999.

Leonard, Jennifer. "Stewart Brand on the Long View." In *Massive Change*. London: Phaidon Press, 2004.

Lévy, Pierre. *Becoming Virtual: Reality in the Digital Age*. Trans. Robert Bononno. New York: Plenum Trade, 1998.

Lim, Bliss. *Translating Time: Cinema, the Fantastic, and Temporal Critique*. Durham, NC: Duke University Press, 2009.

Livingston, Ira. "Darth Vader and Occupy Wall Street: A Twitteressay." Bully Bloggers, November 13, 2011. Accessed March 22, 2012. http://bullybloggers.wordpress.com.

Manovich, Lev. *The Language of New Media*. Cambridge, MA: MIT Press, 2001.

Massumi, Brian. *Parables for the Virtual: Movement, Affect, Sensation*. Durham, NC: Duke University Press, 2002.

Meade, Fionn. "Erin Shirreff." *Kaleidoscope*, no. 8 (Fall 2010).

Meillassoux, Quentin. "Potentiality and Virtuality." In *Collapse II*, ed. R. Mackay. Oxford: Urbanomic, 2007.

Moody, Rick, and Michael D. Snediker. "On the Doctoral Dissertation of One Electroacoustic Musician (Fragments)." *Journal of Popular Music Studies* 24.1 (2012).

Mori, Masahiro. "The Uncanny Valley." Trans. Karl F. MacDorman and Takashi Minato. *Energy* 7.4 (1970).

Muñoz, José Esteban. "Feeling Brown, Feeling Down: Latina Affect, the Performativity of Race, and the Depressive Position." *Signs* 31.3 (2006): 675–88.

Murray, Timothy. *Digital Baroque: New Media Art and Cinematic Folds*. Minneapolis: University of Minnesota Press, 2008.

Nakamura, Lisa. *Cybertypes: Race, Ethnicity, and Identity on the Internet*. New York: Routledge, 2002.

Nietzsche, Friedrich. "On Truth and Lie in a Nonmoral Sense." In *The Portable Nietzsche*. Trans. Walter Kaufmann. New York: Penguin, 1954.

Oudart, Jean-Pierre. "Cinema and Suture." Trans. Kari Hanet. *Screen* 18.4 (1977–78): 35–47.

Pamuk, Orhan. *Istanbul: Memories and the City*. Trans. Maureen Freely. New York: Random House, 2004.

Petzold, Charles. *The Annotated Turing: A Guided Tour through Alan Turing's Historic Paper on Computability and the Turing Machine*. Indianapolis: Wiley, 2008.

Phillips, Adam. *On Flirtation*. Cambridge: Harvard University Press, 1994.

Raszl, Ivan. "Interview with Rob Janoff, Designer of the Apple Logo." *Creative Bits*, August 3, 2009. Accessed August 11, 2011. http://creativebits.org/interview/interview_rob_janoff_designer_apple_logo.

Rheingold, Howard. *The Virtual Community: Homesteading on the Electronic Frontier*. Cambridge, MA: MIT Press, 2000.

Robbe-Grillet, Alain. "From Realism to Reality." In *For a New Novel: Essays on Fiction*. Trans. Richard Howard. New York: Grove Press, 1965.

Rodowick, D. N. *Reading the Figural, or, Philosophy after the New Media*. Durham, NC: Duke University Press, 2001.

Sammons, Ted. "I Didn't Say Look; I Said Listen: The People's Microphone, #OWS, and Beyond." *Sounding Out!*, November 21, 2011. Accessed March 22, 2012. http://soundstudiesblog.com/.

Shields, Rob. *The Virtual*. London: Routledge, 2003.

Silverman, Kaja. "The Author as Receiver." *October* 96 (2001).
———. *Flesh of My Flesh*. Stanford: Stanford University Press, 2009.
———. "Suture." In *The Subject of Semiotics*. New York: Oxford University Press, 1983.
———. *World Spectators*. Stanford: Stanford University Press, 2000.
Simmel, Georg. "Coquetry." In *Das Abenteuer und andere Essays*. Frankfurt am Main: S. Fischer Verlag, 2010.
———. "Sociability." In *On Individual and Social Forms*. Chicago: University of Chicago Press, 1971.
———. "Sociability as the Autonomous Form of Sociation." In *The Sociology of Georg Simmel*. Trans. Kurt H. Wolff. New York: Free Press, 1950.
Smithson, Robert. "A Sedimentation of the Mind (1968)." In *The Collected Writings*, ed. Jack Flam. Berkeley: University of California Press, 1996.
Sobchack, Vivian. *Carnal Thoughts: Embodiment and Moving Image Culture*. Berkeley: University of California Press, 2004.
Sontag, Susan. "Bergman's *Persona*." In *Ingmar Bergman's* Persona, ed. Lloyd Michaels. Cambridge: Cambridge University Press, 2000.
Sophocles. *Sophocles II: Four Tragedies*. Trans. David Grene. Chicago: University of Chicago Press, 1957.
Stoppard, Tom. *Rosencrantz and Guildenstern Are Dead*. New York: Grove Press, 1967.
Strachey, Christopher. "The Thinking Machine." *Encounter* (October 1954): 25–31.
Torlasco, Domietta. *The Heretical Archive: Digital Memory at the End of Film*. Minneapolis: University of Minnesota Press, 2013.
Trinh T. Minh-ha. *The Digital Film Event*. New York: Routledge, 2005.
Turing, Alan. "Computing Machinery and Intelligence." *Mind* 59 (1950): 433–60.
———. "On Computable Numbers, with an Application to the Entscheidungsproblem (1936)." In *The Essential Turing: Seminal Writings in Computing, Logic, Philosophy, Artificial Intelligence, and Artificial Life*, ed. B. Jack Copeland. Oxford: Oxford University Press, 2004.
Turing, Sara. *Alan M. Turing*. Centenary edition. Cambridge: Cambridge University Press, 2012.
Tyler, Parker. "Dragtime and Drugtime; Or, Film à la Warhol." *Evergreen Review* 11.46 (1967).
Ultra-red. "Mission Statement." 2000. Accessed April 2, 2012. http://www.ultrared.org/mission.html.
Vogt, Adolf Max. *Le Corbusier, the Noble Savage: Toward an Archaeology of Modernism*. Trans. Radka Donnell. Cambridge, MA: MIT Press, 1998.
Wardrip-Fruin, Noah. "Digital Media Archaeology: Interpreting Computa-

tional Processes." In *Media Archaeology: Approaches, Applications, and Implications*, ed. Erkki Huhtamo and Jussi Parikka. Berkeley: University of California Press, 2011.

Welter, Volker M. "From Disc to Sphere." *Cabinet*, no. 40 (Winter 2010–11).

Winterbotham, F. W. *The Ultra Secret*. London: Weidenfeld and Nicolson, 1974.

Wollen, Peter. "Godard and Counter-Cinema: *Vent d'Est*." In *Narrative, Apparatus, Ideology*, ed. Philip Rosen. New York: Columbia University Press, 1986.

Zach, Richard. "Alan Turing and the Decision Problem." Lecture at the University of Calgary, January 24, 2012.

Žižek, Slavoj. *The Ticklish Subject: The Absent Centre of Political Ontology*. London: Verso, 1999.

INDEX

www.ingramcontent.com/pod-product-compliance
Lightning Source LLC
LaVergne TN
LVHW010614100826
845148LV00014B/2968